Prague

Cities of the Imagination

Cities of the Imagination

Prague

A cultural and literary history

Richard Burton

Interlink Books
An imprint of Interlink Publishing Group, Inc.
New York • Northampton

First published 2003 by
INTERLINK BOOKS
An imprint of Interlink Publishing Group, Inc.
46 Crosby Street, Northampton, Massachusetts 01060

Library of Congress Cataloging-in-Publication Data

Burton, Richard D. E., 1946–
Prague : a cultural and literary history / by Richard Burton.
p. cm.— (Cities of the imagination)
Includes bibliographical references.
ISBN 1-56656-490-5
1. Prague (Czech Republic)—Civilization. 2. Prague (Czech
Republic)—Description and travel. I. Title. II. Series.
DB2622.B87 2003
943.71'2—dc21
2002156604

Drawings by Nicki Averill

Cover Images: Baseline Arts; Catriona Davidson

Printed and bound in Canada by Webcom

To request our complete 40-page full-color catalog,
please call us toll free at **1-800-238-LINK,** visit our
website at **www.interlinkbooks.com**, or write to
Interlink Publishing
46 Crosby Street, Northampton, MA 01060
e-mail: info@interlinkbooks.com

Contents

CHAPTER FOUR
Theater, Music, Nation

CHAPTER FIVE
Prague Modern, 1900-1948

CHAPTER SIX
In Durance: Prague Under Communism, 1948-1989

CHAPTER SEVEN
Martyrs And Puppets

CHAPTER EIGHT
From Velvet To Velcro: 1989 And Since

Foreword

"Nobody told me," I whispered in amazement as I explored the streets of Prague in the misty October of 1965, lit by glimmering lamps. "Nobody told me," I repeated as I left my student hostel on Strahov Hill and wound my way down the slopes of Petřín, a panorama of roofs, spires, towers and bridges spread before me. Nobody told me, nobody had told me that the next months of my life would be spent in an environment more enchanting than my childhood fairy tales.

They had told me, of course, of the rigors of life under Communism: the shortages of fresh food and other commodities, the lines, bureaucracy and surliness, the fears beyond the heavy doors of the police, the ears that listened and the eyes that read. All that was true, and over the years I grew to know it intimately: I saw lives ruined, families broken, friends corrupted. Let no one be nostalgic about Communism. By the time I encountered it (at least) it had become a self-serving apparatus of control, a pataphysical machine whose only object was to remain in power. But the strength of an independent spirit mercifully showed itself in a few green shoots, pushing their way up through the asphalt of the Communist jungle and threatening to burst into flower.

This was the Prague I knew in the 1960s; great men still lived, or at least those who remembered them. It was a world where things were changing for the better, where Cuban oranges could be bought *right through the winter*, where journals were eagerly scanned for new essays by Václav Havel, Milan Kundera, Ludvík Vaculík and Ivan Klíma. A few years later, after Gustáv Husák's normalization had stripped the land bare, the new growth spread in a more moss-like, lichen-like way than the earlier confident blades. It flourished in places sheltered from the searchlight of public life—home seminars, research institutes, shabby Houses of Culture, even the bars of the Socialist Union of Youth. It became axiomatic that stapled sheaves of carbon-copied typescript offered a more absorbing read than elegantly produced books. The almost-professional, almost-official publications of the Jazz Section are now collectors' items. For as long as it could hold out, the Jazz Section gave its membership—and vastly greater readership—a window on a wider world, of experimental music, art and literature. Its range was not only international; it taught a new generation of Czechs about their own avant-garde past.

As Milan Kundera reminded us, it was memory that the Communists most feared. If, in the 1960s, the urge had to been to catch up with the latest in Western culture, in the 1980s young intellectuals turned to their own past. Theater students avidly studied under their professors the techniques and practices of the inter-war theater director E. F. Burian—himself a committed Communist, but condemned by his lords and masters as a "formalist". Kafka's work was surreptitiously revived, an adaptation of his *Amerika* performed on the bare stages of suburban venues when it was impossible to buy his works in bookstores.

In this period, the second city Brno kept pace with Prague as a center of the independent culture, whose survival was the focus of our efforts. It was a flame to be kept alive, and was fueled by all our resources: not only philosophy and political science professors trying to behave like tourists, not only the latest academic literature smuggled in as "airport reading", but—as the 1980s reached their climax—the new-found-land of information technology. "Subversive" feature films could be shown at informal "home cinemas", entire books translated onto easily concealed diskettes, oral history recorded on audio and video. In those days, all this carried a risk: children banned from education, the humiliation of strip-searches, prison sentences for damaging the name of the Republic. In those days in Prague we avoided using the telephone, peered from the back windows of cars to see if the StB was following, and (with good reason) assumed the microphone under the table. But they were breathtaking days, the summer of '89, the gatherings in bookstores, studios and theaters when democracy, still wary of the grim memory of 1938, 1948 and 1968, hovered tantalizingly out of reach.

Those mass meetings of November 1989, frosty breath rising in the orange-colored air—those meetings were part spontaneous, part dramaturgically organized. Backing up the playwright Václav Havel was a whole team of theater workers whose collective experience kept the crowds entertained, reflective, and above all good-humored. Deep emotions were tapped with the reappearance of Alexander Dubček and other figures from the past, with Marta Kubišová's songs recalling the Prague Spring.

Has Prague lost its charm and mystery in this last decade of reconstruction? No, in many ways it has regained what was slowly slipping into forgetfulness. There is so much still to find out about its buildings, about those who lived in its houses and drank coffee in its cafés. It is emerging first in Czech and now in English, in the book you have in your hands. Alongside the restoration of democracy, the rehabilitation of the innocent and the restitution of property, this has been one of the great glories of the last decade—the opening-up of the fascinating and complex world of Czech art and architecture, theater and film, music and literature. It is still possible to sidestep the turgid columns of sightseers, the harsh lights and loud music, and disappear down crooked lanes into little squares and parks. That is where I will find you, dear Reader, in your ones and twos and threes, sitting in the shade of the linden trees and tentatively uncovering the layers of cultural history. I shall join you, with Richard Burton's book in my hand, and discover Prague all over again.

—Barbara Day

Acknowledgements

I am grateful to the following for their help in the preparation and writing of this book: Suzanne Berry, Ilya Boháč, Šarka Dalton, Barbara Day, Lída Engelová and Margaret Ralph. My principal debt, though, is to James Ferguson for the enthusiasm with which he responded to my unsolicited proposal for a book about Prague. Anyone who knows the literature on Prague will see how much I owe to Angelo Maria Ripellino's *Magic Prague*; other sources are acknowledged in the section on further reading at the end of the book.

Prague From Above: A Note for First-Time Visitors

Prague is not a linear city like New York, nor does it, like Paris, grow out in concentric circles from a central core. Much of it is maze-like, whence the importance, frequently insisted upon here, of the image of the labyrinth in the literature and painting it has inspired. The present study respects that maze-like structure and views the city essentially from street level. The present "bird's eye view" of the city that follows—this being Prague, the bird in question can only be a *kafka*, a jackdaw—is intended only to provide the most basic guidelines for the first-time visitor to the city, not a study of its underlying structures (Prague, rather than Paris, was the true home of structuralism), more a synopsis of the principal sectors into which the city is divided.

Most short-term visits to Prague will turn upon the always crowded axis that links Old Town Square (Staroměstské náměstí) on the east (right) bank of the River Vltava to the Castle complex (Hradčany) high on the west (left) bank opposite, the two halves of the city being linked by the unmissable, unmistakeable Charles Bridge (Karlův most). Almost everything that the first-time visitor is likely to want to see is located on, or within a short distance of, this consistently interesting, and often breathtaking, spine of the city.

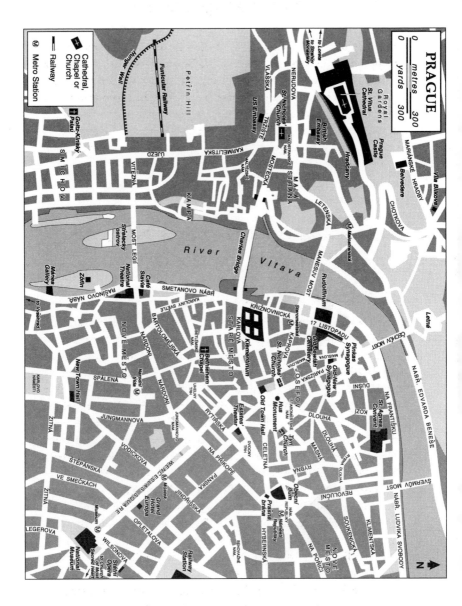

PRAGUE

0 metres 300
0 yards 300

✠ Cathedral, Chapel or Church
═══ Railway
Ⓜ Metro Station

to Loreto
to Strahov
Monastery

Funicular Railway

Hunger Wall

Petřín Hill

Royal Gardens

St. Vitus Cathedral

Prague Castle

MARIÁNSKÉ HRADBY

Belvedere

Vila Bílkova

CHOTKOVA

VLAŠSKÁ

NERUDOVA

St. Nicholas Church

British Embassy

Hradčany

US Embassy

TRŽIŠTĚ

MALOSTRANSKÉ NÁM.

LETENSKÁ

Malostranská Ⓜ

MANESŮV MOST

Letná

KARMELITSKÁ

MALÁ STRANA

MOSTECKÁ

MAL.TRŽIŠTĚ

ÚJEZD

VÍTĚZNÁ

SMÍCHOV

Goltz-Kinský Palace ✠

KAMPA

Střelecký ostrov

MOST LEGIÍ

Charles Bridge

River Vltava

Rudolfinum

ČECHŮV MOST

NÁBŘ. EDVARDA BENEŠE

Mánes Gallery

Žofín

RAŠÍNOVO NÁBŘ.

National Theatre

Café Slavia

SMETANOVO NÁBŘ.

KAROLINY SVĚTLÉ

Staroměstská Ⓜ

KŘIŽOVNICKÁ

17 LISTOPADU

Old-New Synagogue

Pinkas Synagogue

MAISLOVA

ČERVENÁ

JOSEFOV

NA FRANTIŠKU

St. Agnes Convent

ŠVERMŮV MOST

NÁBŘ. LUDVÍKA SVOBODY

to Vyšehrad

NOVÉ MĚSTO

NÁRODNÍ

BARTOLOMĚJSKÁ

Betlémské nám.

Bethlehem Chapel

Náprstek Iríds

KARLOVA

STARÉ MĚSTO

Klementinum

KAPROVA

St. Nicholas Church

PAŘÍŽSKÁ

Jewish Cemetery

DUŠNÍ

KOZÍ

DLOUHÁ

DLOUHÁ

MÁSNÁ

RYBNÁ

NA PŘÍKOPĚ

New Town Hall

SPÁLENÁ

NÁRODNÍ

BENTLÉMSKÉ TŘÍ

UHELNÝ TRH

RYTÍŘSKÁ

Estates Theatre

Hus Monument

STAROMĚSTSKÉ NÁM.

Týn Church

Old Town Hall

CELETNÁ

Týn dům

Obecní dům

Prašná brána

NÁM. REPUBLIKY Ⓜ

REVOLUČNÍ

NOVÉ MĚSTO

SOUKENICKÁ

KLIMENTSKÁ

NA PORÍČÍ

JUNGMANNOVA

Jungmannovo nám. Ⓜ

DYČKOVY TŘÍ

NA PŘÍKOPĚ

PANSKÁ

Museum Estates Square F.E.

JINDŘIŠSKÁ

HYBERNSKÁ

SENOVÁŽNÉ NÁM.

VODIČKOVA

ŠTĚPÁNSKÁ

VE SMEČKÁCH

ŽITNÁ

ŽITNÁ

LEGEROVA

WILSONOVA

National Museum Ⓜ

Museum

Grand Hotel Europa

OPLETALOVA

Railway Station

Státní Opera

Sacred Heart

to Sacred Heart or Holešovice

JUNGMANNOVA

KARLOVO NÁM.

N →

The Old Town (Staré Město)

The Old Town consists of a tangle of narrow streets wound around the large open expanse of the Old Town Square, the site of three of Prague's most famous landmarks: the Old Town Hall whose world-famous astronomical clock gathers huge crowds on the hour, to watch the curiously disquieting procession of its clockwork apostles, the unforgettable silhouette of Tyn Church immediately opposite, with, at the center of the square, the huge monument to Jan Hus (1370-1415), in every sense the pivotal symbolic figure of first Bohemian, then Czechoslovak, and now Czech Republican history.

Josefov (the "Jewish Quarter")

The one-time "Jewish Quarter" or "ghetto", known officially since 1850 as Josefov, is a small knot of streets within the larger maze of the Old Town, with, again, three principal focuses of interest: the so-called Old-New Synagogue (Staronová synagoga), the Pinkasova synagoga which, in 1958, was transformed into a memorial to the 77,297 Czech Jews killed in the Holocaust, all of whose names are inscribed on its walls, and, most memorably of all, a maze within a maze, the extraordinary Old Jewish Cemetery (Starý židovský hřbitov), the only one of its kind, and certainly of its size, still remaining in Europe.

Malá Strana

Crossing over the statue-lined Charles Bridge from the Old Town, will bring the visitor into Malá Strana, the Little City or "Side", which, to the north, spreads up the hill to the Castle and, to the west and south, up the wooded hill of Petřín. The focal point here is the cobbled square of Malostranské námĕsti, just off which looms the great church of St. Nicholas (sv Mikuláš), without doubt the finest Baroque church in the city. From the north of the square leads off the street of Nerudova, famous for its numerous decorative house signs, whose steepish incline will take the visitor to the entrance to the Castle.

Hradčany

Hradčany is the name given to the whole complex of streets, squares and buildings on top of the hill, with, needless to say, the Castle itself (the Hrad) as its monumentally overwhelming focus. The Castle consists of three connecting courtyards with, at its center, the huge St. Vitus Cathedral whose tallest steeple, floodlit at night, can be seen from virtually every point in the city. The Castle is in reality a city within—or rather above—the city, with numerous small squares and alleys of which the Zlata ulička (Golden Lane) attracts a constant stream of visitors with its row of diminutive servants' houses, romantically, but, alas, wrongly, believed to be the home of the teams of alchemists recruited from across Europe by the possibly deranged, but curiously sympathetic Emperor Rudolf II (1576-1612), the last Holy Roman Emperor to actually live in the Castle. Beyond the Castle complex itself spread further streets and squares that form the setting for Milos Forman's film *Amadeus*, with, at the western end of the district, two of the most memorable buildings in Prague: Strahov Monastery (Strahovský klášter) and the baroque extravaganza of the Church of Loretta. To the north of the Castle, it is only a short walk to the Vila Bílková, home of the greatest modern Czech sculptor František Bílek (1872-1941), which houses a superb collection of the artist's carvings in stone and in wood.

The New Town (Nové Město)

Back on the east (right) bank of the Vltava, the New Town spreads east and, above all, south of the Old Town as far as Vyšehrad (see xiv). The New Town was actually founded as long ago as 1348 by Emperor Charles IV, but now contains few buildings antedating the mid-nineteenth century. Its northern portions are the principal shopping and entertainment center of Prague, and almost everything that the short-term visitor is likely to want to see and do is situated on the thoroughfare that marks the division between the Old and New Towns (Národní třida in the west, Na příkopě in the east) and on the great Wenceslas Square (Vaclavské náměstí)—more a broad boulevard than a square—which, midway along the Národní-Na příkopě axis, branches off perpendicularly to the south. Three streets then, each of which terminates with one of the most memorable post-Baroque buildings in Prague. At the Western end of Národní, next to the river, stands the great National Theater (Národní divadlo), nineteenth-century symbol of Czech nationhood before it became a political nation, with, immediately opposite it, probably the most famous café in Prague, the

Czech Surrealists' one-time headquarters, now greatly changed, the Café Slavia. At the opposite end of Na příkopě to the east, overlooking Naměstí Republiky, stands the quite magnificent Obecní dům (Municipal House), one of the finest Art Nouveau buildings in Europe, while the great esplanade of Wenceslas Square culminates, at its southern end, in another of Prague's totemic monuments, the National Museum (Národní muzeum), fronted by a gargantuan statue of the national symbol of symbols Wenceslas (Václav) the First, murdered by his brother Boleslav the Cruel in 929 and founder of the Czech tradition of martyrdom that climaxes in the philosophy student Jan Palach who, in January 1969, set fire to himself in front of the statue of Wenceslas in protest against the Soviet invasion of his country the previous year.

Vyšehrad

Some considerable way south of Wenceslas Square, and overlooking the river, stands the medieval fortress of Vyšehrad (High Castle). Unmemorable in itself, it is worth visiting for its National Cemetery where most of the Czech Republic's great artists, writers and musicians (but not Kafka, Hašek or Janáček) are buried. The suburb of Vyšehrad also contains a small number of villas constructed in the cubist style between 1911 and 1914, virtually the only such buildings in Europe (see Chapter Five).

Other Districts

There are sites of interest in the outlying suburbs of Prague, but nothing that need distract or detain the first-time visitor to the city. North of Hradčany, on the western (left) bank of the Vlatva stretches Prague's famous Letna Park, a vast plateau overlooking the city, notable now for its gigantic red metronome erected on the former site of the belatedly demolished, ninety-foot high, 14,200-tonne reinforced concrete statue of Stalin which, for a brief period (1955-62), held the whole of the city captive under its Big Brotherly gaze. Further to the east, but still on the west bank of the river, lies the suburb of Holešovice, whose principal attraction for the visitor is the fine functionalist Veletržní palace, home of Prague's largest, but variable, post-1800 Czech painting and sculpture. Moving back to the eastern (right) bank, the suburb of Vinohrady, located to the southeast of the New Town, contains, within a few hundred yards of each other, three of the most striking modernist churches, above all Josip Plečnik's "pre-post-modern" masterpiece, the Church of the Most Sacred Heart of Our Lord (Nejsvětější Srdce Páné). Some distance still further to the east stretch Prague's vast cemeteries; the remains of Franz Kafka are buried in the family vault, along with those of his insufferable father from whom, in death as in life, he was unable truly to separate. Finally, the once "red" working-class suburbs of Žižkov (in the northeast of the city, on the right bank) and Smíchov (South of Petřín Hill, on the left bank) are also worth visiting, though Smíchov—the principal home of Prague's substantial Romany community—is regarded by some as a no-go area on account of its beggary, street crime and occasional violence.

Czech Pronounciation for the Faint-Hearted

Czech is, as its native speakers will proudly inform you, a totally phonetic language: the trouble is that many of its constituent sounds present lips, tongues and mouths accustomed to English with almost insuperable problems of articulation, while the English ear will struggle in vain to pick out more than a few comprehensible combinations of phonemes. The following is offered only as the most rudimentary and approximate guide, and the interested reader is referred to the relevant pages of Rob Humphrey's *Rough Guide to Prague* for further tips on how to pick his or her way through the notorious "traffic jams of consonants" (Patrick Leigh Fermor) with which, to the outsider, the Czech language is congested.

Consonants
When *unaccented*, consonants are pronounced more or less as in English, with the exception of *c*, pronounced as in the *ts* of boa*ts*; *ch* is like the *ch* in Lo*ch* Lomond. Problems begin with the appearance of the *haček*,

the inverted circumflex (ˇ) which frequently surmounts the consonants *c,n,r,s,* and *z̆* (and, more rarely, other consonants as well). The effect of the *haček* is to add something akin to the English *h* to the consonant it hovers over. Thus:

č is like the *ch* in *ch*icken

ň is like the *n* in *n*uance

š is like the *sh* in *sh*op

ž is like the *s* of plea*s*ure if it occurs in the middle of a word, but it is pronounced like the *sh* of *sh*op if it comes at the end

ř is reputedly the most difficult sound of all, even for Czechs, being a combination of *r* and *z̆*, as in the name of the composer Antonín Dvořak, pronounced approximately *D – vor- jhak.*

Vowels

Again, *unaccented* vowels closely resemble one of the possible pronunciations of their English equivalents, with the disorienting exception of *a*, which is pronounced like the *u* in c*u*p. *E (e)* is always like the *e* in p*e*t, *i* like the *i* in p*i*t, *o* is pronounced as in n*o*t and *u* like the *oo* in b*oo*k.

The addition of the *haček* transforms ě into *ye* (as in *ye*s), while the equivalent of the French acute accent (´) transforms *á* into f*a*ther, *é* into f*ai*r, *í* or *ý* into s*ea*t, *ó* into d*oo*r and *ú* (sometimes written as ů) into f*oo*l.

In general, all letters are pronounced as separate entities, and the stress of every word is on the first syllable.

Now practice by saying, in quick succession, *Na příkopě, Staroměstské náměstí* and *Nejsvětější Srdce Páně*—but stand well clear of your nearest and dearest as you do so.

INTRODUCTION

Prague, we are told, is the most "magical", the most "mystical" city in Europe, the continent's one-time capital of astrology and alchemy, its ghetto the birthplace of the mysterious and menacing Golem and home to all manner of esotericism, hermeticism and witchcraft. The proverbial Mother of Cities, Prague is said to have given birth, succor or refuge, over the centuries, to a succession of remarkable sons who, in their contrasting ways, embody this or that aspect of her manifold genius: the melancholic and obsessive Emperor Rudolf II (1576-1611), living in Howard Hughes-like reclusion in the huge castle, the Hrad, that towers over the city, having supposedly gathered the pick of Europe's alchemists about him in his relentless quest for the Philosophers' Stone. Or the sublime Mozart (1756-1791) whose *Don Giovanni* was premiered in Prague in 1787 and one of whose finest symphonies, the thirty-eighth, is named after the city. Or, closer to our own time, the tortured and tortuous Franz Kafka (1883-1924), himself a man much preoccupied by castles, and his almost to the month contemporary Jaroslav Hašek (1883-1923), alcoholic creator of the doltish but somehow always triumphant Good Soldier Švejk whose cloddishness—innate or feigned, one is never *absolutely* sure—is held to embody the Czech people's own spirit of survival-by-acting-dumb throughout its centuries-long history of foreign domination and oppression.

Such, at any rate, are the most common figures and images—and something, too, of the style—that make up the conventional picture of Prague and which the city's huge tourist industry promotes for all they are worth, and all will be given consideration in the chapters that follow, though in some instances with rather more skepticism than is often the case. Much —far too much— has been said and written of "magical Prague", of a city seemingly given over, for long stretches of its history, to nothing other than alchemical experiment, cabbalistic speculation and Rosicrucian sophistry, a local specialty being the making of weird zombie-like creatures that promptly turn against their inventors or, like the original Golem, lie sleeping for centuries somewhere in the maw of the city, preparing to wreak a terrible vengeance on either its citizens or enemies. That Prague has a "magical" or "surreal" dimension is not to be denied and the city would be the poorer—and not just in respect of its revenue from tourism—without its mystical and fantastical accretions. To dwell unduly on these aspects, as do even some of the finest books on the city, even the finest of all, Angelo Maria Ripellino's remarkable *Magic Prague* (1973), much drawn on here, is, however, not only to ignore the intense rationality and humanity of many of its most representative citizens but also to draw a veil of exoticism and wizardry over the distinctly un-magical reality the city has lived through, not just in the distant past, but, above all, between 1948 and 1989, the memory of which seems to have been miraculously—indeed magically— expunged from at least the conscious and openly expressed mind of the city.

For over four and a half centuries, brief intervals apart, Prague, once the capital of the dominant power, Bohemia, in the center of Europe, was itself the dominated pseudo-capital of a dominated nation: dominated first from Vienna under the Habsburg and later Austro-Hungarian Empires (1526-1918), then, following its ignominious betrayal at Munich, from Berlin (1939-45), and, finally, with varying degrees of openness and directness, from Moscow (1948-89). When, in 1526, the Bohemian nobles chose as their king the Habsburg Ferdinand I, they unwittingly condemned their country and capital to increasing marginalization, which became outright domination after 1620 when, in the first major engagement of what came to be known as the Thirty Years' War, the by now predominantly Protestant Czechs were defeated by the army of the Catholic Habsburgs at the battle of the White Mountain (Bílá Hora) on the western outskirts of Prague, near the site of the present international airport. The battle lasted just over an hour, and, in effect, determined the fate of Prague, and of the lands over which it remained nominal capital, for the next four hundred years.

White Mountain was, Czech patriots said, the *finis Bohemiae*, the end of Bohemia, and from that date until the "Velvet Revolution" of 1989, Prague knew only twenty years, the years of the First Czech Republic

(1918-1938), of genuine independence. It was followed by three years of fragile and diminishing freedom (1945-8) that ushered in four decades of Communist autocracy, either open and brutal (as in the 1950s) or more insidiously contaminating and corrupting (the 1970s and 1980s), broken only by eight months of exhilarating experiment (January-August 1968). This was the extended "Prague Spring" now apparently obliterated from the city's conscious memory, at least—which ended with the arrival of Soviet tanks on the night of August 21-22 that year. These events, and others related to them, are not so much background as foreground, for in all of them, as we shall see, writers, artists and intellectuals played a crucial, indeed often determining, role. No European city's intellectual and artistic life—not even Paris'—has been as thoroughly *political* as that of Prague, and not just under Communism, but from the very birth of the so-called Czech national revival (*národní obrození*) in the early nineteenth century, which, though some of its earliest proponents were, paradoxically, German-speakers, soon became a movement of the Czech-speaking Prague intelligentsia before all else.

Thus, if Prague is the city of Rudolf II, Mozart, Kafka and Hašek, it is also, and inseparably, the city of Thomas Garrigue Masaryk (1850-1937)—"TGM" to all Czechs—lawyer, philosopher, sociologist, literary scholar, a humanist, rationalist and democrat to the core, and founder and first president of the independent nation of Czechoslovakia that was born, or re-born, after almost four centuries of Austrian hegemony, in October 1918. It is also, alas, the city of two out-and-out dictators of contrasting hue, men whose actions and beliefs, though sharply opposed, stood everything that Masaryk had fought for on its head. First, Reinhard Heydrich (1904-42), Nazi supremo of what was left of the Czech lands after their dismemberment at Munich and the secession of Slovakia as a quasi-independent, fascistic state. And second, Klement Gottwald (1896-1953), the Stalinists' Stalinist, who, in February 1948, engineered the so-called "elegant coup" that brought the Czech Communist Party to power more or less democratically (or at least without direct Soviet military intervention). Heydrich was assassinated by Czech patriots in June 1942, prompting the Nazis' destruction of the village of Lidice, about twenty miles northwest of Prague, in revenge, while Gottwald survived to preside over the notorious Prague show-trials of the early 1950s and, in the process, to create what was probably, until the early 1960s, the most repressive European Communist state other than the Soviet Union itself.

But, then, again, Prague is also the city, though not the native city, of Alexander Dubček (1921-92), both agent and symbol of his country's quest for that political Philosophers' Stone, "socialism with a human face", which, for a few heady months in 1968, seemed indeed on the brink of realization. And then, finally, amidst the appalling bleakness of post-1968 "normalization", it was the city of Charter 77 and of the man who embodied its demands, more outside Czechoslovakia than within, the Prague-born playwright and dissident Václav Havel (born 1936) who, in the Velvet Revolution of November-December 1989, was swept by popular acclaim, followed by formal election, to the presidency of the yet again reborn nation. *Havel na hrad!* (Havel to the castle): for the first time since 1948 the focal point of every panoramic view of the city was occupied by a president who embodied the genuine will of the people.

Political Theater

That the first president of the freed nation was a man of the theater—initially a stagehand, then a reader of scripts and finally a playwright—was by no means as incongruous to Czechs as it sometimes seemed to outsiders; to many insiders, indeed, it seemed like the culmination and fulfillment of a national tradition. From the mid-nineteenth century, the creation of a truly national theater—a theater in which Czech, not German, would be the sole language in use—had been the leading ambition of Czech patriots. Such an ambition was finally achieved, after much delay and the destruction by fire of the original building, when the present imposing Národní divadlo (National Theater) was inaugurated with a triumphant production of Bedřich Smetana's patriotic opera *Libuše* in 1883. It was entirely appropriate that it should be in a theater—not, as it happened, in the Národní divadlo but in the ornate Art Nouveau concert hall of the Obecní dům (Municipal House) on the present Náměstí Republiky—that Czech independence was declared in October 1918. It was entirely appropriate, too, that theaters, particularly the well-known tourist attraction, the Laterna Magika, should have been the improvised headquarters of the movement that finally toppled the Communist regime in November 1989. In the 1920s and 1930s, it had been the Liberated Theater (Osvobozené divadlo) of the celebrated "V + W" (Jiří Voskovec and Jan Werich) that had formed the vanguard of the city's social, cultural and political consciousness, while in the early 1960's, experimental theaters such as the Semafor and the Theater on the Balustrade (Divadlo na zábradlí)—often cramped, improvised affairs, located literally underground in the basement of buildings— played a decisive part in opening the way for the brief awakening of Prague '68.

To the extent that it was for centuries governed from without, Czechoslovakia (since the "velvet divorce" of 1992, the separate states of the Czech Republic and Slovakia) is unusual amongst European nations in that its national identity has had to be continuously reformulated and re-forged, almost in the manner of the formerly colonized and now nominally free nations of the European empires of old. That task of national self-definition and construction has fallen more heavily upon intellectuals in Czechoslovakia, or been assumed more readily and actively by them, than in any other European nation, with the possible exception of Spain. Among those intellectuals, playwrights, theater directors and actors have been particularly prominent in their chosen or imposed role of keepers and voicers of the national conscience. Once more, there can be no case of relegating Czech literature and culture to the "background", for the very good reason that, for almost two hundred years, and especially in Prague, their creators have, by personal choice or constrained by political circumstance, been at the very forefront of national life.

Architecture and Power

All of the political conflicts referred to so far are written into the very form of the city. Prague is renowned above all for the abundance and quality of its Baroque architecture, but few visitors realize that, in terms of Czech history, the Baroque is the style of political and religious domination, being the expression in marble, stucco and gilt of the Austro-Catholic hegemony that was inaugurated in 1526, confirmed by arms in 1620 and consolidated culturally and ideologically through the concerted, Jesuit-led re-catholicization campaign of the next hundred years. Non-Catholics by a ratio of something like two to one at the time of White Mountain, the inhabitants of the Czech lands had, by the early 1700s, been re-incorporated in their majority, if often against their will, into communion with Rome. In its exuberant flaunting of power, the Baroque was both instrument and symbol of that re-conversion. It is thus not surprising that, for many Czech nationalists of the nineteenth and early twentieth centuries, it was the earlier style, the Gothic, introduced into their country by Emperor Charles IV (1346-78), king of Bohemia at the apex of its power, creator of Prague's most famous bridge, its original university and, above all, of the mighty cathedral which, though still incomplete, towered over everything, that seemed to embody the nation's long-lost greatness and freedom. In reality, of course, the Gothic was no less "foreign"—or, better, international—a style than the Baroque, but to Czech patriots it was imperative that Prague possess an architectural style truly its own and that, in the first instance, the cathedral, its unfinished state embodying all too pertinently the unfinished state of the nation, be speedily completed: a Society for the Completion of St. Vitus Cathedral was formally set up in 1859. Thus, if all Czech art is, by virtue of the country's problematic history, of necessity political, it is in the architecture of Prague that the impact of history and politics is most to be felt. Prague is, to anticipate, not just the Baroque treasure house beloved of the brochures. It contains some of the finest—though not always the most finely preserved—Art Nouveau, cubist and modernist architecture of any European capital, architecture that was often conceived and created in conscious opposition to the Baroque. The drama and fascination of Prague's physical structure lies in the constant tension—and complementarity—between its straight lines (the Gothic, the modern) and its curves (the Baroque), between the severity and rigor of the former and the superabundance and flamboyance of the latter, which may be read as the architectural expression of the tension—and, once more, of the complementarity—of the contending components of the country's, and the city's historical make-up: Catholic and Protestant, Austrian and Bohemian, "German" and "Slav", *Mitteleuropa* and the Greater Europe beyond. Not for nothing was the so-called national architectural style (*národní sloh*) of the 1920s which sought a higher synthesis of all these components also known by the name of "rondocubism", a marriage of straight line and curve in the cause of national harmony and wholeness.

Signs and Statues

Prague is indeed one of the most legible of cities, even for the visitor who, like the present writer, confronts the Czech language as a virtually opaque mass of intimidating combinations of letters, in which only the magic word *Pilsener*—ironically, the totemic local beer, as quintessentially Czech as Guinness is Irish, still bears its original German appellation—seems to evoke an instant response.

A minor, but significant, pleasure of walking in the older parts of the city is to "collect" the ancient shop- and house-signs that still endow many buildings with an individual identity, transforming them, so to speak, into words that make up the sentence of a street. Thus, tourism-thronged Nerudova that leads from Malostranské Square up to the castle contains, at no. 6, the House at the Red Eagle (Dům U Červeného Orla), an image of the eponymous bird perched on the peak of a mountain; no. 12, the House at the Three Fiddles (Dům U Tří Housliček), the one-time premises of the Edlinger family of violin-makers, duly bears three crossed fiddles against a blue background, while no. 16, once the shop of a goldsmith named Schumann, sports a gold cup, a variation on the chalice motif, which, for reasons to be explained, is to be found at regular intervals in all parts of the city. A golden key and golden cartwheel mark out nos. 27 and 28, gold being an ever-present theme in this alleged city of alchemists, while no. 34, the House at the Golden Horseshoe (Dům U Zlaté Podkovy) bears a painting of St. Wenceslas on horseback, with, at one time, a "real" golden horseshoe on one of the

hooves of his steed. Towards the top of the street there are houses marked out by a red lion with, again at one time, a gold cup in its paws, a lobster which needs repainting in its original green and, most beautiful of all, an elegant white swan against a blue background.

Few streets in Europe can be as semiotically rich, and this is far from an exhaustive count, and excludes the omnipresent images of Madonna and Child and of St. John Nepomuk, Prague's somewhat dubious patron saint, that seem to sprout identically from every other building in the older parts of the city, as though no single recess can be left unfilled. Nor are such signs—long since detached, of course, from the function of the buildings they adorn, now almost all restaurants and gift shops—confined to Malá Strana and the Old Town, for, as we shall see, the Art Nouveau, modernist and "rondocubist" buildings of the New Town, Vinohrady and elsewhere frequently transmit intriguing ideological messages as well.

But it is the human figure that is Prague's signifier par excellence. Few cities can muster quite such a profusion of statues of all sizes; it is hard to miss the huge memorial to Jan Hus (c. 1372-1415) in Old Town Square, and the still more massive monument to František Palacký (1798-1876), Hus' earliest and greatest historian, and principal leader of the nineteenth-century revival, on the square named after him. Then there are the thirty-odd evenly spaced statues on Charles Bridge, each laden with heavy iconographical significance, or the countless prophets, saints, bishops, martyrs and other ecclesiastical worthies that stare down unseeingly from equally numberless churches and monasteries. Or the statuettes and other figurines—Madonnas and Child by the hundred, Wenceslases and Nepomuks by the score—that seem to cling to every available crevice and cornice. And this is only the outside of buildings. Inside, in churches and galleries, the human figure reigns once more supreme: harrowing crucified Christs that bleed more profusely than elsewhere, Madonnas unequalled in the intensity of their grief, flamboyantly weeping and swooning Mary Magdalenes, bishops skewering their foes with the sharp end of their crosiers, ecstatic martyrs surveying the mangled parts of their bodies, like St. Agnes carrying her own severed breasts on a salver in the Loretta, all smothered in impossible swarms of swooping angels and more fluttering pudgy-faced cherubs than the eye, or the stomach, can take. And, returning to the street, it starts again: the plethora of wide-eyed dolls and puppets in shop-windows, the shelves of unblinking *Bambini di Praga*, cloned in every tawdry detail from the much-revered Christ-doll in the Church of Our Lady of Conquests, and, most famous of all, the twelve clockwork apostles that, every hour on the hour, shuffle past on the Old Town Hall tower, blindly nodding down on the craning heads, staring eyes and flashing cameras of the hundreds of spectators gathered beneath them.

Prague is a city fascinated, even obsessed, with automata, with statues, puppets and other creatures—the Golem and the Commendatore of *Don Giovanni* among them—that move menacingly on the marches between life and death, inhabited by some uncanny alien spirit that their human inventors seek in vain to control. It is no accident, surely, that the term "robot" derives from a Czech word for slave or serf, (*rab*), and that robots, word and thing, made their first appearance on, precisely, a Czech stage, in Karel Čapek's 1922 play *R.U.R.* and acronym for "Rossum's Universal Robots" that seems to hint at "USSR." Some of these proliferating figures have names, like Nepomuk and Hus, and deliver an intelligible ideological message, while others mutely create an atmosphere of menace, melancholy or merriment. All, though, provide links in a coherent urban text which, with a little historical knowledge, can be "read" by the patient and willing observer, as, without further ado, the chapter that follows sets out to show.

CHAPTER ONE

How to Read Prague

Old Town Square

Let us begin where most visits to Prague either begin or end: on Old Town Square, Staroměstské náměstí. The square is defined by two unforgettable buildings, both begun under the reign of John of Luxembourg (1310-46), known to English (and Welsh) history as the blind King of Bohemia slain at the battle of Crécy while fighting for France and whose motto—*Ich Dien* (I serve)—was co-opted for use by future Princes of Wales. To the west rises up the single 180-foot high tower of the Old Town Hall, with its world-famous astronomical clock, dating from around 1400, to which were added in 1490 the intricate clockwork figures of the twelve perambulating apostles and, beneath them, four automata representing, from left to right, worldly vanity (a man admiring himself in a mirror), miserliness (once unmistakably intended to be a Jew, but shorn of his stereotypical beard when the clock was reconstructed in 1945), a skeleton with hourglass tolling a bell, and a be-turbaned Turk who contrives to look both idle and threatening. The work, originally of a Master Hanuš who, according to legend, was blinded with a red-hot poker after completing his

masterpiece lest he repeat it for another city elsewhere, the clock displays the two most feared and despised Others of the medieval Christian *polis*: the infidel, the avaricious, Christ-murdering Jew, along with a decidedly effeminate male and the enemy of enemies, Death.

Immediately across the square, the spectacular twin towers of the Church of Our Lady before Tyn leap into the sky, the unique silhouette of their spires enhanced by the clusters of pinnacles, baubles, and stars with which they are primped out. On the gable between the two towers is mounted a refulgent golden relief statue of the Mother of God, the sun's rays streaming out from her as, crowned and besceptered, she stands in triumph upon an inverted half-moon: the city's hope and protection against the enemies held up for derision on the clock tower opposite. But, as we shall see, she is a relatively recent addition, a direct result of the Austro-Catholic victory over Protestant Bohemia at the Battle of White Mountain (1620), itself a long-term consequence of the life, teaching and, above all, the death of the man whose vast memorial stands—or, rather, spreads out for it is substantially longer and broader than it is high—at the center of the square: Jan Hus.

Jan Hus: Tragedy and Triumph

The pivot of the square, Hus is also the pivot of the history of the Czech lands, and his monument, whether festooned in flags or shrouded in black, the central icon, since its inauguration in 1915, of the splendors and miseries of the country, and the city, he has come to embody. Born around 1370 and appointed professor of philosophy at Charles University in 1398, Hus had, by his early thirties, achieved eminence as the most charismatic preacher in Prague, a man capable of attracting congregations of up to three thousand to the newly constructed, and intentionally spacious and uncluttered, Bethlehem Chapel on the present square of that name a few hundred yards to the south of Staroměstské náměstí. Here, speaking in Czech rather than German or Latin, he berated the institutional Church for what he saw as its comprehensive betrayal and perversion of the true teaching of

Christ. He attacked the pomp and circumstance of its offices designed, he proclaimed, to exclude all participation by the laity, the extravagance of its vestments and treasures, its collusion with secular power and underwriting of inequality and poverty, its shameless sale of indulgences and blatant use of the confessional as a mere palliative to sin rather than as the instrument of its uprooting and removal.

For Hus and the many preachers and prominent laymen who shared his views (Jakoubek of Stříbro, Hieronymus of Prague, Jan Příbram, Jan of Rokycana, Peter of Mladoňovice), one practice above all epitomized the corruption of the Church, namely the denial to the laity of the Blood of their Saviour, the consecrated wine which, in established church liturgy, only the officiating priest drank from the chalice, before distributing the bread of Christ's Body to those in the congregation deemed worthy to receive it. Hus and his followers believed that Christ's Blood, like His Body, was sacrificed and given for all, and, accordingly, both clergy and laity should receive communion under both kinds (*sub utraque specie*, that is, in both bread and wine), hence the name Utraquists which was in due course given to them. So crucial was the chalice, freely offered to, and drunk from, by all, to their beliefs and liturgical practice, that they adopted it as their emblem and eventually, when their beliefs led to war, as the escutcheon on their shields and the banner under which they went into battle. Images of the chalice, almost always picked out in gold, are to be found everywhere in Prague, and have their distant prototype in the chalice used in the first Utraquist mass celebrated at the tiny church of St. Martin-in-the-Wall, almost opposite the reconstructed Bethlehem Chapel, in 1414. To be Czech is, in some way, to partake of the chalice: not for nothing do we first encounter the Good Soldier Švejk in a pub called U kalicha, on Na bojišti in the New Town, now given over to the triune cult of Švejk, beer and the euro, packed every evening with congregations of tourists as vast, it seems, as those that thronged to Bethlehem Chapel half a millennium ago. But these pilgrims presumably know and care little about the theological and liturgical controversies that rent fifteenth- and sixteenth-century Bohemia apart.

Hus did not see himself as a religious—and still less, as a social—revolutionary, and did not himself advocate generalized communion in both kinds. Nonetheless, the vehemence of his preaching, and the enthusiastic response it evoked in his listeners, who, like his opponents, cut across all classes of society, inevitably brought him into conflict with both Church and State. The first was embodied locally by Archbishop Zbyněk Zajíc of Prague, the second in the person of the notorious drunkard Wenceslas IV (1378-1419) who, originally sympathetic, turned against Hus when the preacher began to attack the sale of indulgences of which the Crown was a major beneficiary. Hus was summoned to an ecclesiastical council at Constance in Switzerland where, called upon to retract his incendiary criticisms of Church practice, he remained faithful to his motto of *Pravda vítězí*, Truth prevails, and was duly burned at the stake as a heretic on July 6, 1415. His leading follower, Master Hieronymus of Prague, was similarly dealt with on May 30, 1416.

The extraordinary monument to Hus, part Rodinesque, part Art Nouveau, is the work of Ladislav Šaloun (1870-1946) and its inauguration was timed to coincide with the five hundredth anniversary of Hus' martyrdom, in 1915. It shows Hus and a group of his followers standing on what might be the peak of a mountain—mountains being a key figure in the iconography of Czech nationalism, from the Hussite capital of Tábor (after Mount Tabor, the site of Christ's Transfiguration), seventy miles or so to the south of Prague, to the cataclysmic defeat at White Mountain (Bílá hora) that marked the so-called *finis Bohemiae* until its resurrection almost three hundred years later. Hus stands clearly apart from his followers, fully upright while they are mainly bent down, kneeling or recumbent. He looks to the south, more or less in the direction of Bethlehem Chapel, and wears a full-length cloak and the symbolic cap of the heretic about to undergo death. He is the lone and heroic messiah-cum-martyr, whose isolation contrasts strongly with the amalgamated mass of his huddled supporters, one of whom holds the inevitable chalice. A mourning figure lies supine at his feet, while behind him, presumably embodying the future Czech nation, still not realized half a millennium after his death, a mother sits with two children, suckling the younger at her breast.

The words *Pravda vítězí* are engraved in huge letters at the monument's base, along with similarly rousing citations from the work of Jan Amos Komenský (1592-1670), known internationally as

Comenius. He wrote what might be described as the Czech *Pilgrim's Progress*, *The Labyrinth of the World and the Paradise of the Heart*, in 1623, five years before the author, scholar, humanist and ordained minister of the Hussite-derived Community of Brethren, went into exile from Bohemia, never to return to the land of his birth. Endlessly represented in nineteenth- and early twentieth-century painting and sculpture, most famously in the statue that stands outside the Prague home of the sculptor and mystic František Bílek (1872-1941), the flight of Comenius emblematizes the *finis Bohemiae* and, continuing the martyrdom of Hus, forms a further link in the Czech nationalist myth of despair, diaspora and darkness in the wake of White Mountain. To carry the myth into the present, and to show that out of disaster a new dawn is born, the base further commemorates "8 V 1945" and the deaths of two partisans Hynek Šlosar (aged 34) and Karel Janeček (38) who perished that day in the fight for control of the Old Town Hall, marking the end of the German occupation of the city.

But Hus is not just a symbol of Czech tragedy and triumph in the face of *external* enemies. His statue may have been smothered in swastikas by the Nazis when they took possession of Prague in March 1939, but the part that he and his image have played in the country's *internal* politics is even more significant by dint of being fundamentally ambivalent. Like Joan of Arc, who has been used by both right and left, collaborators and resisters, as a French national icon, so the life and death of Jan Hus have been contested ideological territory, lending themselves to co-option both by the regime in power and by the opponents of that power. In the late 1940s and 1950s, when the newly installed Communists were locked in combat with the Catholic Church, Hus and the Hussite tradition of opposition to Rome were taken over by the otherwise aggressively atheistic ruling regime. It was the Communists who, between 1950 and 1953, were responsible for the scrupulous reconstruction of Bethlehem Chapel which, having been bought by the Jesuits in 1661, had been demolished when they, in their turn, in an ironic repetition-cum-reversal of the flight of Comenius, had been expelled from the Czech lands by the Austrian Archduchess Maria Theresa in 1773. The fact that the German Anabaptist Thomas Münzer, regarded as a proto-Communist by the regime, had also preached at the chapel in 1521 was further justification for rebuilding the fountainhead of Czech Ultraquism as a disguised Stalinist shrine to the struggle not just with Catholicism but, ultimately, with Christianity as such.

Having turned the Hussite tradition against their adversaries, the Communists could not, however, prevent its being given a further twist of the ideological ratchet and turned back against them by other, later opponents. The essence of Hussitism was opposition to the hierarchies and corruption of power, leading to a fundamental

Bethlehem Chapel

ambiguity in the many works of art—novels, plays, paintings, sculptures, music—which, under the Communist regime, celebrated his martyrdom and that of many of his followers. Take, for example, the impressive choral work *Epistola de M. Hieronymi de Praga supplicio* by Svatopluk Havelka (born 1925), first performed in 1984, which sets to music a letter written by a member of the Council of Constance, one Poggio Bracciolini, on the subject of the trial and execution of the Hussite Hieronymus of Prague in 1416. Poggio's letter records verbatim the preacher's speech of self-defense before his accusers and includes such incendiary denunciations (in Latin in both the original and musical setting) as the following:

> *What iniquity is this! Three hundred and forty days have I been kept in a dismal and dank dungeon, in filth, squalor, excrement, in shackles, in want and lack of all things… I myself am but a little man, feeble and faint, whose head is now at stake… Thus also St. Stephen was stoned to death by a pack of priests, the Apostles all were condemned to death not as men innocent and good but as rebels of the people, defamers of the Lord and evil malefactors of villainies…*

No half-aware listener to Havelka's composition—and Czech audiences under Communism were alert as no others to possible sub-texts and allegories—could mistake the analogies between 1416 and, date of all dates, 1984. Signatories of Charter 77 were being routinely harassed and excluded from public life, its leading figure Václav Havel had only recently been released, for reasons of health, from four years in prison and another Chartist, the philosopher Jan Patočka had, like a latter-day Socrates (also referred to in Hieronymus' speech), died after being ruthlessly interrogated by the secret police in March 1977. The whole of Havel's political philosophy of "living in the truth", discussed in detail in Chapter Six, was a deliberate echo of Hus' own *Pravda vítězí*. Likewise, his conception of "the power of the powerless", elaborated in a famous essay of that title published in *samizdat* form in 1978, deals, precisely, with the possibility of the "little man, feeble and faint" living a life of personal authenticity even under the most total of so-called "post-totalitarian" regimes. "Seek the truth, hear the truth, learn the truth, speak the truth, hold the truth and defend the truth unto death," Hus had instructed his followers. By canonizing Hus as a social and political radical in the early 1950s, the Communists of the time had, inadvertently, opened the way for his becoming the oppositional focus of the 1960s, 1970s and 1980s.

"This nation, do what it may, has Master Jan Hus in its genes," wrote the novelist Bohumil Hrabal (1914-97) in November 1990, a year after the final collapse of the Communist regime. Small wonder, then, that his statue became a place of pilgrimage and shrine during the spring and summer of 1968, especially on the anniversary of his death (July 6) and then, inevitably, a place of collective mourning after the new Bílá hora of August 21/22. Inevitable, too, that in November 1989 and for some months thereafter, his monument was, according once more to Hrabal's testimony, to be seen almost permanently

> *crawling with young people, all over the steps, even on the plinth, anywhere you can sit, you find these young people. Master Jan Hus has rock groups in front of him, young people sitting on the steps writing postcards and greetings from Prague on their knees, even quite tiny children under the eyes of their parents scrambling up under the auspices of various gaunt ascetic mystics, who ushered our nation into a new era in the name of their revered Master. This monument was a kind of promissory note, redeemable only during the Velvet Revolution, when Rafael Kubelík conducted his symphony orchestra in Smetana's Má vlast.*

The Velvet Revolution was the re-conquest of Prague by its citizens, the reinvestment, after forty years of exclusion, of its public spaces by, in particular, those under thirty. Its hero and inspiration was Hus, and it marched, characteristically, to the mingled strains of the Hussite anthem "Ye Who Are God's Warriors", Smetana's 1874-9 masterpiece of Bohemian nationalism, and the once banned music of the local punk rock band, Plastic People of the Universe. Against such a concert of voices and styles, the Jericho of Communism collapsed overnight.

A Tradition of Defenestration

Hus was, at best, a reluctant revolutionary, but the Communists were not wrong in promoting the social and political egalitarianism implicit in his teaching and explicit in the words and actions of many of his followers. After his death, relations between his supporters and the combined forces of Church and State deteriorated rapidly and erupted into open warfare in 1419. At the same time, the Hussites themselves split into moderate and radical factions, the former dominating the Old Town and the latter the New. The conflict came to a head in July 1419 when a mob led by Jan Želivský, the radical preacher at the Church of Our Lady of the Snows close to Wenceslas Square, stormed the New Town Hall on Charles Square and, capturing several town councilors hostile to their cause, threw them to their deaths out of an upper-story window. It inaugurated Prague's unlovely tradition of defenestration, which in various forms has survived up to the present (in 1997 Bohumil Hrabal fell to his death out of a hospital window, allegedly when leaning too far out to feed the pigeons), and led to Želivský becoming, effectively, the religious tyrant of the city until he was overthrown and executed in 1422. A plaque on the Old Town Hall commemorates his name, presumably mounted by the Communists as part of their policy of recuperating Czech religious history for their own anti-religious ends.

The Hussite Wars continued, off and on, until 1436, by which time the moderate faction, under its one-eyed (and eventually blind) military commander Jan Žižka, had both compelled Church and State to recognize its right to receive communion in both kinds and defeated its radical rival. This sect had been based after 1422 in the fortified hill town of Tábor to the south, where, for a time, a kind of primitive

Christian Communism was practiced, complete with sharing of property and, in the extreme case of the Adamites, exponents of integral nudism as a sign of God's grace, of marital partners as well. In 1458 a Hussite supporter, George of Poděbrady, was even elected King of Bohemia, and promptly had a huge golden chalice, underwritten with the equally huge words *Pravda vítězí*, mounted on the frontispiece of Our Lady before Tyn. Just as promptly, the victorious Catholic party had it melted down after White Mountain, refashioning the ore into the triumphalist image of the Virgin mentioned above.

Progressively, the Hussites fragmented into fissiparous sects, most notably the pacifist Community of Brethren to which Comenius would belong, or, in the sixteenth century, amalgamated with the new and fully Protestant churches originating mainly in Germany. In the Bohemia over which Rudolf II (1576-1611) reigned as part of his immense territories, only one subject in eight belonged to the orthodox Roman communion. Rudolf publicly endorsed the various treaties and agreements that granted religious freedoms to Protestant, Hussite and Hussite-derived churches, but privately favored re-catholicization, a policy openly pursued by his successors Mathias and Ferdinand of Styria who became King of Bohemia in 1618. Ferdinand's anti-Protestant measures led directly to the second (or, according to some computations, third or even fourth) defenestration of Prague, discussed later in the section on Hradčany, which, in its turn, led somewhat less directly, to the Battle of White Mountain two years later. Following their defeat, twenty-seven Protestant leaders were executed, beheaded or hanged according to rank, on Old Town Square on July 21, 1621, the public executioner Jan Mlydár establishing some kind of personal best or all-comers Bohemian record that probably stood until the far more terrible bloodbath at Lidice in 1942. The heads of some of the victims were publicly displayed on Charles Bridge for more than ten years, the tongue of one (Johannes Jessenius, rector of Charles University) having been ripped out before he was executed and later nailed to his head. An anonymous pro-Catholic poem, published in 1621, celebrated the bloodbath as follows:

Twelve heads upon the Bridge Tower
were set before men's eyes,

that all the world should witness
and all should recognize
who sinned against the King,
the ill-fated Directors
who caused the suffering.

At the crossroads of the city
the quartered bodies lay:
and others suffered despite,
whose hands were chopped away
to purge their treachery—
the fingers raised in falsehood
that pledged their loyalty.
      ("The Execution")

The victims are commemorated by twenty-seven white crosses set into the pavement in front of the Old Town Hall, close to a plaque marked simply "Dukla" in memory of the pass in Slovakia where 80,000 Soviet troops and Czechoslovak partisans died fighting the German occupiers: truly Czech history is a history of successive martyrdoms and massacres.

Before the Europe-wide war begun by the defenestration of Prague ended in 1648, the city had twice been occupied by invading Swedish troops, the second time just months before the signing of the Peace of Westphalia brought hostilities to a close. Malá Strana and Hradčany were seized, and the occupying force made off with the best part of Rudolf II's fabulous art collection stowed in its wagons: its return to Prague is still a source of bitter dispute between the governments of the two countries. To celebrate the city's deliverance from the Swedes, the municipal authorities erected a column surmounted by the inevitable statue of Our Lady in the middle of Old Town Square where it stood, isolated and unrivaled, until the inauguration of the Hus monument in 1915. Three years later, on the declaration of Czech independence, it was torn down by the celebrating crowd as too blatant a symbol of three centuries of Austrian-Habsburg domination. The poet Jaroslav Seifert (1901-86), the only Czech writer to have received the Nobel Prize for Literature (in 1984), was present at the time, and was amazed many years later to find the head of the Virgin in the home of his fellow poet, the reclusive Vladimír Holan (1905-80):

On a low cabinet by the door
I caught sight of the cast of a female head.
Good Lord, I've seen this before!
It was lying there, resting upon its face
as if under a guillotine.

It was the head of the Virgin Mary
from Old Town Square.
It had been toppled by pilgrims
when exactly sixty years ago
they returned from the White Mountain.

They overturned the column with the four armed angels
on which she stood.
It was nowhere as high
as the Vendôme in Paris.

May they be forgiven.
It towered there as a memento of defeat and shame
for the Czech nation
and the pilgrims were a little high
on the first breath of freedom.

I was there with them
and the head from the broken column
rolled over the pavement
near where I was standing.
When it came to a halt
Her pious eyes were gazing
upon my dusty boots.

Now it came rolling up to me
a second time.

between those two moments lay
almost an entire human life
that was my own.
I'm not saying it was a happy one
but it is now at an end.

Jaroslav Seifert, "The Head of the Virgin Mary" (1978)

Goltz-Kinský palace

There is one other building that requires our attention before we leave Old Town Square for other parts of the city. Just to the east of the Hus monument stands the eighteenth-century Goltz-Kinský palace, designed like so many of the finest Baroque buildings in Prague by Kilian Ignaz Dientzenhofer (1689-1751), also responsible for the Church of St. Nicholas in the northwest corner of the square. The palace has two main claims to fame. First, it was here that Hermann

Kafka ran a haberdashery shop on the ground floor and where his only son Franz attended the German Gymnasium upstairs from 1893 to 1901. More recently, it was from the balcony of the palace that, in February 1948, the Communist leader Klement Gottwald addressed thousands of supporters on the morrow of the "elegant coup"—*Vítězný únor* (Victorious February) in official regime-speak—which ushered in forty-one years of Communist rule. The scene is memorably, if that is the word, captured on the opening page of Milan Kundera's *The Book of Laughter and Forgetting* (1978):

> *In February 1948, Communist leader Klement Gottwald stepped out on the balcony of a Baroque palace in Prague to address the hundreds of thousands of his fellow citizens packed into Old Town Square. It was a crucial moment in Czech history—a fateful moment of the kind that occurs once or twice in a millennium. Gottwald was flanked by his comrades, with Clementis standing next to him. There were snow flurries, it was cold, and Gottwald was bareheaded. The solicitous Clementis took off his own fur cap and set it on Gottwald's head. The Party propaganda section put out hundreds of thousands of copies of a photograph of that balcony with Gottwald, a fur cap on his head and comrades at his side, speaking to the nation. On that balcony the history of Communist Czechoslovakia was born. Every child knew the photograph from posters, schoolbooks, and museums. Four years later Clementis was charged with treason and hanged. The propaganda section immediately airbrushed him out of history and, obviously, out of all the photographs as well. Ever since, Gottwald has stood on that balcony alone. Where Clementis once stood, there is only bare palace wall. All that remains of Clementis is the cap on Gottwald's head.*

Gottwald's borrowed fur hat curiously echoes Hus' heretic's cap, and Clementis' fate is eerily prefigured in the scene of martyrdom commemorated directly beneath him. One night in January 1989, after leaving his favorite watering-hole, *U zlatého tygra* (The Golden Tiger), on Husova street, Bohumil Hrabal was heading back home across Old Town Square when he was struck by the sight of Hus' shadow against the brightly lit pink-and-beige wall of the Goltz-Kinský palace. It was as though the specter of freedom was haunting the balcony from which unfreedom had been proclaimed forty years earlier. At that very moment there came the sound of a flute—a magic flute indeed—that seemed to float up from the very heart of the monument, from the point where its "vertical message unfurls... 'I believe that the rule of the people of Thy cause will return again into Thy hands...'" It is the first of Hrabal's famous "Letters to Dubenka", addressed to the American student April Gifford, "April" in Czech being "duben", the "oak month", and the sound of the magic flute wafting across Old

Town Square on a January night presages all the extraordinary changes of the coming twelve months.

Before taking our final leave of the square, let us glance up Pařížská, the would-be Parisian boulevard that runs out of it to the north, leading across the Vltava to the city's famous Letná Park. There, high up on the hill, a huge metronome oscillates day and night, a figure of post-modern meaninglessness contrasting so markedly with the semiotic density of the city below. But there is point, of a kind, to its pointlessness, for it was on this very site that, for a time, the "world's largest statue" reared up its ninety-foot-high mass of granite, a full 14,200 metric tons of mystification and menace. Designed by Jiří Štursa and sculpted by Otakar Švec, the statue depicted, inevitably, an immense messianic Stalin leading his flock, Czechs on one side, Soviets on the other, towards a Land of Marxist Milk and Honey. Cynical Praguers apparently called it *tlačenice*, the crush, because of the procession's all too close resemblance to the bread lines of the time.

The monument was inaugurated on May 1, 1955, but within a year Stalin had been denounced by Krushchev at the Twentieth Congress of the Soviet Communist Party and, like a bolshevized version of Mozart's Commendatore, the statue remained to haunt the city for a further seven years (not that the unreconstructed Stalinists of the Czech Communist leadership minded a jot) until it was blown up in a series of explosions spread over two weeks in 1962. But by then the Moloch had already devoured the lives of its creator and his wife. In the face of criticisms by friends for his accepting the commission, Švec's wife committed suicide in 1953, and in 1955, just before his work's inauguration, Švec followed suit, reputedly leaving his fee to a school for blind children, in atonement for having inflicted such an eyesore on his fellow Praguers. It is a further link in the theme of blindness curiously present or implied in and around Old Town Square (John of Luxembourg, Master Hanuš and his twelve blind apostles, one-eyed and then sightless Jan Žižka, the unseeing eyes of Jan Hus sweeping the scene, the severed head of Our Lady and those of the Protestant martyrs mounted on Charles Bridge) and confirms the main conclusion of this preliminary reading of one of Prague's principal *lieux de mémoire*: this, before all else, is a city whose history has been marked by sacrifice and suffering, and in which every change of regime—even, as we shall see, its (rightly) much-lauded Velvet Revolution of 1989—has brought in its wake a procession of real or symbolic victims.

Charles Bridge

Having picked his or her way through the labyrinth of streets between Old Town Square and the river, having dodged, insofar as it is possible, the endless distributors of leaflets advertising puppet versions of *Don Giovanni* and performances of *Má vlast* and Dvořák's "New World" Symphony, having uneasily skirted past beggars crouched on all fours in prayerful supplication, a few pathetic crowns or valueless hellers in the plastic coffee cups before them, the visitor debouches onto Charles Bridge. He or she will have followed, knowingly or not, part of the traditional coronation route, the so-called King's Way, that took Kings

of Bohemia from Old Town Square to the Castle on their accession to the throne.

To the right of the cobbled esplanade that leads to the bridge stands a nineteenth-century neo-Gothic statue of Emperor Charles IV (1346-78), who inaugurated the building of the bridge on July 9, 1357 but whose name was not formally given to it until 1870; for half a millennium it was known simply as the Stone or Prague Bridge. The great Gothic tower that gives access to the bridge, the work of the gifted Peter Parler of Gmünd (died 1399) who also built St. Vitus Cathedral, bears mannikin-like statues of Charles IV and his son Wenceslas IV flanking St. Vitus at the center and, above them, two more of Bohemia's numerous patron saints, Adalbert and Sigismund. For ten or more years after 1621, the east face of the tower also flaunted the severed heads of the Protestant martyrs, suspended in iron baskets the better to be seen by the still predominantly non-Catholic population.

What opens up beyond the tower can only be described as the most semiotically loaded, if contradictory, five hundred yards of thoroughfare in any European city. It is necessary to proceed with patience and attention, and to pause before at least a dozen of the thirty evenly-spaced statues that, over the centuries, have overseen the transit of millions from Old City to the Lesser, and vice versa. A schematic plan of their lay-out will make the following discussion much clearer. (It should be noted that the statues with odd numbers are to one's right as one crosses from the Old City to Malá Strana.)

Old Town Bridge

(1)	Madonna with St. Bernard	St. Ivo	(2)
(3)	Madonna with SS. Dominic and Thomas Aquinas	SS. Barbara, Margaret and Elizabeth	(4)
(5)	The Crucifixion	Pietą	(6)
(7)	St. Anne	St. Joseph	(8)
(9)	SS. Cyril and Methodius (formerly St. Ignatius Loyala)	St. Francis Xavier	(10)
(11)	Baptism of Christ	St. Christopher	(12)
(13)	St. Norbert	St. Francis Borgia	(14)
(15)	St. John of Nepomuk	SS. Wenceslas and Ludmilla	(16)
(17)	St. Antony of Padua	St. Francis of Assisi	(18)
(19)	St. Jude Thaddaeus	SS. Vincent Ferrer and Procopius	(20)
(21)	St. Augustine	St. Nicholas of Tolentino	(22)
(23)	St. Cajetan	St. Lutgard	(24)
(25)	St. Philip Benizi	St. Adalbert	(26)
(27)	St. Vitus	SS. John of Matha, Felix of Valois and Ivan	(28)
(29)	Christ between SS. Cosmas and Damian	St. Wenceslas	(30)

Visiting Prague in the late 1890s, the French sculptor Antoine Bourdelle described Charles Bridge as an architectural centaur: Gothic below, Baroque above, the two halves, the bridge and its statues, being separated from each other not only by over three centuries in time but, from the Bohemian point of view, by religious revolution, military defeat, and the comprehensive loss of political sovereignty. But the real situation is even more complicated, for, of the thirty present statues, only fifteen are the actual original works (4-5, 7, 14-17, 19-20, 23-5, 27-9), five are nineteenth-century copies of eighteenth-century originals (6, 8, 11, 13, 18), seven are twentieth-century copies of eighteen-century originals (1-3, 10, 21-22, 26), two are completely new nineteenth-century works (12, 30), and one (9) is an original work completed as late as 1938. Nor, contrary to widespread belief, were the statues erected by the triumphant Austro-Catholics in the *immediate* aftermath of their victory at the Battle of White Mountain. Indeed, it was only in the 1650s that the earliest of the present statues, the Crucifixion (5), was erected, and then only to replace the original fourteenth-century Crucifixion that had been demolished by a well-aimed Swedish cannonball in 1648. The fact that the replacement was a 1628 work imported from Dresden suggests that, at this stage, there was no plan to create anything resembling the present avenue of statues, either for aesthetic or ideological reasons. In 1696, it is true, the new Crucifixion was given an emphatic political, not to say racist, twist when a local Jew was convicted of having turned his back on the statue and bowed (thus, presumably, presenting his posterior to the Messiah—the Christians' Messiah, that is, not his own), and was punished by having to pay for the present gilded inscription which runs in a semi-circle from one tip of the cross to the other and, in Hebrew, declares: "Holy, holy, holy, Lord God of Hosts." The original target of the statuary of Charles Bridge was thus not the Protestant, but a far older, enemy: the Jew.

Nor is it true that all the original statues were Jesuit-sponsored and Jesuit-inspired. Other religious orders—Cistercians, Premonstratensians, Trinitarians, Dominicans, Augustinians—were involved, and at least one of the statues, that of St. Ivo (2) on the immediate left as one enters the bridge from the Old Town side, was commissioned by a secular corporation, St. Ivo being the patron saint of lawyers. Most of the original statues were commissioned, carved and placed in position between 1707 and 1714 under Emperors Joseph I (1705-11) and Charles VI (1711-40) at a time when, possibly because they were involved in a European-wide war (the War of Spanish Succession 1702-13), the

Habsburgs were anxious to placate the non-German populations of their patchwork empire. In 1709, for example, not only were over five hundred churches returned to their original Lutheran congregations in Silesia, but an imperial decree strictly prohibited "all reproach and remembering of long forgotten misgivings as to the Bohemian Estates"—in other words, don't talk about the (Thirty Years') war, it does so upset the Bohemians. A time of relative liberalism and attempted reconciliation was hardly the moment to embark upon a display of Austro-Catholic triumphalism. Whatever their

The "Trinitarians"

ideological message (and they are surely not mere ornamental additions), the statues are most unlikely to be saying anything as crude and provocative as: Get down, you heretics, and stay down.

Things become more curious still when we learn that the sculptor of six of the statues (4, 6, 8, 11, 13, 15), the celebrated Jan Brokoff (1652-1718), was originally a German-speaking Lutheran from Slovakia who claimed to have undergone a conversion to Roman Catholicism in 1682. This occurred even as he was working on the most famous of all the statues, that of the "martyr" John of Nepomuk who would be canonized in 1729 almost four hundred years after his death and be sedulously promoted, and accepted, as the new patron saint of the Czechs. There are suggestions, however, that Brokoff's conversion was more one of convenience than conviction—like so many, in other words, that took place in seventeenth-century Bohemia—and that, deep down, he may have remained loyal to, and returned to, his original Lutheran persuasions. The question is doubly important because Brokoff's two sons, Michael Jan Josef (1686-1721) and Ferdinand Maximilian (1688-1731), were also sculptors of talent—or more than talent in the case of Ferdinand Maximilian—and, singly or jointly, were responsible for seven of the statues (9, 10, 14, 20, 18—Ferdinand

Maximilian alone), 27 (Michael alone), 26 (together). In addition, Ferdinand Maxmilian collaborated with his father on the statue of St. Norbert (13). On his statue of St. Francis Xavier (10), founder of the Jesuit Order in the Far East, Ferdinand Maximilian took the unusual step of depicting himself to the saint's left, as one of his two young assistants, holding his master's biretta but also the Bible, the ultimate source of *Protestant* (but not Catholic) authority. The original was swept away by floodwater in 1890, and only fragments remain, the present statue being a copy completed in 1913 by Vincenc Vosmík. But a 1714 engraving of Ferdinand Maxmilian's original (1711) design shows the sculptor *looking away from* the Jesuits' most revered saint after their founder St. Ignatius Loyola, while his fellow assistant, like the Indian chief who kneels on the plinth, looks fixatedly at him; something of Ferdinand Maximilian's incongruous isolation remains in Vosmík's reproduction. Is the sculptor saying—necessarily indirectly and covertly—that he does not share his Jesuit sponsors' enthusiasm for their number two saint? Is this a critique, rather than a celebration, of Jesuit triumphalism? Is there a crypto-Protestant element present in this work and, by extension, in the whole avenue of statues as well?

Once we entertain this possibility, or something similar to it, "reading" the statues on Charles Bridge becomes decidedly more complex and intriguing. What is consciously constructed at one level— a celebration of Austro-Catholic power—may be being deconstructed at another, deeper, level, either deliberately, or unconsciously through the interplay of the combined, but contending, signifiers present. Or, to put it more simply, the message intended by the statues' (Austro-Catholic) sponsors may not be the same message as that being picked up by their (primarily Czech) "consumers", who, in many cases, were recent, and perhaps reluctant, converts to Catholicism, or maybe not really Catholics at all.

Nepomuk: Ambiguous Icon

Take, for example, the most famous of the statues, that of "Saint" John Nepomuk (15, in Czech Jan Nepomucký). The earliest of the present statues other than the Crucifixion (5) that replaced an earlier work, Nepomuk was raised to his present eminence at the center of the bridge in 1683, a full 38 years *before* his beatification in 1721, followed by almost instant canonization in 1729. There seems little doubt that the Jesuits wanted and needed a *local* Catholic martyr and saint to counter the still powerful memory of Master Jan Hus (to say nothing of the Protestants executed in 1621), that they figuratively sifted through the possible candidates and came up with the dubious and contentious figure of John of Pomuk. The "real" John of Pomuk fell victim to the conflict between Church and State that raged under the reign of the notorious wastrel Wenceslas IV (1378-1419), though neither he, nor, above all, the cause for which he died, was exactly holy in character. In 1393 the conflict between the Emperor and the Archbishop of Prague came to a head over a controversial church appointment, and John of Pomuk, the Archbishop's Vicar General, was arrested and tortured on the Emperor's orders, along with two other church officials, who duly signed an affidavit denying any mistreatment. John, however, died of his wounds before he could sign, and his corpse was thrown off Charles Bridge into the Vltava to get rid of the evidence.

This sordid story of Church-State jostling for power was rewritten as follows by the fourteenth-century Church. John was tortured by the jealous and suspicious Wenceslas when he refused to divulge what the Queen had revealed to him in confession. Still saying nothing, he was thrown, bound and gagged but very much alive, off the bridge, a cluster of stars appearing over the spot in the river where he was drowned: he had said "No" to the Emperor's sacrilegious attack on the seal of the confessional, whence the nickname of Ne-pomuk, the No man from Pomuk, *ne* being, of course, the Czech word for No. His body—or, at least, *a* body—was retrieved and interred; he was used for a time by the Church in its struggle with secular power, but little was heard of him between the end of the fourteenth century and the middle of the seventeenth, when he was discursively resurrected by the Church to meet new ideological needs.

In 1641, at the height of the Thirty Years' War, the Jesuit Jiří Plachý published a biography of Nepomuk in Latin, German and Czech, followed, in 1680, by a eulogistic history by another Jesuit Bohuslav Balbín (1621-88). The fact that Nepomuk had supposedly been martyred in defense of confession was particularly relevant and convenient, for the sacrament of penance was notoriously detested and contested by the Protestant enemy, and, indeed, by their Hussite forerunners. It is to be noted that both of Nepomuk's earliest encomiasts were not Germans but Czechs, Balbín being indeed the author of one of the first defenses of the Czech language, a work which, for political reasons, was not published until 1775. In short, Balbín was an early variety of Czech nationalist, writing of the "once happy but now grievous state of the Kingdom of Bohemia", and ending his defense and illustration of his first language with a rousing quotation from the medieval St. Wenceslas chorale: *Nedej zahynouti nám I budoucím!* Do not let us or our descendants perish! All this suggests, once again, the complexity of what is going on along Charles Bridge. The statues are *not*, to repeat, an attack on Bohemian traditions and identity, but an attempt to co-opt and, if necessary, reinvent those traditions in the cause of the counter-reformation Church and so refashion, but not suppress, Bohemian identity in the interests of Austro-Catholic hegemony. It was less a negation of Bohemian-ness than an attempted recuperation of its past for use in the present and future, a delicate project that opened up the possibility of multiple (mis) readings.

The statue itself is the work of Jan Brokoff, based on a terra-cotta model by the Viennese sculptor Matthias Rauchmüller and brings together the principal iconographical features of the hundreds, even thousands, of Nepomuks that would be produced over the decades and centuries to come: a halo of stars around an inclined and biretta'd head, a stylized palm frond in the right hand, and a large crucifix clutched at an angle across the chest. It is notable, however, that the head of Brokoff's Nepomuk, though still inclined, is perceptibly more upright than that of Rauchmüller's model, and his whole body pose considerably more vertical than that which became current in the eighteenth century, as in the hundreds of Nepomuks turned out by the workshop of Ignác František Platzer (1717-87), which was still operating, and still in the family, around 1900. The standard Platzer-style Nepomuk bends sideways at the waist, often to a depth that defies anatomical possibility. The upper body and head arch over the crucifix which is raised to shoulder height until the saint and his Savior seem almost to kiss. Brokoff's Nepomuk, however, looks straight ahead, holding the crucifix well down his chest. Though frail, he is altogether more sharply defined, more upright, more virile than the mass-produced statues and statuettes, all feminine curves and tearful embraces, that later flooded the market. It still just has something Gothic, dare one say "Protestant", about it.

On the pedestal were mounted two bronze reliefs, almost certainly *not* Brokoff's work, one depicting Nepomuk confessing the Queen while her husband, stroking the head of a mastiff (a reference, presumably, to his violence and addiction to the hunt), looks jealously on. The other shows him being thrown from the bridge while in the foreground—an obvious echo of the Massacre of the Innocents—a soldier attacks a mother and child who have had the misfortune to witness the murder.

The statue undoubtedly aided the campaign for Nepomuk's beatification which duly took place in 1721, two years after his tomb had been opened and, miracle of miracles, his tongue, pink and fresh as on the day he was born, discovered intact in the earth-filled buccal cavity of his skull. The relic—it appears it was really a fragment of brain tissue—was paraded with much pomp and circumstance at the office of beatification, and is supposedly contained in the monumentally ugly solid silver tomb of the "saint" in St. Vitus Cathedral; certainly there is something vaguely fleshy and pink displayed in a glass casket, and an inevitable cherub makes meaningful gestures towards it. How could this miraculously preserved "tongue" not remind at least some history-conscious Praguers of the tongue of the wretched Johannes Jessenius a century before, ripped from his mouth, then nailed to his severed head and publicly exhibited for ten years or more? But, then, did not the "depontification" of Nepomuk curiously resemble the various defenestrations of the city's turbulent past? Was not the whole beatification process a reminder of the martyrdom of Hus, precisely the memory which the Church sought to counter and suppress?

Of the extent and intensity of the cult of Nepomuk over the following two centuries there can be little doubt, even if its meaning remains ambivalence itself. Czech-speakers undoubtedly identified with the pseudo-saint so deliberately manufactured for their consumption, and, typically, Hašek's drunken chaplain Father Katz exhibits "yearnings for martyrdom" in his cups and confusedly asks Švejk to "cut off his head and throw him in a sack into the Vltava." "'Some stars round my head would suit me very well,' he said with enthusiasm. 'I should need ten.'" Beginning in 1771, a Nepomuk festival took place annually in Prague on May 16, and droves of Czech-speaking peasants flocked to the city for the occasion. But whom or what were they celebrating? A fourteenth-century "martyr" or themselves and their Czechness? Almost certainly the latter, if an alleged prayer recorded by the nineteenth-century poet Boleslav Jablonský (1813-81) is anything to go by: "Saint Jan, you who know the value of the tongue [*jazyk*], protect for us our golden jewel, protect for us our language [also *jazyk*]." The key images of tongue, language and alchemical gold are rolled into one: it is in the crucible of the mouth that the Philosophers' Stone of identity is formed. Perhaps, in the mind of both populace and elite, Nepomuk the bogus nay-sayer became the double of the genuine refusenik, Jan Hus, rather than the alternative that the Church clearly planned. A figure intended to strengthen Austro-Catholic hegemony by clothing it in Czech garb became, in time, a symbol of Czech cultural, linguistic and political distinctness. Nepomuk was a hagiological hoax—even the Vatican recognized his spuriousness in 1963—but it was a hoax that catastrophically rebounded against the forces that devised it.

Subversive Statues

Once one starts to look at Charles Bridge in this way, virtually every statue begins to yield ambiguities, double meanings and, if not subversive intentions, then at least potentially subversive results. Thus Ferdinand Maximilian Brokoff's unexplained and unenthusiastic presence undermines the missionary triumphalism of the statue of St. Francis Xavier (10), while that of Saints Barbara, Margaret and Elizabeth (4, Jan Brokoff, 1707) is undercut by the chalice, with its inevitable reminder of Hussitism, that St. Barbara holds. The statue of Saints Vincent Ferrer and Procopius (20, Ferdinand Maxmilian Brokoff, 1712), possibly the finest, artistically, of the whole sequence, is rendered almost comical by the inordinate claims it makes for its subjects. High on their pedestal supported by an emblematic Saracen, Jewish Rabbi and sulking pointy-eared Demon with a curious quiff which the viewer is obviously invited to equate with each other, the two saints tower above an assortment of devils they have triumphed over, or souls they have saved. A plaque over the Turk's turban-clad head declares that St. Vincent brought "8000 Saracenas ad fidem catholicam", while above the subdued hooded Rabbi, the statistic "2500 Judaeos ad Christum" is appended. "Resuscitavit 40" announces another, while St. Procopius scores even higher in the salvation stakes: "Convertuit 100,000 peccatores." Surely some eighteenth-century forerunner of Švejk would have seen through the fatuousness of such claims, and, like the reprobate Jew, have presented his ample bottom to the sanctified pair.

But the most ambiguous of all the statues is that of Saints John of Matha, Felix of Valois and Ivan (28, Ferdinand Maxmilian Brokoff, 1714), none of them exactly familiar names, and with no obvious reason for being brought together. John and Felix were the twelfth-century founders of the Order of Trinitarians which commissioned the statue. Their mother house was at Cerfroy in France, hence the stag (Latin *cervus*=deer) that peers over the pedestal, a crucifix firmly planted between its antlers. The stag in its turn suggested to the sculptor or his sponsors the figure of St. Ivan, a local Bohemian saint whose iconographical signature was a wounded hind. Once again, the intention seems to have been to provide a Bohemian link with two foreign clerics, and so "indigenize" the religious order they founded.

But it is what lies beneath the three saints, on the pedestal, that is so enormously suggestive. The original mission of the Trinitarian Order was to ransom Christians who fell into the hands of the Infidel, and three prisoners are duly presented, wailing and in fetters, locked in a dungeon set into the pediment, while a fiendish guard-dog barks at them through an iron grille. To the left, a pot-bellied Turk, at once sadistic and bored, the very picture of mustachioed corruption, languidly leans against the cell wall, while, above the iron grille, an escutcheon shows two prisoners being unchained by a visiting angel. Higher still, a broken pair of handcuffs dangles from the hand of St. Felix. As a parable of oppression, reclusion and (eventual) liberation, the massive monument could hardly be bettered, but, like all parables, not least parables in stone, it by definition permits more than one interpretation. The imprisoned Christians could all too easily be read as an image of conquered Bohemia (and, later, of Nazi- or Soviet-dominated Czechoslovakia), while it would take little imagination to substitute the Austrian, the Nazi or the Communist, either local or foreign, for the overweight oriental who holds them in thrall. And so it turned out in 1948 (ironically), 1968 and 1989: on each occasion the iron grille was torn off by demonstrators, and the three howling prisoners metaphorically released.

More generally, any image of suffering and woe—and Charles Bridge is an open-air chamber of martyrological horrors—could be turned against its authors and read as an allegory of the state of the nation that was a nation no more. Specifically, the equation of the crucified Christ and defeated Bohemia (and, correspondingly, of Golgotha and White Mountain) became almost a cliché of nineteenth-century Czech nationalism, and, as we shall see, was widely used by Czech artists under both Nazi and Communist domination. And then there is the question of style. Generally, all the statues are lumped together as "Baroque", but there is a huge difference between the statues made by Jan and Ferdinand Maximilian Brokoff and, in particular, the Saint Lutgard (24, 1710) by Ferdinand Maximilian's great rival, Matthias Bernard Braun (1684-1738). A brilliant sculptor, Braun was Italian-trained and patently an admirer of Bernini, and his St. Lutgard is a Teresa of Avila transported from Rome to the banks of the Vltava. His subject was a blind thirteenth-century Cistercian nun (note the motif of blindness once more) who, in an ecstatic inner vision, saw the wound in her Savior's side open up, and His heart pass into hers, and hers into His. Only one of Christ's hands is nailed to the Cross, while the other enfolds the nun in passionate embrace. It is a typical piece of Baroque erotico-mystical fusion, in which a feminized Christ and female disciple swoon rapturously together, and on-looking cherubs buss each other in imitation of their bliss. St. Lutgard's robes ripple with Bernini-esque suppleness, as she lovingly places her hand on His knee: their eyes meet and merge as only lovers' do.

Nothing could be further removed from the severe, at times almost rigid, dignity of the Brokoffs' sculptural style, in which straight lines predominate over curves, and whose whole character is reflective rather than emotive. There is nothing in any of their statues of the unadulterated Jesuit triumphalism that positively *erupts* in the Dientzenhofers' Church of St. Nicholas in Malá Strana, built between

1704 and 1755. Here Platzer's St. Ignatius gleefully spears some hapless recumbent with a gilded thunderbolt, St. Cyril of Alexandria bludgeons another with the butt of his crozier, various other heathens and heretics are trampled under foot, and hordes of gamboling *putti* clap their little hands at the thrill of it all. Moreover, apart from Jan Brokoff's Pietą (6), a lifeless, conventional work even in the original, and his group statue of Saints Barbara, Margaret and Elizabeth (4), all of the female-dominated statues on the bridge, above all those featuring the Madonna, are by Braun or the competent but uninspired Matthias Wenzel Jäckel. The Brokoffs' work is unquestionably more "masculine" than "feminine"—even Jan's three female saints have a severe and angular aspect—and only once, in Ferdinand Maximilian's St. Cajetan (23, 1709), did they indulge in the stone "bobbles" so beloved of an out-and-out Baroque sculptor like Braun. Overall, the Brokoffs' work might be described as much more Bohemian-Gothic than Italian-Baroque, closer to the *Sondergotik*, or "special Gothic", of Peter Parler's Cathedral than to the Dientzenhofers' masterpieces of extravagance, as though in them some residual Protestantism were struggling against the plethoric over-the-top-ness of the counter-reformation vision and style. This, of course, did not stop their work being classified as Jesuit-inspired propaganda in stone, and when Ferdinand Maximilian's fine St. Ignatius Loyola (1711) was swept off the bridge by a flood in 1890, Czech nationalists insisted that it be replaced not by a copy but by the politically correct missionaries to the Slavs, Saints Cyril and Methodius (9), a very dull work by Karel Dvořák, ten years in the making, that was finally mounted in its present position during the Czechs' *annus horribilis*, 1938.

Hradčany: Nationhood and Diversity

Whereas Charles Bridge only reveals its inconsistencies of style and vision on close inspection, even the most casual observer quickly grasps that the castle and cathedral are an almost impossible patchwork of styles, the latter wholly encased in the former, with only its huge steeples visible when viewed from the city below. The castle complex is bricolage from beginning to end—how could it be otherwise when it took almost a millennium to reach its present stage?—and it is easy to list, and decry, its most obviously discordant features:

- A fine Romanesque chapel, the Basilica of St. George, has been encased in a russet-and-cream Baroque facade, so that interior and exterior are utterly at variance with each other.

- The cathedral's highest steeple, the south tower, is Gothic to start with, turns Renaissance about two-thirds of the way up, and is topped by a Baroque cupola added four hundred years after the foundations were laid.

- The western half of the cathedral was begun 450 years after the eastern half was completed, work having been suspended at the outbreak of the Hussite wars and not resumed until 1873, fourteen years after a Society for Completing St. Vitus Cathedral had been set up.

- In the eighteenth century, the ancient walls of the castle were given a green-and-white cladding in the neo-classical style which effectively destroyed the castle *qua* castle, transforming it into an elegant royal residence in which, however, no king or queen ever actually lived.

- The cathedral was conceived by a Gothic architect from northern France (Matthias of Arras, d. 1352), and continued by a rather different kind of Gothic architect from Swabia (Peter Parler, d. 1399); when work was resumed after an interval of four and a half centuries, it was directed by a succession of Czech architects (Josef Krunner, Josef Mocker, Kamil Hilbert) who each had a very different conception of his task.

- The castle was given its neo-classical veneer by an Italian, Niccolo Pacassi (1716-90), who destroyed any Bohemian character it had, and when, in 1918, the castle was at last occupied by a Czech president, that president, Tomáš Masaryk, confided the task of renovating the by now dilapidated complex not to a Czech architect, or even a Slovak, but to an eccentric and unclassifiable outsider from ... Slovenia, one Josip Plečnik (1872-1957), now widely viewed as a "pre-post-modernist" of genius, who added more than a few stylistic oddities of his own.

All this is to say that Kafka's decentered allegorical castle, all outbuildings and no keep, always open in theory but impenetrable in fact (for the very good reason that there is nothing to penetrate) seems a model of order and coherence compared to the Hrad. Even now it is difficult to believe that the President of the Czech Republic actually *lives* there, secreted away like some cyber-age Rudolf II in a remote penthouse or wing in one of the many parts of the complex that are closed to the public, even though the courtyards, it seems, are open every hour of the day and the night. What or whom are they protecting, the handsome young guardsmen clad in their stylish blue uniforms designed—as is, of course, only proper under a post-modern president, a man of the theater—by Theodor Pistek, the Oscar-winning costume-designer of Miloš Forman's *Amadeus* which was shot, needless to say, on Hradčany itself? And who but a local rock musician (Michal Kocáb) could have composed the self-mocking fanfare that, every day at noon, is delivered by a brass ensemble from a first-floor window in the first courtyard? Is there anything other than facade and fashion-show, irony and pastiche? Is there any substance behind all this style?

But it was precisely its just sustainable hotchpotch of competing elements that made the castle complex so telling a replica of the motley, multi-ethnic, multi-lingual nation that, after three centuries of "darkness" (*doba temná*) was born, or reborn, in 1918. And it was Plečnik's (and perhaps Masaryk's) genius to have realized that its heterogeneities needed to be both accentuated and ironized, rather than glossed over, if it was to succeed as the more than symbolic heart of the new nation. According to Milan Kundera, speaking at the celebrated Fourth Writers' Congress in June 1967, the real beginning of what is known simplistically as "Prague spring", what defined (the then) Czechoslovakia was precisely its lack of definition, the "unobviousness", to use his word, of its existence. Hence the need for it to be continuously constructed and re-constructed through, in particular, the activities of its cultural, artistic and intellectual élites and hence too, though Kundera did not say this, the more or less continuous threat to its survival posed by this or that of its constituent groups, the so-called Sudentenland Germans and the Slovaks in the 1930s, the Slovaks again in the 1970s and, this time decisively, after 1989. What had had to be so painfully constructed could, all too easily, be deconstructed. In the same speech, Kundera evoked the irony of two most popular national beers, Budweiser (*not*, needless to say, the American decoction that masquerades under that name) and Pilsener, still being referred to by their original German names rather than as Budvar and Plzen. Indeed, Pilsener even adds the word "Urquell" (< German Ur = earliest, Quelle = source), as though its ultimate source, its true *fons et origo* is, even now, not Czech (or Bohemian) but *German*. If even the national nectar—and Czechs are by far Europe's heaviest *per capita* consumers of beer—is still, eighty years plus after independence, known by a word from the ex-occupier's language (Austrian then German), what does this tell us about Czech "national identity"?

The problem, and the accompanying irony, was there from the very beginning of the so-called national revival (*národní obrození*) of the late eighteenth and early nineteenth centuries. There is the initial irony that the seminal work on the Czech language, and the primary source of the Czech national idea, was written in German by a scholar with a German name (Josef Jungmann, 1773-1847) using the ideas of the German linguistic nationalist Herder. Similarly, the name of the author of *the* Czech-language novel of the nineteenth century, *Babička* (1855), Božena Němcová (1820-62), means literally, "Božena the German woman", and Smetana, often seen as "the most Czech" of Czech composers, actually spoke German as his first language. From the work of Jungmann and, in a more qualified form, of the great historian of Hussitism, František Palacký (1798-1876) derived the language-centered concept of Czech nationality that was to predominate throughout the nineteenth century. For this school of thought, to be Czech was to speak Czech and the history of the still-to-be-(re)born Czech nation consisted, in Palacký's words, of "the constant contact and conflict between the Slavs on the one hand and Rome and the Germans on the other." But, if only Czech-speakers were Czechs, where did this leave the millions of German-speakers who lived within the historic frontiers of Bohemia and Moravia, not to mention the tens of thousands of mainly German-speaking Jews also resident for centuries within those same frontiers, a very high proportion of them in Prague itself?

In 1918, the situation became even more complicated when the nation (re)born after three centuries of darkness consisted not, as most nationalists had expected, of just Bohemia and Moravia, but, for complex geopolitical reasons that will not be gone into here, of Slovakia as well. Historically, Slovakia had been administered as part of the Hungarian half of the Austro-Hungarian Empire, and had had no dealings of importance with Bohemia and Moravia, which had come directly under Vienna. The Czech and Slovak languages were closely related, and mutually intelligible, to each other but whether each was a separate language or, if not, which was a "dialect" of which was endlessly, and fruitlessly, debated. More important was the fact that Slovakia brought with it further linguistic minorities in the form of its Magyar-speakers in the south and Ruthenian (Ukrainian) speakers in the far eastern tip on what was now the Polish frontier. Czech nationalism had been founded on the identification of language and nation, but what actually emerged was a patchwork of languages and ethnicities: Bohemians, Moravians, Slovaks, Germans, Jews, Hungarians, Ruthenians.

There was, as it happened, an alternative to the "linguocentric" conception of Czechness that had been formulated by Jungmann and his school. This had been elaborated by Bernhard Bolzano (1781-1848) who, in a series of essays written in Czech, defended a pragmatic notion of Czech nationhood founded on the simple fact of residence: "The land in which you live is your homeland." As his name indicates, Bolzano, a mathematician, philosopher and theologian, was of mixed Czech, German and Italian origin, perhaps descended on his father's side from the many Italians who had been drawn to Prague by the massive post-1620 reconstruction as stonemasons, carpenters, painters, gilders and silversmiths. There is, keen readers of Kafka will recall, a Titorelli in *The Trial* and a Sordini in *The Castle*. Such a man would have little truck with a concept of Czech nationhood that saw it simply as a centuries-long conflict between Czech and German, whose nationalism was replete with dubious historicism and mysticism (ironically of Herderian, i.e. German, origin) and whose mono-lingualism implicitly, and often explicitly, excluded literally millions of non-Czech-speaking residents of the historic Bohemian and Moravian lands from full membership of the (still hypothetical) Czech nation. While in no way minimizing the tensions between German and Czech, Bolzano also pointed to instances of interaction and collaboration between them. Retrospectively, it is clear that Bolzano was defending, with the historical and philosophical means at his disposal, what would now be called a multi-ethnic, multi-lingual and multi-cultural definition of Czechness in which, in a democratic polity, the component groups could both retain their identity and contribute to a necessarily mixed and complex national culture.

St. Vitus Cathedral: Splendors and Miseries

When nineteenth-century Czech nationalists looked up from the Old or New towns towards Hradčany, how could they not see its dilapidated, half-finished and unoccupied state as the precise image of the wretched condition of their non-nation, and of themselves as eternal non-citizens? Thus Karel Hynek Mácha (1810-36), often called the Czech Byron, as he contemplated the "silent sleepers" in the absurdly truncated cathedral:

At the foot of each sleeping monarch a carven lion lies prone

As though spent its strength and anger, it crouched there, turned to stone.
The shadow of Bygone Glory and the Daemon of Midnight Fear

Hovered o'er the dishonoured dust of my fathers and made their sojourn there
And a sudden Ague palsied their most unhappy son.

His lips writhed back in terror, and the power of his limbs was gone.
   "Prague Cathedral" (trans. Hugh Hamilton McGoverne)

The impotence of the erstwhile and still-to-be nation deprives its "unhappy son" of his manhood. He, like the cathedral, is semi-formed, incomplete, suspended in some limbo-land between life and death, part pre-pubescent child and part living corpse.

Melancholy is the Czech's natural condition, says Bohusch, the hero of an early story by the Prague-born (and, of course, German-speaking) Rainer Maria Rilke (1875-1926): "They scarcely know how to walk than they see the gloomy figure of John of Nepomuk in front of their door, holding the crucified Christ in their arms." To which Rezek, the nationalist hero of the companion-story, *Brother and Sister* (1899), replies:

> *Our people is still in infancy. I often I say to myself that our hatred of the Germans is not at all political but rather, how shall I say… human. Our resentment comes not from the fact that we are obliged to share our homeland with the German, but that we are growing up under the thumb of a people of adults, it is that which makes us melancholic.*

The cathedral, says Bohusch, is "a signal", at once enduring and lacking: an allegory of the splendors and miseries of Czechness. Small wonder, then, that many Czech nationalists regarded the completion of the cathedral as a necessary precondition to the attainment not just of nationhood but of full adult manhood itself, or that the formation of a Society for Completing St. Vitus Cathedral in 1859 is widely regarded as second in significance only to the inauguration of the National Theater (see Chapter Four) in the annals of Czech reconstruction. Rarely have an architectural and a political project acted in such close concert together.

Typically, though, it was not until 1873 that the actual work of reconstruction began, and it was still not fully completed when the cathedral was formally re-consecrated in 1919 on the (supposed) thousandth anniversary of the foundation of the first Christian edifice to occupy the site, once a temple to the pagan god Svantovit whose name survives, given a Christian veneer, in the dedication to St. Vitus, *svatý Vít* in Czech, healer of epilepsy and other convulsive disorders. The founder of the first church was none other than Wenceslas (Václav), not a king, good, bad or whatever, but, like all early rulers of Bohemia, a mere prince who was murdered by his pagan younger brother Boleslav, also in 929. Wenceslas' mother Drahomíra had already

murdered *her* mother Ludmila, and Wenceslas would be canonized before the end of the tenth century by Vojtěch, Archbishop of Prague, who himself was martyred not long after, joining (as St. Adalbert) Wenceslas and Ludmila to form a trinity of martyr-saints presiding over a self-styled "nation of martyrs". Repenting of his crime and becoming a Christian, Boleslav himself promoted the cult of his brother and had his remains interred in the Church of St. Vitus, where subsequent members of the dynasty, the mighty Přemyslids, first as princes then as kings of Bohemia, paid homage to him as patron saint of the nation. When the Přemyslid line became extinct in 1306, succeeding monarchs were even more anxious to clothe themselves in the martyred saint's mantle, and Charles I of Bohemia, alias Holy Roman Emperor Charles IV, bolstered his family's dubious claim to the Bohemian throne by embarking, in 1344, on the complete rebuilding of the church as a shrine to St. Wenceslas. Charles it was who, through his great architect Peter Parler, constructed the Chapel of St. Wenceslas over the alleged site of the saint's original tomb and had the shrine garnished with no fewer than 1,372 semi-precious stones to mark the year of its consecration and to symbolize the bejeweled New Jerusalem of Revelations 21: this truly was dynasty-building with a vengeance.

The chapel gives entrance to the coronation chamber above which, since their return from Vienna in 1868, has housed the Bohemian crown jewels behind a door with seven different locks—another Biblical echo—held by seven separate people, beginning with the President of the Republic himself. On only eight occasions since 1900 (most recently in 1993, following the Czech Republic's "velvet divorce" from Slovakia) has the treasure been open to the public, and, according to tenacious legend, death awaits anyone who, like the assassinated "Reichsprotektor" Reinhard Heydrich in 1942, seeks to gain unauthorized access to it.

Following White Mountain, the cathedral was "repossessed" by the Austro-Catholic victors who, as later on Charles Bridge, did not so much seek to suppress the Wenceslas cult as infiltrate it and recruit it into the counter-reformation cause. On the other hand, they could hardly be expected not to commemorate their victory, and this they did through a superbly carved sequence of wooden relief panels encircling the altar depicting the different phases of their triumph. The silver monstrosity housing the alleged remains of Nepomuk now conceals much of the work, but the most accessible panel shows the Protestant armies in retreat from White Mountain under their fly-by-night "Winter King", Frederick of the Palatinate, crossing Charles Bridge from Malá Strana to the Old Town, and thence into exile. Mounted in 1630, it bears the superscription "Irruit super eos formido et pavor" (Fear and dread fell upon them, Exodus 15: 16, tense changed from future to past as if prophecy had been fulfilled), as the whole of Protestant Bohemia seems to flock in terror across the Vltava. But, characteristically, even this image of Austro-Catholic triumph, like the later image of St. John Nepomuk, could be turned against its instigators. How could the image of exodus not suggest to Bohemian Protestants the Children of Israel in captivity in Egypt or Babylon, with themselves cast as the new Chosen People?

When work was resumed on the cathedral after an interruption of four centuries, the policy was to "rebohemianize"—not, to be sure, to "reprotestantize"—the building in every particular, to rededicate it as much to the cult of the emerging Czech nation as to that of Wenceslas himself. The western half of the cathedral was built using a sandstone that would rapidly age, so that the "join" between the two parts is barely apparent, thus fulfilling in stone the nationalists' overriding project: to re-establish the interrupted continuity of the nation, to join past to present in one seamless whole. The interior was studded with suitable nationalist slogans: *Praha Matka Měst* (Prague Mother of Cities) above the south door, and, inevitably, Hus' *Pravda vítězí* beside the Wenceslas chapel. Gradually the remains of earlier kings of Bohemia were brought together to join those of the Habsburgs Ferdinand I (1526-64), Maximilian II (1564-76) and Rudolf II (1576-1612) in the crypt beneath the so-called *castrum doloris* (castle of grief) commissioned by Rudolf, in the center of the nave. Modernist sarcophagi, designed by Kamil Roškot in the early 1930s, provide an incongruous final resting-place for the remains of Charles IV, his four wives and the Hussite King George of Poděbrady (1458-71). Inside the south transept is a memorial (by Karel Pokorný) to the thousands of Czech legionnaires killed between 1914 and 1918 fighting against the Austro-Hungarian empire of which they were citizens. (During the First World War, some 120,000 Czechs and Slovaks, mainly deserters and prisoners of war, enlisted in the Czechoslovak Legion and fought against the Austro-Hungarian Empire and its ally Germany on the eastern front, in Italy and in France.) A typically striking wooden carving entitled "The Crucified One" (1899) by the heterodox Catholic-cum-theosophist-cum-nationalist František Bilek is as much an image of martyred Bohemia as it is of Christ, in keeping with the widespread vision of Czech history since White Mountain as a repeated re-enactment of Gethsamene and Golgotha.

The cathedral's magnificent stained glass windows, installed at intervals between 1866 and 1966, those in the old eastern half mainly in the 1870s, those in the new western half mainly in the 1920s and 1930s, are, in their way, as instructive an iconographical sequence as the statues on Charles Bridge. Mingling Christian and nationalist images, the windows foreground, as one would expect, the themes of suffering and sacrifice, with the iconic figures of Wenceslas, Ludmila, Adalbert and Nepomuk (but not Hus, still too controversial for a Catholic cathedral) standing beside Saints Stephen and Barbara in a kind of national-apostolic succession of violent death. Alfons Mucha's imposing *Allegory of the Slav Nation* (1928-31) in the Hora Chapel traces the Christianization of the Slavs from Saints Cyril and Methodius down to Wenceslas and Ludmila before concluding, somewhat bathetically, "God be praised, glory to the country, in honor of art, donated by Slavie Bank"—or the Slavie Mutual Assurance Co. and Bank, to give the donors their full title.

As though to underline the close connections between Czech nationalism and Czech business (and perhaps inadvertently undermining some of the cathedral's eloquence), almost all of the windows in the new western half have commercial or industrial sponsors. Thus František Kysela's teeming *They that sow in tears shall reap in joy* (1927-9) was sponsored by the First Bohemian Mutual Assurance Co. to mark its centenary: the images of fire, flood, hailstorms, injury and old age seem like so many advertisements for the company's policies. Finally, and not without irony, the Prague Municipal Insurance Co. donated Max Švabinský's *Last Judgment*: did the Municipal offer coverage against Hell? Švabinský's composition brings together virtually every Bohemian ruler of consequence from Wenceslas IV, George of Poděbrady and Ferdinand I, under whom the country passed under Habsburg control; the victor of White Mountain, Ferdinand II (1619-37), is, however, conspicuously absent, or perhaps he features as one of the damned. Unhappy symbol, Švabinský's masterpiece was installed in its present position in 1938.

The cathedral unabashedly celebrates Czechness. Or, to be even more precise, it celebrates the splendors and miseries of *Bohemian-ness*. How adequately, though, did it serve between 1918 and 1938, and again between 1945 and 1993, as the more than merely metaphorical hub of a multi-ethnic, multi-lingual state successively known as the Czechoslovak Republic, Czecho-Slovakia (note the politics of the hyphen), the Czechoslovak Socialist Republic and, in its final avatar before the Velvet Divorce, as the Czechoslovak Federal Republic? The cathedral proclaims Prague to be the "Mother of Cities": how did that go down with Slovaks accustomed to revere Bratislava? Did Hus' *Pravda vítězí* (in Czech rather than Slovak) have for the country's ultra-Catholic east the same inspirational ring that it had for the increasingly anti-clerical and free-thinking west? Most important of all, what did the cathedral say to the hundreds of thousands of German-speaking citizens of the new republic, not all of whom, by any means, considered themselves to be "Sudetenland Germans"—a Nazi-invented ideological fiction—and of whom not a few were prepared, in 1938, to fight for *their* country—unlike their Czech-speaking president and his French and British "allies"? Could they find any *positive* image of themselves, any recognition of *their* contribution to national life, in the cathedral's blatant casting of the Bohemian as eternal victim, and of the German and Austrian as equally eternal aggressor? And, of course, the cathedral had no place at all, not even as mythical Christ-murderers, for the country's substantial Jewish minority.

Prague Castle

President Masaryk may well have sensed the danger of too strident an assertion of Bohemian uniqueness at the heart of the new nation's holy of holies. It could have been this that prompted him to entrust the task of renovating the castle (as opposed to the cathedral) not to a Czech, or even a Slovak, but to a complete outsider, albeit a Slav, from Slovenia. Plečnik's additions to the external fabric of the castle (many of his finest creations are inside, and closed to the public) may seem lacking in both seriousness and substance, but their effect is, by some miracle, both to bind it into a visual unity and to accentuate its stylistic heterogeneity. Thus the two colossal flagpoles in the first courtyard pull the whole space into sharp focus and break up the monotony of Pacassi's facade with contrasting colors and materials, the deep varnished brown of the poles set off by their gilded bases and tops. In the third courtyard, Plečnik placed a deliberately incongruous marble obelisk by the southwest corner of the cathedral. It has no more meaning than the famously non-significant obelisk on the Place de la Concorde in Paris, but again it gives focus and perspective to an otherwise uninteresting enclosure. By adding the so-called Bull Staircase that leads down from the courtyard to the Jižní zahrady (South Gardens) below, Plečnik set off Pacassi's flat neoclassicism with an ironic allusion to the recently excavated and restored palace at Cnossos. In the gardens themselves, a further enigma is posed by the combination of two sandstone obelisks and a huge granite bowl. By deliberately jumbling the architectural codes rather than reducing them to a bland homogeneity, Plečnik gave to the castle complex the irony, the ambiguity and the playfulness that the cathedral so demonstrably lacks. In so doing, he hints at the multifariousness of the new state and at its essentially constructed character. Far from constituting an integrated ideological whole, cathedral and castle actually propose sharply contrasting images of what it is—or rather was—to be a citizen of the Czechoslovak Republic. Cathedral is to castle as Jungmann to Bolzano: monolithic versus multiple, the romance of "roots" versus the prosaic reality of residence, the mystical cult of a perhaps imaginary past versus an ironic sense of the present.

Historically, however, Czechoslovakia was progressively to lose its composite, pluralistic character. Its Jewish minority was effectively

annihilated between 1942 and 1945 and, in a still controversial move, its much larger German- speaking population was "relocated"—in reality expelled—in 1945-6. During this period two and a half million "Sudetenland Germans" without a proven record of anti-Nazi resistance were transported to Germany, at one time at a rate of six trainloads of 1,200 passengers per day, their property having been confiscated without compensation and redistributed to Czech-speaking Czechs who in due course became one of the bedrocks of Communism. (There was also an attempt to remove the country's Hungarian-speaking minority, but this was finally abandoned.) Finally, to the extent that the "Velvet Divorce" was engineered by both Czech and Slovak politicians, 1993 may be seen metaphorically as the victory of cathedral over castle, the end, pending the arrival of new minorities (see Chapter Eight), of a whole tradition of ethnic and linguistic symbiosis.

Imprisonment and Liberation

Visible from everywhere during the day, and now also dramatically floodlit at night, the cathedral and castle haunt the imagination of Prague, not least because of the doubleness of their meaning. On the one hand, they stand for power, for the glories of the Bohemian past and for the immense possibilities of its future, for liberation, not just political liberation from external or internal oppression, but spiritual and psychological liberation from the labyrinth of the city below. On the other, they symbolize impotence, the darkness and emptiness of long tracks of history (1620-1918, 1939-45, 1948-89), and the curious interconnection throughout Czech history between physical unfreedom and artistic creation. At the castle's northeastern tip stands, for example, the Daliborka, the tower so named after its earliest and most famous prisoner, and yet another emblematic Czech martyr, the young Duke Dalibor, incarcerated there in 1496 and executed two years later. According to legend, Dalibor learned to play the fiddle while in prison, drawing crowds to the foot of the tower by the rapturous beauty of his playing. It was this characteristic trinity of themes—external constraint, internal freedom and violent death—that provided the subject of Smetana's archetypal nationalist opera *Dalibor* (1868), discussed in Chapter Four.

Another tower, the Prašná věž (Powder Tower), was the laboratory of Rudolf II's internationally recruited team of alchemists and occultists, including the Englishmen John Dee (1527-1608) and the notorious hoaxer Edward Kelley (1555-95) whose malfeasances led to imprisonment and torture. The alchemists are wrongly said to have lived, like diminutive Vulcans, in the tiny dolls' houses on Zlatá ulička (Golden Lane, once known as Alchimistengässchen) of which the surrealist Vítězslav Nezval (1900-58), a frequent visitor, wrote as follows:

In the Golden lane in the Hradčany
Time almost seems to stand still
If you wish to live five hundred years
Drop everything take up alchemy

When that simple miracle comes to be
our rivers will exhale their gold
Farewell farewell charlatan say hello
For us to the coming century

The cottages were in fact servants' quarters, though they later served as crucibles for the verbal alchemy of Jaroslav Seifert (at no. 6) and Franz Kafka who, in 1916, wrote a number of short stories, including *A Country Doctor*, at no. 22 which was rented at the time by his younger sister Ottla. Physical enclosure, imaginative release: it is one of the constants of the Czech experience, from Duke Dalibor to the imprisoned future president Václav Havel.

A more sinister Czech theme, likewise destined for a long history, is also inseparable from the castle, though it did not actually originate there. On May 23, 1618, a posse of outraged Protestants led by the German-speaking Count Mathias Thurn marched up the hill to the castle to protest against an array of anti-Protestant measures promulgated by the new Emperor and King, Ferdinand II. There they confronted the emperor's representatives. A "discussion" ensued at the climax of which two of the emperor's men, Jaroslav Martinic and Vilém Slavata (note the Czech names: Bohemia's religious and political conflicts were never *simply* a matter of nationality), were seized and thrown out of the chancellery window. When their secretary, Johannes (or Filip) Fabricius, tried to sneak out, he too was tossed into the fosse below. All three survived the fall, because—said the Protestants—they had landed on a dung-heap below or—the Catholic retorted—because the Blessed Virgin Mary had spread out her celestial mantle to catch them. A remarkable painting of the 1620s in the Jiřsky Klášter (St. George's Convent) shows the three men drifting down to earth sustained by angelic parachutes. They hold lighted votive candles in their hands (Slavata later received the noble title of "von Hohenfall", Baron High-Fall), and a skeleton, representing death, turns away in frustration at their escape; he would have more than enough compensation in the thirty-year-long, European-wide conflict that the failed lynching triggered off. Such was the second (or third, or even fourth) defenestration of Prague, but, as we shall see, by no means the last. Obsessed by thoughts of suicide by self-defenestration or, failing that, of "jumping out of [a] high window, but on to rainsoaked ground, where the impact won't be fatal," Kafka regularly slept with his bedroom or hotel room window open, and not just for reasons of health, but as combined threat and temptation.

Inside the Labyrinth

Leaving to a later chapter the most famous castle in literature, let us conclude this reading of Hradčany with an earlier masterpiece. This time written not in German but Czech, Jan Amos Komenský's strikingly entitled *The Labyrinth of the World and the Paradise of the Heart* (1623), has a still more expansive sub-title:

> *That is, A BRIGHT PORTRAYAL showing that in this world and in its works there is nothing but confusion and staggering, floundering and drudgery, deceit and fraud, misery and sorrow, and finally weariness and despair with all: but that he who remains alone with the Lord god, comes to the full and complete peace of mind and of joy.*

We have already encountered Komenský (1592-1670), the fourth, with Wenceslas, Hus and Nepomuk, of Bohemia's great quartet of martyrs, though Komenský's fate was not violent death but exile. Mass-produced images of Komenský abound in nineteenth- and early twentieth-century Bohemia, showing him leaving his homeland in 1628, clutching the Bible of Kralice in one hand and *The Labyrinth of the World* in the other. They were often so sentimentally and melodramatically portrayed that Jan Werich (one half of the "V + W" satirical partnership at the Liberated Theater in inter-war Prague—see Chapter Four) always had one such image pinned to his dressing-room mirror as an example of the kind of nationalistic kitsch that he and his colleague Jiří Voskovec were attacking. But Komenský himself was a remarkable man, spending over forty years in often impoverished exile, mostly in England, Sweden and Holland (where he died—another frequently illustrated scene— sitting in a chair before the incoming sea at Naarden). He also published a succession of didactic and pedagogical works in Latin, notably his ambitiously entitled *De rerum humanarum emendatione consultatio catholica* (*General Discourse on the Reform of Human Affairs*, 1644-62), in which some have seen the distant origins of Europeanism. But *The Labyrinth of the World* is in Czech and is directed primarily at fellow members of the Bohemian Community of Brethren. It is also, as Angelo Maria Ripellino has brilliantly shown, the foundational work of Czech literature in which are contained *in nuce* three of that literature's archetypal characters and themes: the figure of the pilgrim (as found later in Kafka's land-surveyor and investigating dog, or in the recurring prowlers of Prague in expressionist and surrealist writing), the labyrinth (continued in Kafka's extraordinary story *The Burrow* (1923), as well as in the Mirror Maze on Petřín Hill, or in the maze-like involutions of the original Laterna Magika) and the castle itself.

The Labyrinth begins with an imposing panoramic vision of order, as the Pilgrim looks out from a tower over the city and its castle, the kind of vision still just possible today from the mini-Eiffel Tower built on Petřín Hill for the 1891 Prague Exhibition:

> *The city itself, as I perceived, was divided into innumerable streets, squares, houses and buildings both large and small. Towards the east, I saw a gate, from which an alley ran towards another gate facing the west. The second gate opened upon the streets of the city. I counted six principal streets running from east to west, parallel with each other. In the midst of these streets was a very large ring or marketplace. Farthest towards the west, upon a steep and rocky*

eminence, stood a lofty, magnificent castle towards which the inhabitants of the city frequently gazed.

He is approached by a "Mr. Search-all, nicknamed Ubiquitous" who offers to lead him to the castle—not that a guide would seem necessary, given the city's rectilinear lay-out. The situation is already incipiently Kafkaesque, and becomes more so as the rectilinear pattern of the city is revealed to be totally illusory. The streets intersect and run into each other, and in no time at all Pilgrim and his companion are drawn into a labyrinth where all is masquerade, conflict and confusion, where as many languages are spoken as in the tower of Babel and where the only universally recognized value is money and the market. Ubiquitous renews his promise to lead Pilgrim to the center of the maze where, he says, "at the hub of everything else, stands the residence of Wisdom, the queen of the world." But they go through courtyard after courtyard thronging with people of every trade, craft and calling, from manual laborers "scorched and blackened like Moors" to grammarians, mathematicians, astronomers, astrologers, musicians, metaphysicians (all these a likely comment on the court of Rudolf II), and still the center eludes them. Are they inside the castle or not? If they are, it is no less labyrinthine than the city outside, with its endless staircases, underground passages and cellars such as that in which Pilgrim sees "several rows of fireplaces, small ovens, kettles and glass instruments, all shining brightly." Meanwhile, scores of wizened, scorched troglodytes argue with each other as to whether the fires are too hot or not hot enough as they pour liquids from one phial to another, some going blind or suffocating in the process. It is the den of the alchemists, and, after them, Pilgrim and Ubiquitous encounter droves of Rosicrucians selling books with title like *The Christian Cabala*, *The Castle of Primordial Matter*, *The General Tri-Trinity*, and *The Triumphal Pyramid*. But the Jews, the Muslims and, above all, the Christians are no better, all of them gluttons, wantons or worse, all of them selling their spiritual wares to the highest bidder. The rabbis are depicted "wagging their heads and [giving] out sounds not unlike those of howling wolves," the priests "lying on feather beds and snoring" or "gorging themselves with food and drink to speechlessness."

And so it goes on. Every religion or pseudo-religion, cult, sect or coven is revealed to be wanting. Soldiers, knights, the wealthy, the learned, the pleasure-seeking, all are the same. All wear masks to conceal their gross appetites, all pursue power under the guise of principle, all are for sale, and neither the castle nor its inhabitants has any center. At the end of his journey which, in true Kafkaesque style, has led him from nowhere to nowhere, Pilgrim looks into his own deepest self—and here any analogy with Kafka abruptly ends—and finds the true God, the God of the Communion of Brethren, to be indwelling in what Komenský calls his *centrum securitatis*. The Labyrinth of the world may lack a center, but not the Castle of the Soul, and by leaving the one and entering the other, Pilgrim achieves, as the subtitle promises, "full and complete peace of mind and of joy". Kafka's novels and stories have a Comenian stucture without the happy Comenian outcome, for here the mind and heart of the pilgrim are at least at labyrinthine as the city and castle, and there is no way out—any more than there is a way in: "There is a goal, but no way; what we call a way is only a wavering."

Chessboard City

A patchwork, a hybrid, a jigsaw, a mosaic: these are some of the images that Angelo Marie Ripellino applies to Prague in his brilliant study of the city, and all are appropriate provided that they are emptied of any implication of disorder or chaos. For the miracle of Prague is that, architecturally, it is both heterogeneous and coherent, that it juxtaposes contrasting structural elements in a discursively meaningful way, and that it succeeds in combining them without either blurring their distinctiveness or merely bodging them together. Looking out over Prague from Petřín Hill around the time that it became once more the capital of an independent nation, the future Nobel prize-winning poet Jaroslav Seifert (1901-86) captured the city's remarkable unity-in-diversity by comparing it to "a chess board at the beginning of a game": "The king and queen stood over there, here was the golden rook. The apartment houses and villas were the pawns... The chessmen on the board moved slowly, deliberately before my eyes." It is the perfect analogy: different pieces—Gothic, Baroque, neo-Renaissance, neo-Gothic, Art Nouveau, modernist—moving differently yet all combining in a patterned yet infinitely variable game. It all points, as being the proverbial "Mother of Cities", it should, to some broader or higher differentiated unity: "At that moment I felt that I was holding Europe in my hands."

Appropriately enough, Prague contains some of the world's greatest collections, not just of pictures, but, at the National Museum on Wenceslas Square and the Strahov Monastery on Petřín Hill, of all manner of natural phenomena. Shells, fossils, crystals, insects, pickled two-headed foetuses and similar *lusus naturae*, even (at Strahov) a pair of whales' penises are arranged, in all their disparateness, in some kind of order, like a *mise en abysme* of the city itself.

Unfortunately, nowhere in Prague is there an example of the work of the artist who, though not a native of the city, or even a Czech, captures better than any other, in a metaphorical rather than realistic manner, the structured diversity of its interlocking forms. The artist in question is the Milan-born Giuseppe Arcimboldo (1527-93) who came to Prague in 1562 as one of Ferdinand I's accredited court artists, perfected his art under Maximilian II and attained his zenith at the court of Rudolf II, all of whose weird and wanton imagination seems compressed into his work. All the Arcimboldos in Prague seem to have been sold or stolen by marauding Swedish invaders in 1648. The best collections are now in Paris, Munich, and—to the fury of Czechs who regard them and other looted art-works as Bohemia's Elgin Marbles—in Sweden.

Arcimboldo's great invention, along with a rich array of automata, was the *tête composée*, human faces and heads made up from the fitting together of natural and, more rarely, man-made objects so as to emblematize the four seasons or the four elements, themes that he painted over and over again. Flowers and fruit are coupled together to create humanoid puppets of spring and autumn respectively, while shoals of fish or flocks of birds somehow combine in anthropomorphic figurations of water and air, all painted in a way that allies microscopic exactitude with conjunctions and contrasts of truly surrealistic shockingness. Most famous of all is the portrait of Rudolf II as Vertumnus, the Roman god of vegetation and transformation, that Arcimboldo painted as a parting gift for the Emperor after he returned to his native Milan in 1587. It is the most extraordinary assemblage of fruit and flowers imaginable—Rudolf's nose is a pear, two apples form his cheeks, and a pair of cherries (or tomatoes?) his lower lip. Word and thing punning together, ears of corn stick out from his head, while grapes, onions, pumpkins and turnips transform him into a human cornucupia, suggesting a universe of matching microcosm and macrocosm, in which nature mutates and morphs from one shape to another, all the time preserving an underlying unity of structure. It is an art of juxtaposition and composition which would surface two and a half centuries later in the collages and *objets trouvés* of Prague's highly individual version of international surrealism (see Chapter Five). A poem (not by Arcimboldo but by one Don Gregorio Comanini) accompanying the painting has Vertumnus declare: "There's diversity within me/Though despite my diverse aspect, I am one." It could be the voice of Prague itself speaking, even if, not altogether inappropriately, it does so here in Italian, the language of hundreds of imported craftsmen, rather than in the Czech, German, Hebrew or Yiddish that, at one time, made Prague one of the most polyglot cities in Europe. The making and unmaking of this remarkable *guláš* of languages and cultures is the subject of the chapter that follows.

CHAPTER TWO

Ghetto, Golem, and Germans

Jewish Prague

The "Mother of Cities" to the nineteenth-century Czech nationalist tradition, Prague had for over two hundred years been known throughout the Jewish diaspora by the still more exalted name of "City and Mother of Israel". It was as though it was not merely a metropolis of Jewish culture, scholarship and commerce but a very fragment of the Promised Land itself. There had been Jews in Prague since the end of the tenth century, but it was only in the wake of the anti-Jewish measures promulgated by the Third and Fourth Lateran Councils (1179 and 1215) that they began to be confined to the area north and west of Old Town Square that since the late eighteenth century has been known officially as Josefov, but which is still loosely referred to as the "Jewish city" or even as the "ghetto", even though it has not contained any substantial Jewish population for well over a century.

In 1254 Přemysl Otakar II issued a *Statuta Judaeorum* that imposed spatial and occupational restrictions on the city's Jewish population while at the same time extending to them royal protection in the event of Christian attack. Henceforth, Jews were defined as *servi camerae*, servants of the royal chamber, directly subject to the King but without the right to permanent residence in either city or country that could be revoked at any moment. Confined at night into their designated precinct of the city, they could only venture out during the day if wearing the cap or badge that declared their non-Christian identity. They were excluded from guild membership (and so, officially, from the practice of crafts) and allowed to trade only in such commodities as furs, leather, old clothes and—crucially—money, the lending and changing of which was forbidden to Christians under the blanket condemnation of usury. Royal protection did not prevent 3,000 Jews being massacred over Easter in 1389, some of them in the Altneuschul

(Old-New Synagogue) itself. But the monopoly on the money trade greatly enriched at least a minority of the community, which in its turn led to a *de facto* alliance between the Jewish elite and the King and nobles who needed the financial services it provided.

By the end of the fifteenth century, as the ban on usury weakened, Christians began to encroach on areas of economic activity previously restricted to Jews, and Jews, in their turn, began to engage in crafts and areas of commerce that brought them into conflict with the guilds. Several decades of acute tension ensued, punctuated by recurring anti-Jewish riots (1514, 1516, 1517, 1533) and by attempts by the burghers to have the entire community expelled (1507, 1524). These the King and his nobles were usually able to resist, though on at least two occasions (1541-43 and 1557-59) all but the elite were driven into temporary exile in Poland. What finally secured the Jewish position in Prague was Rudolf II's decision, in 1584, to transfer his seat of power from Vienna to Hradčany. The move created still greater opportunities for the great Jewish banking families (the Maisels, the Horowitzes, the Bassevis) who were able to use their power to protect and advance the rest of the community. Jewish immigrants began to arrive in Prague from Italy, Germany, Poland and Hungary, attracted both by economic opportunities—Jews were officially permitted to work in gold and silver in 1628—and by the relative security the city could afford. The ghetto remained but, within its walls, an expanding and prosperous Jewish community began to live what they and posterity came to regard as a Golden Age in their history.

Synagogues and Cemetery

Most of the surviving Jewish monuments in Prague date, at least in their original form, from this period, causing the one-time "New" Synagogue—completed around 1280—to be renamed "Old-New" to differentiate it from the more recent additions: the Pinkas Synagogue (completed 1535) built by Aaron Meshullam Zalman Horowitz and now the city's Holocaust memorial; the High Synagogue (completed 1568) built by Mordechai Maisel whose fortune, at his death in 1601, was valued at a stupendous 500,000 guldens and whose private synagogue, the Maiselova, also survives, though in a form which, after several re-buildings, the most recent between 1893 and 1913, bears

"The Old-New Synagogue"

little resemblance to the original; and the Klausen Synagogue, built by Maisel to honor the Emperor Maximilian II's visit to the Prague ghetto in 1573 and rebuilt in the Baroque style after fire swept through the whole district in 1689. The completion of the Jewish Town Hall, also financed by Maisel and famous above all for the "anticlockwise" Hebrew clock that so haunted the French poet Guillaume Apollinaire when he visited Prague in 1902, made the ghetto a virtually self-governing, self-sustaining city-within-a-city. The ghetto was disliked by the Christian world that pressed up against its six-gated walls, yet was sufficiently powerful to fly its own municipal standard—reputedly the first to feature the Star of David—as a sign of its prosperity and quasi-autonomy.

If the ghetto was, as Jews throughout the diaspora said, the "metropolis of Israel", then its cemetery was a further mini-city set into its walls, its internal structure as intricate and bewildering as the maze of alleys that twisted about it: a labyrinth-within-a-labyrinth-within-a-labyrinth wholly typical of Prague. Like many of the houses in the city itself, the tombstones often bear symbols of their residents' one-time occupations: scissors for tailors, a mortar and pestle for pharmacists, hands raised in blessing for rabbis, and so on, while others provide rebus-like equivalents of well-known first or family names, a bear for Dov (Bär in Yiddish) or a fish for Karpeles as though nothing in this city can be permitted to remain semiotically neutral. Maisel's own tomb bears the image of a mouse, and it is one of the most imposing of the 12,000-odd that lean this way and that in the necropolis he helped to expand, with thousands more bodies lying layer upon layer under the surface.

The earliest tombstone, dating from 1439, belongs to the poet and scholar Avigdor Kara who survived the 1389 pogrom to write a *kinah*, or elegy, commemorating its victims, while the most recent dates from 1787, when the cemetery was closed on the orders of Emperor Joseph II. Almost every personality who illuminated the history of Jewish Prague between those two dates is buried in the cemetery: the printers Gersom Kohen, Mordechai Katz and their descendants who, between them, created Prague's European-wide reputation for the publication of Hebrew literature lie there. As does the historian and astronomer David Gans (1541-1613) whose *Nechmad ve-naim* (meaning "Lovely and Agreeable") shows the influence of his friendship with Kepler and Brahe. The mathematician, philosopher and physician Joseph Schlomo Delmedigo (died 1655) and the scholar David Oppenheim (died 1736) whose library forms the basis of the collection of Judaica at the Bodleian Library in Oxford, are among the cemetery's residents.

Prague's renown as a center for Jewish mystical studies also dates from the late sixteenth century, when its position and relative security made it a refuge for scholars fleeing persecution in other parts of Europe, notably Spain. Major works on the Kabbalah and Zohar were published by, among others, Mordechai ben Abraham Jaffe (c. 1530-c. 1614). Jomtob Lipman Heller (1579-1654), elected Chief Rabbi in 1627, published a still authoritative commentary on the Mishnah between 1614 and 1617 before being banished from Prague for alleged defamation of the Christian faith. The grave, dating from 1605, of

Rivka (Rebekka) bat Meir, author of the now lost *Nurse of Rebekka* as well as of poems and hymns, shows that literary and scholarly activities were by no means an entirely masculine preserve.

The most famous and imposing tomb, though, is that of Rabbi Judah Löw ben Belazel (c. 1520-1609), Chief Rabbi of Prague from 1594 to his death, the continuing potency of whose memory is evidenced by the coins and pebbles holding down *kvittleh*, or messages of supplication, that are still left on his grave. To distinguish, at this distance, between the "real" Rabbi Löw and his mythical accretions is next to impossible, save in one particular: there is absolutely no historical link between him and the myth of the Golem, to be discussed shortly, with which his name is now almost automatically associated. Nor is there any evidence, despite one documented meeting (in 1592), of any mystical or magical collaboration between him and Rudolf II. Although there are links between the cabbalistic, hermetic and alchemical world-views, the Rabbi's reputation as combined magus, mystagogue and thaumaturge is a much later, and probably nineteenth-century, creation. But Löw's standing as a speculative philosopher, mystic and educationalist of more than local import is fully justified by his fifteen extant works which reveal, in the words of a leading scholar on the period, a "characteristic Cabbalist and Hermetic striving for harmony, set in something of the ecstasy of the mystic." The great twentieth-century Jewish scholar Gershon Scholem regarded him as a direct precursor of Hasidism, the mystical form of Judaism now chiefly associated with the name of Martin Buber (1878-1965) who, as we shall see, was to exercise a decisive influence on later Jewish thinking in Prague.

Germanization and Anti-Semitism

A major change in the situation of the Jewish population of Prague (which, by that time, accounted for a substantial majority of the Jews in Bohemia) took place in 1781 when, as part of his policy of imperial modernization and unification, Emperor Joseph II issued a so-called Patent of Toleration which, as well as extending considerably the economic and other freedoms of Jews, required that German replace Yiddish as the language of the ghetto and that "normal schools" be set up to disseminate the new medium. Not only did Jews readily accept "Germanization"—the old *Mauscheldeutsch* of the ghetto barely survived the passing of the ghetto itself in 1848—but they themselves became agents of the broader imperial policy of "Germanizing" the Czech-speaking population of Bohemia as well. As such, they drew closer to, and, especially after 1848, were increasingly accepted by, the non-Jewish German-speaking population of Prague from which they had previously been clearly differentiated on religious, linguistic and residential grounds, with major consequences, and complications, for their future standing in the city. It was, of course, absolutely no coincidence that the first strivings of Czech nationalism took place in the late eighteenth and early nineteenth centuries against the background of concerted Germanization. Nor was it by chance that nationalism was focused, then and later, on the defense of the Czech language, which had to be virtually reinvented in its written form in the process.

In the course of the nineteenth century, language and what we would now call ethnicity (and which the Czech *buditelé*, or "awakeners", called nationality) came increasingly to mean the same thing, with the inevitable consequence that non Czech-speakers, be they Christian, Jewish or whatever, found themselves collectively extruded from the body of the emerging, but still hypothetical, Czech nation. According to the dominant Jungmann-inspired school of Czech nationalism, only Czech-speakers were authentic Czechs. The fact that many Czech-speakers also spoke German, and vice versa, was simply disregarded in the ethno-linguistic heat of the moment, and non-Jewish German-speakers, who had previously defined themselves as "Bohemian" or "Austrian", now found themselves categorized as "Germans" by an increasingly vocal and hostile Czech nationalist elite, many of whom, as we have seen, were paradoxically more "at home" in German than in Czech. The overwhelming majority of German speakers in Bohemia lived, of course, *outside* of Prague, leaving the "German" minority in the city in a precarious situation indeed, especially as more and more Czech-speakers flooded in from the country. It was not so much that Prague's German-speaking community formed an alliance with the (by 1840) predominantly German-speaking Jewish population, which actually outnumbered it by about two to one, but that the two groups were simply lumped together by the Czech-speaking majority.

Since the 1781 edict also required that Jews take German surnames (the Kafkas, then in South Bohemia, being a rare exception to the rule), Jewish-owned shops would be regarded—and, on occasion, attacked—as being "German", and vice versa. When the ghetto walls were pulled down after 1848, German-speaking Jews moved into parts of the city already containing significant German-speaking minorities where, by and large, they were welcomed for the demographic and economic reinforcements they brought. By the late nineteenth century, religious practice—and often religious belief—was in decline among both sections of the German-speaking minority and, though intermarriage was rare, the last remaining barrier between them became effectively invisible to the outsider's eye. "Germans! Jews!" wrote the journalist Willi Haas of *fin-de-siècle* Prague in 1958, "they were nearly identical at that time for Czech Prague and both, Germans and Jews, were equally hated."

Merging with the city's "Germans" thus brought Prague Jews no security at all. Indeed, it made them doubly vulnerable, as anti-Germanism and anti-Semitism combined to target them as both "Germans" and "Jews". If Prague Jews encountered little prejudice among the old Prague-born "German" bourgeoisie, they did among "Germans" from the west of Bohemia living, working, and, above all, studying in the city; Jews were decidedly unwelcome in the German student organizations at Charles University.

Things came to a head in December 1897 when, in an effort to conciliate the Czech-speaking majority, the imperial government headed by Count Casimir Badenia issued a decree giving equal standing to Czech and German in the Bohemian crown lands, a move that predictably precipitated riots in the predominantly German-speaking regions in the west. The measures were withdrawn, whereupon, and equally predictably, Czech-speakers rioted in Prague and for several days rampaged through the city, attacking and looting shops with German names. Many Jewish-owned shops were thus automatically ransacked, though not Hermann Kafka's haberdashery on Zeltnergasse (Celetná) off Old Town Square, concealed and protected by its owner's Czech-sounding name meaning "jackdaw" or "rook". His son Franz, aged fourteen at the time, would later recall in a letter to Milena Jesenská written on the occasion of a later (1920) anti-German/anti-

Semitic riot, the terror of being confronted by a rioter screaming *Jste žid?* (Are you a Jew?) "Don't you see how in *jste* the fist is drawn back to gather strength? And in *žid* the punch flies forward, willingly and unfailingly? Such are the side-effects that the Czech language often has for the German ear."

Two years later, in 1899, Jews were targeted as such when, in the small Czech-speaking town of Polna on the borders of Bohemia and Moravia, a Jew named Leopold Hilsner was accused of murdering the nineteen-year-old Christian Anežka Hrůzová. The motive, it was claimed, was not sexual but religious, for the victim's body had allegedly been drained of its blood, the blood of a Christian virgin being, according to centuries-old anti-Jewish obsession, an essential ingredient in the making of Passover bread. Thanks to an intervention by the ubiquitous Thomas Masaryk, Hilsner's death sentence was not carried out, and he was released from prison in 1918 on the declaration of Czech independence. But the affair rumbled on, and as late as 1965 Bohumil Hrabal was forced to retract a veiled allusion to the likely real culprit, one Petr Pešák, made in his novel *Dancing Lessons for the Elderly and the Advanced* (1964). Nothing would be more naïve than to look for a "source" for *The Trial*, but the sixteen-year-old Franz Kafka can hardly have been unimpressed by the plight of a fellow Jew arbitrarily and unjustly accused of an almost unutterable crime. It is against this turbulent background that the story of the Prague Golem can best be understood.

The Golem

What, first of all, is the Golem according to ancient Jewish magical-mystical tradition? In his authoritative study, *On the Kabbalah and its Symbolism* (1964), Gershom Scholem defines it as a "man-like creature, produced by the magical power of man," a replication of, and in some ways a challenge to, the original creation of man narrated in Genesis 2:7: "And the Lord God formed man of the dust of the ground, and breathed into his nostrils the breath of life; and man became a living soul." The word *golem* itself only occurs once in the Bible (in Psalm 139:19) in the general sense of unformed or amorphous, and this was assimilated by Jewish scholars to the *adamah* (= earth, clay) from which God fashioned the primal man Adam, breathing into his inanimate form his *neshamah*, his spirit or breath, so that the clay effigy becomes a "living soul", an admixture of the telluric and the pneumatic, from which the spirit will be removed at death, consigning the body once more to the realm of the formless. In making the Golem, the magus repeats the stages of the initial creation, first modeling a doll-like replica of a human being out of mud or clay and then, at once an imitator and rival of God (whence the danger of the whole proceedings), breaths into the model's nostrils. On receiving the magician's *nefesh*—his "motor soul" rather than his spirit (*neshamah*)—the model comes to "life". Like the curiously similar figure of the *zombi* in Haitian voodoo (though this involves the resuscitation of an actual corpse), it performs whatever tasks, usually of a humdrum domestic character, that the magician orders it to do, growing larger and larger as it does so until finally it is deactivated by the removal of the *nefesh*. The infusion of the *nefesh* is usually figured by the magician's inscribing the word EMETH (= Truth) on the creature's forehead which propels it into action. When he wishes it to stop, the magician merely removes the letter "E" (the *aleph*), leaving the word METH (= He is dead), whereupon the Golem reverts to its corpse-like condition from which it can be "resurrected" by the simple replacement of the *aleph*. In a further version of the myth, the creature is activated by the placing of a piece of parchment bearing the name of God (the *shem*) under its clay tongue, and deactivated by its removal.

The motif of the tongue is suggestive, if nothing else, of the miraculously surviving tongue of St. John Nepomuk or of the all too real severed tongue of the unfortunate Johannes Jessenius, from whom, incidentally, Milena Jesenská's father claimed direct descent; Kafka often reproached Milena for preferring German to her native Czech tongue.

It is, perhaps significantly, the parchment version of the legend that came, at some point in the eighteenth or nineteenth century, to be associated with Rabbi Löw. According to legend, the rabbi always removed the parchment from under Josef's (or Yossel's) tongue on

Friday nights so that he/it could "rest" on the Sabbath. One Friday he forgot, and Josef rampaged through the ghetto, until the rabbi was able to corner him and somehow extract the *shem* from the raging creature's mouth. Finally, Rabbi Löw permanently deactivated him and consigned Josef's inert remains to the attic of the Old-New Synagogue where, according to legend, he sleeps on, awaiting resuscitation. (There is a clear parallel here with the legend that Wenceslas was sleeping beneath Blaník Mountain and would shortly awake to deliver the city of its Austrian (or German or Soviet) occupiers.)

This story is in its turn given a Frankensteinian twist in the numerous tales of the Golem's turning against its creator, either killing him of its own "free will" or, alternatively, crushing him under its collapsing weight when the *aleph* or *shem* are removed inopportunely. The Golem is, in short, a living statue, an earthy version of the puppets, automata, dolls and robots that figure so prominently in the collective imagination of Prague, an over-sized Jewish equivalent, too, of the *homunculus* of alchemical theory and practice. That it should be precisely in Prague that the myth of the Golem "lives on", banalized certainly for tourist consumption, cannot be regarded as a simple coincidence.

A creature of the ghetto, the Golem began to haunt the Prague imagination at precisely the time that the ghetto itself disappeared once and for all. When, in 1849, Jews were finally emancipated from all occupational and residential restrictions, the walls of the ghetto were pulled down, and only a minority of the old *Judenstadt*'s population chose, or were compelled by poverty, to remain in the area now renamed Josefov—presumably after Emperor Joseph II and not Josef of the Golem legend. As Jews moved out into other parts of the city, particularly, as we have seen, those where there were already significant German-speaking minorities, so a new, mixed and, above all, pauperized population moved in: that congeries of street peddlers, beggars, prostitutes, vagabonds, criminals and other "marginal elements" which, ironically, was conventionally known in the nineteenth century by the adopted French term, *la Bohème*. The former ghetto, once a functioning community, rapidly degenerated into a slum district offering insalubrious refuge to all and sundry who packed into its increasingly dilapidated tenement houses. By 1890, when the Old

Town had a population density of 644 persons per hectare, in Josefov the figure was 1,822, of whom, by now, only a fraction—perhaps twenty percent—were actually Jews. It could not go on, and, beginning in 1890, the whole district, apart from the Jewish town hall, the principal synagogues and the cemetery, were razed to the ground. Its labyrinth of alleys and lanes was replaced by intersecting rectilinear streets, which, it was hoped, would become a new residential and shopping area for the rising middle class. It never quite worked out that way, and—tourists and visitors excepted—Josefov remains a somewhat dull and deserted part of the city, a far cry, at any rate, from the elegant *faubourg* that the Haussmann-inspired city planners envisaged a century ago.

The *Assanierung* of the ghetto, as it was known, also cleared the ground for all kinds of literary fantasy, ranging from the romantic to the paranoid, as to what it had been like. This was not so much on the part of Jewish writers (who, having literally or figuratively escaped the ghetto were not anxious to return to it, even in imagination) as of their "German" counterparts with whom, in other respects, they had so much in common. The "ghetto" was a constant reference point for the *Jung-Prag* school of writers, which came together even as the "ghetto" was being taken apart, and particularly for its leading figure Paul Leppin (1878-1945), editor of the journals *Frühling* and *Wir* in which the group—German-speakers, but not, for the most part, Jewish—published its work. None of the writers concerned had any experience of the actual (that is, pre-1850) ghetto, and some of them, including Leppin himself, were barely old enough to have known the very different Josefov of the second half of the century, their semi-ignorance acting, of course, not so much as a deterrent as an incentive to private and collective fantasy-weaving. The opening of Leppin's story, "The Ghost of the Jewish Quarter", dating from the early 1900s, is typical of the group's blend of realism and reverie:

> *In the centre of Prague, where tall airy apartment buildings now line the broad streets, there stood—but ten years ago—the Jewish Quarter: a steep, gloomy maze of narrow streets from which no weather could blow the stench of decay and dank, moulding walls and where, in summer, a poisonous breath streamed forth from the open doors. Odours of filth and poverty vied with each other; a*

dull, brutal corruption flickered in the eyes of the children who grew up there.
The streets led at times into low, arched viaducts, through the entrails of a house
and beyond, or turned suddenly athwart, finally ending before some blind wall.
The sly-faced hawkers piled their second-hand wares on the uneven flagstones in
front of the shops and cried out to those passing by. Young women with painted
lips lolled in the doorways, laughing coarsely, hissing in men's ears, lifting their
skirts to display gold and chartreuse stockings. Aging bawds with grizzled hair
and slackened jaws called out greetings from the windows, clapping, winking,
and chortling in eagerness and gleeful satisfaction whenever a man entered their
net and drew near.

The point is, of course, that what is being evoked here was no
longer in any meaningful sense the "Jewish quarter" of the city (though
it still contained a significant Jewish population) but the slum district
that it became *after* the "exodus" of the 1850s and 1860s. Crime,
prostitution and squalor have become inherently Jewish, and the city's
classes dangereuses have, in the process, been comprehensively semitized.
This conflation of crime, vice and "race" provides the clay from which
the new myth of the Golem was formed, in the wake of, and partially
in response to, the riots of 1897 and Prague's own mini-Dreyfus affair,
the trial of Leopold Hilsner in 1899.

The revived legend seems first to have appeared in print in a
novel in Hebrew, dating from around 1909, entitled *The Miraculous*
Deeds of Rabbi Loew with the Golem and supposedly based on an
apocryphal "Manuscript in the Library of Metz". The novel was
published by one "Judah Rosenberg", who may also have been its
author, though, in the era that produced *The Protocols of the Elders of*
Zion, the possibility of its being an anti-Semitic hoax cannot be
excluded. The gist of the novel is that the rabbi created the Golem to
combat accusations of Jewish ritual murder, an obvious allusion to
the Hilsner affair. It is most unlikely that this work had any influence
on the most famous re-working of the Golem theme, begun in 1907,
published in serial form in 1913-14 and finally as a novel the
following year, selling 200,000 copies within a few months and
inspiring one of the earliest Czech expressionist films, made by the
German actor-director Paul Wegener (1874-1948) in 1914. In fact,
Wegener made three films on the Golem theme (1914, 1917, 1918),

starring himself in the title role, having made his name as an actor in *The Student of Prague* (1913). He later married the Czech actress Lyda Salmanová (1899-1968).

The author of *The Golem* was the Viennese-born Gustav Meyer, later Meyrink, illegitimate son of Baron Karl Varnbüler von und zu Hemmingen and a Bavarian-Jewish actress Maria Meyer who had him baptized and raised as a Protestant. Meyrink came to Prague in the early 1890s as a director of the Meyer and Morgenstern Bank. He promptly had a nervous breakdown and attempted suicide, before an occultist pamphlet slipped under his door reputedly pointed the way out of his misery. Meyrink became the founder member of a "Theosophical Lodge of the Blue Star", had some frosty dealings with the spiritualist Rudolf Steiner (1861-1925), when he visited Prague, and plunged into the familiar *fin-de-siècle* package of esotericism, mysticism and drugs, to which, being in Prague, he added the study of the Kabbalah and alchemy. A correspondent of Annie Besant and disciple of the bogus German mystagogue "Bô Yín Rč", he was also one of the earliest westerners to practice Hatha Yoga. He fought duels, was imprisoned, failed to set up a puppet theater with a friend and, leaving Prague for Bavaria, published short stories and novels of which *The Angel of the West Window* (1927), about Rudolf II's imported alchemist and sorcerer John Dee, and, above all, *The Golem* are still read today. If anyone invented the fiction of "magic Prague", it was Meyrink.

There is no point in attempting to summarize the "plot" of *The Golem*; it is as shambolic, improbable, and full of zany coincidences as the author's own life, in part a deliberate parody of the *roman noir* of the time. Far better to read it on the level of the images that run through the text like Wagnerian motifs: spiders, dolls, sleepwalkers, tarot cards, chess pieces, all of them suggesting a world in which everyone is both manipulator and manipulated, in which every apparently "free" action is determined and over-determined by a multitude of forces, in which the structure of the self—"who is the 'I' now?"—becomes deeply problematic as it fissures and fragments or dissolves pantheistically into the not-self. This is a world in which the non-human is anthropomorphized and the human is drained of its substance by vampiristic objects. The very houses of the ghetto take on a life of their own, their doors "black gaping mouths in which the tongues had rotted away": that archetypal Prague image once again, as predictable as the labyrinthine alleys of the ghetto and the martyrs' statues on Charles Bridge, plus the inevitable "defenestration scene" when one of the characters throws the head of a puppet out of a window, so reminiscent is it of that of the Golem.

The novel is in fact as much about puppets as the Golem, or, rather, the puppet is no more than a mini-Golem made out of wood and operated by strings, just as the Golem is a giant clay marionette invisibly controlled from afar by a magician-puppeteer. And, of course, the novel, originally entitled *The Eternal Jew*, abounds in anti-Semitic stereotypes, from the fourteen-year-old nymphet Rosina, a typical member of the "red-headed tribe" with her "teasing smile and waxy, rocking-horse face" and red eye-lashes as "repulsive as those of rabbits" to the junk-dealer Aaron Wassertrum, all "fish's eye and gaping hare-lip". These and many other such, all live—if that is the word—like "so many toads under their stones" in the "thousand filthy nooks and crannies" of the ghetto, so drained of humanity that "there is no one living anywhere in the Ghetto capable of laughing cheerfully."

In this world of dissolving, unstable and proliferating identities, the Golem does not so much intrude as an alien or supernatural force as grow spontaneously out of it as its natural embodiment. The strength of Meyrink's novel is that the Golem as such never really appears. He/it is always the product of this or that character's fevered perception as though we all of us carry a Golem (or Golems) within us, an excrescence of the collective as much as the individual psyche. Meyrink's Golem "represents" nothing. If he/it "stands for" anything, it is "the paralyzing dread at an inexplicable, shapeless nothing that eats away the boundaries of our thought." The terror and hatred that the Golem inspires is our own self-terror and self-hatred projected outwards, an inverted self-image towards which, as towards all self-images, we are narcissistically and self-destructively drawn: "We can only hate something as deeply as I do, if it is part of ourselves." Thus when the narrator is taken to be the Golem by others, they are merely projecting on to him the hidden Golem in themselves, just as, far more disturbingly, he finally recognizes himself in the Golem: "And across the room he sat, he... I... myself."

The Golem, it transpires, is not so much amorphous as polymorphous like the "polymorphous life" (Leppin, *Severin's Journey into the Dark*, 1914) of the city of which it is the creature. Each individual, each community models its Golem out of the *'adamah* of its own fears and obsessions, fires it in the furnace of its repressed desires and breaths into it those psychic forces that it cannot accommodate or control in itself. Meyrink's Golem is not an allegory but a symbol, meaningless in itself but capable of receiving and embodying an infinity of meanings. Written in German by a (disguised) half-Jew in a city ridden with all manner of anti-German and anti-Semitic phobias, could it be that the unutterable Other of *The Golem* is none other than, precisely, the Czech?

Prague "Germans"

All this leads us back to the most problematic of the three communities that made up the *Dreivölkerstadt*, "the city of three peoples", not the Czechs or the Jews, but the non-Jewish German-speakers, that minority within a minority, outnumbered three to one by German-speaking Jews, and twenty to one by Czechs in 1889, rising to forty to one in 1910. Moreover, the combined German-speaking community was rapidly losing its Jewish component to Czech. In 1890, 74 percent of Prague Jews declared German to be their first language, compared with 45 percent a mere ten years later; for prudential as well as practical reasons, Prague's Jews, Hermann Kafka amongst them, were beginning to align themselves with the majority language group. In the early 1860s Czechs gained control of the Prague City Council and, in 1892, inflicted a traumatic blow on their rivals by replacing bilingual street signs with signs in Czech only. To rub salt in the ideological and linguistic wound, the old Gothic script was replaced by Roman, and the new red, white and blue plaques—the color of the nation in formation—simply nailed on top of the traditional Bohemian brown and gold of the former mixed-language signs.

Everywhere, social space was being colonized by the rising majority and populated with symbols of its numerical, moral and ideological strength, pending its acquisition of actual political power. At every turn, German-speakers were confronted with the inescapable fact that, for the Czech-speaking majority, nation (*národ*) and country (*vlast*) were *not* the same thing, that a people could have been for generations in the *vlast* and still not be authentic members of the *národ*. Some German-speakers simply reinvented themselves as Czechs, including, ironically, the two founders of the fervently nationalist gymnastics society *Sokol* (The Falcon), Miroslav Tyrš (born Friedrich Emanuel Tirsch) and Jindřich (formerly Heinrich) Fügner. Those who refused the convenience of an ethnolinguistic make-over began to feel more and more like aliens in their own native city.

Nor, unlike their fellow German-speakers in the west, did the Prague Germans have the option (as some future "Sudentenland" Germans were doing even before 1914) of identifying with Berlin rather than Vienna and of simply leaving Prague and its German-speaking remnant to sink into the Czech-speaking majority. The slogan *Heim in's Reich* (Back Home to the Reich) had, then and later, *Los von Prag* (Out of Prague) as its inevitable corollary. The German-speakers began to feel increasingly beleaguered as, even in their communal "heartland" around Wenceslas Square and Am Graben (Na příkopě), their proportion of the population fell from half in 1850 to just under a third in 1900 and then to a mere fifth in 1910. In desperation, they clung to their cultural bastion, the German Kasino on Am Graben, which was regularly targeted by Czech demonstrators, formed their own *Deutscher Turnverein* to challenge the domination of *Sokol* (significantly, Konrad Henlein, future leader of the Sudetenland Germans, began life as a gymnastics instructor) and, above all, sent their children to German-language schools. This they did even if, like the school Franz Kafka attended in the mid-1890s, it meant going past a rival Czech-language school displaying a bust of Komenský and a banner declaring (in Czech) "A Czech child belongs in a Czech school!"—a warning and exhortation to those Czechs who persisted in sending their children to German-speaking schools. That some Czech parents were prepared to risk censure and do this indicates that the old *Dreivölkerstadt* had not totally trisected, or even bisected, into its component parts, but inter-community relations were undoubtedly tense in pre-1914 Prague, though some considerably way short of a *mitteleuropäischer* version of Belfast or Beirut.

There were regular stone-fights between German and Czech children on the streets (Kafka's friend Oskar Baum was actually blinded by a blow from a pencil box in one such street battle), and Sundays saw almost institutionalized confrontations between German and Czech student organizations around Wenceslas Square. German smokers allegedly refused to light their cigars with Czech School Society matches, and Czech smokers naturally did likewise with the German equivalent. Even writers, who might have bridged the widening gap between the two communities, tended to congregate at separate cafés, the Czechs at the Café Union, the Germans, both Gentile and Jewish, at the Arco. "One lived in the same city," wrote Franz Carl Weiskopf of the time, "saw the others daily. One heard them, spoke their language, even if only when compelled to. One dealt with them repeatedly, but one did not love them, know them, or want to know anything of them."

Things became even more problematic in 1918 when, within days of independence being declared, the statue of the Madonna on Old Town Square was torn down by demonstrators as too stark a reminder of "three hundred years of German occupation". Two years later, in November 1920, amidst city-wide anti-German/anti-Jewish demonstrations, the German-language Estates Theater was "taken over" by a Czech-speaking mob, and its resident actors, technicians and staff thrown out on to the street. That very night, a performance of the archetypal Czech national opera, Smetana's *The Bartered Bride*, was ostentatiously mounted, the audience presumably blind to the irony of its composer's first language being German and to the fact that his librettist, Karel Sabina (1813-77), was subsequently revealed to be an Austrian police informer (see Chapter Four).

Despite this, the Czech state, especially as embodied in the person of "TGM", did its utmost to incorporate the German-speaking minority into the new nation, and there is clear evidence of a decline in "negativism"—the refusal by many Bohemian Germans even to recognize the existence of the Czechoslovak Republic—in the course of the 1920s, until the Nazi seizure of power and the rise of Henlein's Sudetendeutsche Partei sent the whole process into reverse. But Prague "Germans" viewed with misgivings the proposed integration of "Sudetenland" into the Reich which could only leave them more vulnerable and exposed, and there were some, not all of them Communists, who remained committed to Czechoslovakia up to, and beyond, September 1938. Johannes Urzidil, founder of the significantly named Protective Union of German Writers in the Czechoslovak Republic, spoke for many of his community when he described himself as "hinternational", living "behind national identities, not merely above or below them."

For all this, the bulk of Prague's non-Jewish German-speaking population welcomed the arrival of the Nazi occupying force in March 1939 and their own incorporation in the so-called Protectorate of Bohemia and Moravia. Parts of the city were symbolically re-germanized, German street names returned, and Prague was promoted as a "center of German culture", indeed, in anticipation of today's tourist brochures, as "Mozart's second home"; in a ceremony heavy with symbolism, Smetanovo nábřeží was renamed after Mozart. But these were semiological trifles, and in no way implied a return to pre-1860 power for the German-speaking minority. Under its figurehead Czech-speaking president Emil Hácha, the Protectorate was run by and from the Reich in the interests of the Reich—not that this prevented Prague's tiny German-speaking rump from being dispatched westwards in 1945-46 along with their supposed fellow Germans from the fictional "Sudetenland".

Zionism and Migration

Barely distinguishable before 1914, the German and Jewish populations of Prague began to move somewhat apart during and after the Great War, though never to the extent, before 1939, of being clearly and absolutely separable one from the other. One reason for the emerging demarcation was the spread of Zionist ideas among the Jewish intelligentsia, particularly those members of the Jewish student association, Bar Kochba, who attended Martin Buber's famous Three Lectures on Judaism in 1909-10 and who, for the first time, heard an alternative to their own instinctive assimilationist assumptions vigorously spelled out. There were not many of them—Max Brod said that "if the ceiling of a certain café (the Café Gieringer) collapses, then it's the end of all Prague Zionism"—but their influence would grow after 1918 and increasingly challenge the traditional Germanocentrism of the Jewish elite. The influence of Izak Löwy's travelling Yiddish theater on Kafka is also well known, and Kafka's own preoccupation with Judaism and with his own Jewishness towards the end of his life—the 1920 anti-Semitic riots touched him directly—is symptomatic of a growing ethnic and religious self-consciousness amongst Prague Jews as a whole.

Another factor was the influx of eastern European Jews into Prague after the outbreak of war in 1914. These were mainly refugees from Polish Galicia who spoke Yiddish, looked and dressed "Jewish" in a way that the old Prague community certainly did not, and whose religion was most definitely not something to be pursued discreetly in private; many were also openly and passionately Zionist. The rise of fascism in Europe, including, to a limited extent, in Czechoslovakia itself, also lent itself to ethnic and religious differentiation within the German-speaking community. The home-grown fascist party, General Radola Gajda's numerically insignificant *Vlajka* (The Flag) did its best to revive the old bugaboo of Jewish ritual murder.

Nonetheless, the impression persists that, compared to inter-war Poland, Hungary or Romania (to say nothing of Germany, Austria and even France), Czechoslovakia was not, the 1920 riots apart, virulently or aggressively anti-Semitic. What happened in the Czech lands after 1940—Slovakia, headed by the undoubtedly anti-Semitic Catholic cleric Josef Tiso, is another matter entirely—happened at the instigation of the occupier alone, with no evidence of tacit, let alone active, support on the part of sections of the local population. But what happened has nonetheless no parallel in the history of the European holocaust.

Terezín: Holocaust and Music

The brute statistics are terrible and typical enough. Of the 118,310 people in the "Protectorate of Bohemia and Moravia" classified as "Jewish"—the figure includes a large number of Jewish refugees from Germany and Austria—in March 1939, 26,111 were able to emigrate, 14,045 survived the war and 78,154 perished at German hands. Invidious though it is to single out individual casualties, it should be recorded that all three of Kafka's sisters (Elli, Ottla, and Valli) died in the camps, as did Milena Jesenská, though she was interned and killed as a political prisoner and not as a Jew.

These stark figures conceal the extraordinary story of Terezín (Theresienstadt), a massive and probably impregnable fortress-town some forty miles to the northwest of Prague, built in the 1780s by Joseph II and named after his mother Maria Theresa, ominously so, since she it was who had instigated the most recent would-be "final solution" to the Bohemian Jewish problem by banishing the whole Jewish population of Prague from 1745 to 1748. Terezín consists of two fortresses, separated by about a mile, and located on opposite sides of the River Ohře. The *Malá Pevnost* (Small Fortress) to the east was the first to be commandeered by the German occupiers and from June 1940 was used as an internment center by the Prague Gestapo, receiving between then and May 1945 some 32,000 detainees (including 5,000 women), mainly Czech political prisoners, some of them Jews, Communists, members of *Sokol* and resistance groups like *Věrní zůstaneme* (We Remain Faithful), with more and more foreign nationals arriving towards the end of the war. The French surrealist poet Robert Desnos (1900-45) was one of the last of the 2,500 prisoners who perished in the fortress itself, with a further 8,000 dying in concentration camps elsewhere.

But it is the *Hlavní Pevnost*, or Main Fortress, to the west that is the more remarkable, first because its appearance—brick buildings laid out on a rectilinear plan, with avenues, squares and even parks—so defies the conventional huts-and-barbed-wire image of the concentration camp; second because of the truly devilish deceptive use to which it was put by the Nazis; and finally, both because of and despite all of this, on account of the extraordinary works of art—plays, paintings and, above all, music—that were created there between 1941 and 1945. In all, 139,654 people, almost all of them Jews but not all of them Czechs, entered the Main Fortress between November 1941 and May 1945. Of these 33,419 died on the site, and 86,934 were deported "to the east", principally to Auschwitz, where the overwhelming majority were killed; 17,320 detainees were liberated by the Soviet army at the end of the war. At least 15,000 children under the age of 15 passed through the "camp", of whom two—the novelists Arnošt Lustig and Ivan Klíma—survived to give accounts of their extraordinary experiences.

At first, the purpose of the camp was simply internment, and for a time detainees lived more or less side by side with the fortress's 3,000 or so permanent residents. These, however, were moved out in mid-1942, and the fortress became a "Jew-only" ghetto, nominally administered by the inmates themselves, but in reality serving as a transit center for eventual dispatch to the east. Under the overall control of S.S. Hauptsturmführer Dr. Siegried Seidl, a 32-strong "Council of Elders" (*Ältestenrat*) headed by Jakob Edelstein, the former secretary of the Socialist Zionist Party in Prague, was responsible for much of the day-to-day running of the camp, and it was the council which, with Nazi approval, organized the *Freizeitgestaltung*, or Administration of Free Time Activities, under whose aegis the *Kameradshaftsabende*, or fellowship evenings, took place, featuring plays, concerts, even operas performed by the inmates themselves. All the time prisoners were being transshipped to the east and new prisoners arrived, until, at the end of 1943, the Nazis conceived the fiendish idea of using the fortress as a model exhibit with which to deceive the International Red Cross as to the true nature and purpose of their concentration camp system. A policy of *Verschönerung*, or "beautification", was embarked upon, and the whole site was given the air of a spa-town, a fortified Marienbad just for the Jews, complete with park, rotunda and even a café. Bogus currency and stamps were issued to give the impression of a functioning, self-regulating community, and, on its arrival, the Red Cross inspection team was treated to a special performance of the children's opera *Brundibár* (Bumble Bee), written by the inmate-composer Hans Krása (1899-1944), and to a jam session at the café by the resident Ghetto Swingers, under their leader, the pianist Martin Roman. The visit was captured on film under the title *Der Führer schenkt den Juden eine Stadt* (The Führer donates a town to the Jews), with such success that the inspection team was *twice* comprehensively hoodwinked by the fiction of normality, in June 1944 and again as late as April 1945, and submitted positive reports to headquarters.

It is important to stress that, apart from the painters (whose work was often literally too close to the bone), the artists of Terezín were not generally working clandestinely, but with the approval, and often the active encouragement, of their Nazi oppressors. Nor were they normally amateurs, but in many instances from among the cream of the nation's professional artists: the noted cartoonist Bedřich Fritta (1906-44), the painters Leo Haas (1901-83), Ferdinand Bloch (1888-1944) and Otto Ungar (1901-43), the singers Anny Frey, Nella

Eisenschimmel, Lisl Hofer, Karel Berman and Walter Windholz, and the ballerina Kamila Rosenbaumová who both danced in and choreographed a range of stage works from *Brundibár* to the review *Long Live Life*. Musicians included the pianists Bernard Kaff (1905-44), Edith Steiner Kraus (born 1913) and Alice Herz Sommer (born 1903), the violinists Egon Ledeč (1889-1944) and Karel Fröhlich (born 1917), leader of the Terezín Quartet, and two notable child prodigies Pavel Kling (violin, born 1928) and Zuzana Růžičková (harpsichord, also born 1928). Writers such as Peter Kien (1919-44), Ilse Weber (1903-44) and Georg Kafka (1921-44) composed sketches, short stories, poems and plays, and the archetypally Czech art form of puppetry was kept alive by Jaroslav Dubský, Fredy Hirsch and Zdeněk Jelínek.

Dominating everything was Karel Ančerl (1908-73), perhaps the greatest Czech conductor of the twentieth century, and principal conductor of the Terezín string orchestra. Music of all styles and periods was performed, including works by Jewish and other "degenerate" composers that could not be heard in Prague at the time, and compositions were often interpreted—by performers and audiences in their respective ways—as reflections of the prisoners' present and future situations. Thus when Bernard Kaff performed Mussorgsky's *Pictures at an Exhibition* in June 1944, his rendering of the piece's radiant finale "The Great Gate of Kiev" was felt, over optimistically, to portend the imminent arrival of the liberating Red Army. What, on the other hand, it meant to hear the soprano Hilde Aronson-Lind perform Mahler's *Kindertotenlieder* in the summer of 1943 in a camp packed with doomed children can only be said to beggar description. Finally, a significant omission: not a note of Wagner was sung or played at Terezín throughout the duration.

But it is the composers of Terezín who have attracted most attention, and four of them, Pavel Haas (1899-1944), Hans Krása (1899-1944), Victor Ullman (1898-1944) and Gideon Klein (1921-45) have, thanks to Decca's enterprising *Entartete Musik* ("Degenerate Music" series), belatedly attained the fame they deserve. All save Klein had established themselves as composers before the outbreak of war, and Haas, as befitted Janáček's star pupil at the Brno Conservatory, was already renowned as a composer of chamber music. His *Suite for Oboe and Piano* (1939), written in immediate response to the Nazi takeover of the country, is notable for its use of themes from the St. Wenceslas Chorale and the Hussite battle-hymn "Ye Who Are God's Warriors"—a telling example of a Jewish composer identifying himself fully with the Czech nationalist tradition. Haas' output at Terezín was relatively sparse: a chorus for male voices (*Al S'fod*) based on poems in Hebrew by the Zionist Jakov Šimoni who was inspired by clashes between Jewish settlers and Palestinian Arabs in 1936-39 ("Do not lament, do not cry, when things are bad, do not lose heart, but work, work!"), an orchestral piece dedicated to Ančerl (*Suite for String Orchestra*), and a song-cycle written for his friend Karel Berman. This last piece, using Czech translations of Chinese texts, moves from melancholy and nostalgia to what, to this listener, sounds like a forced and sarcastic outburst of joy, hardly surprising in a work written between February and April 1944, six months before Haas' departure for Auschwitz.

Far more productive was the Silesian-born Victor Ullman, a pupil of Schönberg, who completed no fewer than twenty works while in Terezín, most notably the one-act opera (in German), *Der Kaiser von Atlantis oder der Tod dankt ab* (The Emperor of Atlantis, or Death Abdicates), to a libretto by fellow inmate Peter Kien. The opera, scored for five singers and a thirteen-piece orchestra, has a sub-text so obvious that it scarcely merits the preposition "sub": the wicked Emperor of Atlantis, Kaiser Überall, orders Death to lead his army into war whereupon Death goes on strike, Chaos ensues, and order is only restored when the Emperor himself submits to Death. Ullman laces his work with knowing musical winks to his sophisticated audience: an opening trumpet-call from Josef Suk's great *Asrael Symphony* (1907, Asrael being the Jewish Angel of Death), a minor-key send-up of *Deutschland über alles* in the middle and, at the climax, a chorus adapted from Martin Luther's *Ein' feste Burg ist unser Gott*.

The most famous Terezín opera, Hans Krása's *Brundibár* referred to above, also has a somewhat more concealed political sub-text which, given that the opera ran for an incredible 55 performances, was presumably never "cracked" by the Nazi authorities. The plot is well summarized in Joža Karas' *Music in Terezín 1941-1945*, the work primarily responsible for the rediscovery of all the composers discussed here:

The story of the opera deals with two children, Pepíček and Aninka (Little Joe and Annette), who have a sick mother. The doctor prescribed milk for her, but there is no money to buy it. Seeing the organ-grinder, Brundibár, as he plays on the street corner, the children begin singing, to the annoyance of the passers-by and Brundibár, who chases them away. Three animals—a dog, a cat, and sparrow—come to their aid. Together with the neighborhood children, they all sing a charming lullaby. People are touched and reward them with money. However, in an unguarded moment, Brundibár steals it. All the children and animals chase him and recover the money. The opera ends with a song of victory over the evil organ-grinder.

The opera had actually been written in 1938, to a text (in Czech) by Adolf Hoffmeister and was first performed in secret at a Jewish orphanage in Prague in November 1941, in the absence of the composer, the designer (František Zelenka) and the originally intended conductor (Rafaël Schächter) who were all by that time in Terezín. When the children themselves were dispatched to the camp in July 1943, the opera was revived and made immediate "stars" of the six principal singers, all of whom duly perished "in the east": Piñta Mühlstein (Pepiček), Greta Hofmeister (Aninka), Zdeněk Omstein (Dog), Ela Stein (Cat), Maria Mühlstein (Sparrow) and, above all, Honza Treichlinger, an orphan from Pilsen, who played the part of the mean organ-grinder Brundibár. A photograph survives of the children performing before the Red Cross committee, and to listen to Krása's buoyant, vibrant music on one of several modern recordings, and to the optimism and energy of the singing of the children, is to reflect, *inter alia*, on the connection between confinement and creativity to which we have already alluded. Lest the meaning of the work be lost on its original audience—and there was, surely, little chance of that happening!—the last lines, as the children celebrate Brundibár's undoing, was changed from "He who loves so much his mother and father and his native land is our friend and he can play with us" to "He who loves justice and will abide by it, and who is not afraid, is our friend and can play with us." Czech art is never greater than when it draws inspiration from constraint.

Of the 14,000 or so Czech Jews who survived the war, only 5,000 remained in the country at the time of the Communist takeover in

1948, and more still left when the regime revealed its "anti-Zionist" (i.e. anti-Semitic) character at the time of the show-trials of the early 1950s. Of the fourteen party cadres tried for "sabotage" or "espionage" in November 1952, eleven were listed as being "of Jewish origin", including the alleged ringleader, former party secretary Rudolf Slánský. A small Jewish community remains in Prague, principally composed of senior citizens: truly, as one holocaust survivor wryly observed, the Golem "has let us down once too often. Like him, we seem to be destined to return to lifeless clay. But what beautiful monuments we are leaving behind."

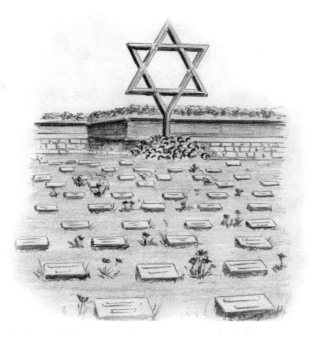

CHAPTER THREE

Josef K. and Josef Švejk: Trials and Triumphs

Vyšehrad Castle

Next to Hradčany, or perhaps even surpassing it, among the holy places of Czech nationalism is the castle of Vyšehrad (meaning "High Castle"), located on a rocky eminence just south of the New Town, a couple of miles upriver from Charles Bridge. It is by tradition the site of the earliest Slav settlement in the Prague region, upon which Krok, a descendant of the mythical Ur-Bohemian Čech, built the first castle, from which, in due course, his youngest daughter Libuše, the country's one-and-only female ruler celebrated in Smetana's eponymous opera (1881, see Chapter Four), set out to found the city of Prague itself. Not for nothing was Bohemia's first scientific journal, founded by Josef Jungmann and others in 1821, given the name *Krok*.

Vyšehrad quickly lost importance to Hradčany, though it continued to be the starting-point of the traditional coronation route (*králová cesta*) followed by each new king of Bohemia, and was effectively recreated in the nineteenth century as the matrix and shrine of Czech identity, whose composite, constructed and, at times, downright bogus character is no more evident than here. The most visible part of the complex is the Church of Saints Peter and Paul, whose successive reconstructions capture in microcosm the history of the nation. Upon the site of the Romanesque original, a Gothic structure was erected under Charles IV, which was completely rebuilt in the Baroque style between 1723 and 1729, as part of the thoroughgoing "Jesuitization" of the city. No self-respecting Czech nationalist could accept so "alien" a structure, and between 1885 and 1887, under the direction of the same Josef Mocker who was in charge of the cathedral project, the whole Renaissance and Baroque interior was ripped out and replaced by polychrome decorations in the neo-Gothic style. Even this was not enough for the architectural hard-liners, and in 1902 the Baroque facade was replaced by an (inevitably) neo-Gothic substitute by František Mikeš, and the entire edifice crowned by two ugly, open-work spires whose discordant bulk mars the whole panorama of the city.

To the south of the church lies a grassy oblong, at each corner of which stands a gargantuan statue by the sculptor Josef Václav Myslbek (1843-1922), best known for his statue of Wenceslas on Wenceslas Square (see Chapter Six). Hewn, rather than sculpted, between 1889 and 1897, these nationalist colossi were first mounted on Palacký Bridge, and were moved to Vyšehrad between 1848 and 1870 when the bridge had to be modified to provide a new access road. Each statue monumentalizes a couple drawn from Czech nationalist myth: Libuše and Přemysl, founders of Bohemia's first ruling dynasty, Lumír and Píseň, the first the Czech version of Orpheus and the second his Muse (Singer and Song: one sees yet again how fundamental music is to Czech national identity), and Ctirad and Šárka, who may be said to have inaugurated the Prague tradition of suicide-from-a-height when, having tricked Ctirad to his death and fallen in love with him in so doing, she threw herself off a cliff in the valley to the northwest of the city that now bears her name. The fourth statue depicts two warriors named Záboj and Slavoj, so mythical that there is no mention of them anywhere prior to the early nineteenth century when, as though on cue, they were conveniently "discovered" or, more accurately, invented and duly took their place in the carefully assembled mosaic of Czech national identity. Before all else, Vyšehrad is a monument to what has been called "invented tradition" or "imagined community", the whole site proof in stone of the truth of Ernest Renan's dictum that "historical error [or, in this case, hoax] is an essential factor in the formation of a nation."

Curiously, but not inappositely, it was the "discoverer" of the story of Záboj and Slavoj, one Václav Hanka (died 1861) who was the first to be buried in what is now Vyšehrad's centerpiece, the national cemetery. Beginning in 1817, Hanka "discovered" several sets of manuscripts that he claimed dated from between the tenth and the thirteenth centuries, the most important of them becoming known as the Dvůr Kralové manuscript after the Bohemian town where it was allegedly found. The supposedly ancient texts contained, written in Old Czech, poems about known and as-yet unheard-of Bohemian heroes and heroines, and seemed (and were certainly intended to by their "discoverer") to place Czech literature on an equal standing with German. These were the authenticating Homeric poems of an authentic nation, the *Niebelungenlied* of the future *národ*. In 1858 Hanka was accused of forgery by one of Prague's leading German-language newspapers and sued successfully for libel; the paper's editor was Jewish, and the controversy over the manuscripts is said to have been one cause, among many, of the anti-Jewish/anti-German riots of 1861. It was not until more than twenty years after Hanka's death that his manuscripts were shown conclusively to be an elaborate fraud, thanks to the philologist Jan Gebauer (1838-1907) and—displaying yet again the extraordinary range of his talents—Tomas Masaryk, who revealed for the first time his distaste for the essentialist myth-, language- and ethnicity-based nationalism of the Jungmann-Palacký school. But the controversy refused to die down. When another inveterate hoaxer, Jaroslav Hašek, creator of the Good Soldier Švejk, formed his bogus "Party of Moderate Progress within the Bounds of the Law" in 1911, the defense of the "genuineness of the manuscripts" was one of the major planks of his mock manifesto.

Vyšehrad Cemetery

Hanka may have been an inauspicious beginning, but the cemetery, as it gradually filled over the ensuing decades, is undeniably impressive, both more and less than Prague's open-air version of Paris' Panthéon, for it is reserved solely for artists, intellectuals and scientists, with mere politicians conspicuously excluded. If Václav Havel is eventually buried at Vyšehrad, it will be as the playwright and emphatically not as the President of the Republic. Here are to be found almost all of Bohemia's, and some of Moravia's, artistic "greats": composers (Smetana, Dvořák, Fibich), singers (the superbly named, and appropriately passionate, Ema Destinová), sculptors and painters (Myslbek and Šaloun, creators of Wenceslas and Jan Hus respectively, Alfons Mucha and Bohumil Kafka), architects (Josef Gočar) and writers (Božena Němcová, Jan Neruda, Karel Čapek). Some lie in individual graves, others are buried together in the huge Slavín monument, erected in 1893, which, in all, contains the remains of more than fifty Czech writers, painters, musicians and sculptors.

Most potent of all, though not the most visually impressive, is the grave of Karel Hynek Mácha (1810-36) whom we have already encountered as the doomed author of the long poem *Maj* (1836) and traditionally regarded as the "founder" of modern Czech poetry (much as Němcová is the "founder" of the Czech novel, and Smetana the "founder" of its music). Like all "new nations", Czechoslovakia was obsessed with origins, foundation and inauguration. Mácha had died, and been buried, at Litoměřice in western Bohemia, but when that region was absorbed into the Reich in March 1939, his body was exhumed and brought back to Prague, the poet's native city, where, after a massively attended funeral procession through the streets, it was reburied at Vyšehrad. It was Prague's equivalent of the return of Victor Hugo's remains to Paris in 1840, but in a spirit of national mourning as much of national pride. Nowhere more powerfully than Vyšehrad demonstrates the centrality of art and artists to Czech national consciousness: it is the artist, not the politician, the creator of fictions rather than the dealer in facts, who is the true *buditel*, or awakener, of the sleeping beauty of the nation. Significantly, the student demonstration that triggered the collapse of the Communist regime in November 1989 began at the grave of Karel Hynek Mácha.

In view of all this, it is disconcerting to find that the four greatest Czech artists of the late nineteenth and twentieth century are not buried at Vyšehrad. The sculptor František Bilek is buried at his home of Chýnov near Tábor. Opera composer Leoš Janáček, who was in any case more of a Moravian than a Czech, and almost all of whose works were premiered in Brno rather than Prague, is buried in the Moravian capital and is not, for that and other reasons, discussed in this book. But, exact contemporaries, Franz Kafka and Jaroslav Hašek were both born and brought up in Prague, and Kafka, at least, rarely left the city except on holiday until the onset of tuberculosis forced him to seek extended treatment elsewhere. He died at a sanatorium near Vienna and is buried in the New Jewish Cemetery in Prague, in the same grave as his father and mother, who survived him by seven and ten years respectively. Hašek, after returning to Prague in December 1920 after five eventful years in war- and then revolution-torn Russia, soon left the city for the small town of Lipnice a hundred miles or so to the southwest where he proceeded rapidly to drink himself to death, all the time writing, or dictating, the final version of *The Good Soldier Švejk*. In the absence of other information, it is assumed here that he is buried in the town where he died.

Kafka and Hašek

Kafka's reputation, reviled or repressed in Communist Czechoslovakia, has never been higher, either internationally or in his own native city which, after rejecting or ignoring him for decades, has now, with the help of the Prague tourist board, enthusiastically embraced him. His stereotyped image adorns coffee cups, T-shirts and other such merchandise, and you can meet for coffee at the Café Milena, the Café Franz, even the Café Samsa (after Gregor Samsa, the insect-hero of *Metamorphosis*). Hašek, on the other hand, after having been feted by the Communist regime as an active supporter of the Bolshevik cause, and enshrined for tourist consumption at *U kalicha* (one of the few *pivnice* in Prague at which, despite its prominence in his novel, he did *not* regularly get drunk), is probably now in abeyance. He is little read, though more often referred to, outside the Czech Republic, and even there perhaps with greater reserve, or a less passionate identification, than in the past. Švejk is the icon of an unfree society, and his story of survival by being, or feigning to be, dumb may have less to tell, and less power to delight, a society which, in 1989, was, for the first time in fifty dismal years, at last freed from the assorted ideologues and fanatics, informers and spies, who populate the pages of Hašek's rambling epic of human stupidity.

So precisely do Kafka and Hašek contrast with, and complement, each other that their lives may almost be tabulated as a series of binary opposites:

KAFKA	HAŠEK
Born in Old Town (Staroměstské náměsti)	Born in New Town (Skolská Street, near Charles Square)
Jewish (non-believing)	Catholic (non-believing)

German-speaking	Czech-speaking
Dominated by father	Father died when he was thirteen
Never married	Bigamist
No defined political beliefs	One-time anarchist, later supporter of Bolshevik cause
Hardly published in lifetime	Prolific producer of short stories and articles

Even physically, they were as Laurel to Hardy: Kafka abstemious, vegetarian, almost anorexic even before the onset of tuberculosis, Hašek an alternately loud-mouthed and sullen beer-drinker, weighing a reputed 336 pounds towards the end of his life. Whereas Kafka was sharp-eyed and almost maniacally alert, Hašek was slow and slovenly, with heavy hoods over his world-weary eyes. They were, one may assume, totally unknown to each other (though Max Brod was a champion of the writings of both), yet both were vitally concerned with the question of power, and how to survive it when one is powerless. The most famous novel of each centers around an unjust accusation: of disrespect to the portrait of His Imperial Majesty in the case of the character Josef Švejk; of everything, anything and nothing in that of Joseph K. Both, in short, were provincial subjects of the Austro-Hungarian Empire, on opposite sides in the riots of 1897 as in practically everything else, yet united in their sense of helplessness in the face of authority. And both, after their death, achieved the rare feat of giving their name, or the name of their principal fictional creation, to the international vocabulary, though what precisely is meant by "the Kafkaesque" or by "Švejkism" is not easily defined, explaining the need for the words in the first place.

Kafka's Prague

Since his political rehabilitation and adoption by the Prague tourist industry, Kafka has been thoroughly reinserted into the life of the city. So thorough has been his reassessment, in fact, that, where he was once praised (by non-Czechs) for the "universality" of his vision, he is now seen (and not just by Czechs) as a Prague writer not only first and foremost but also through and through. The new orthodoxy is, needless to say, an improvement on the old, but still lends itself to frequent simplifications and occasional gross reductions. It is naïve, for example, to say that Kafka's castle is "based on" Hradčany or that the cathedral in the penultimate chapter of *The Trial* is a transcription or transposition of St.Vitus Cathedral. Equally, however, both structures have some bearing on Kafka's verbal constructions, just as it is difficult to believe that he would have written *The Great Wall of China* without the example of Charles IV's so-called Hunger Wall or *Hladová zed* that reaches down from Petřin almost to the Vltava and was built in the 1460s, supposedly to provide work for the destitute; it seems likely, however, that the wall was principally financed by the expropriation of Jewish-owned property.

Much, too, is made of Kafka's "double", "triple" or even "quadruple" exile within Prague society: as a Jew among Gentiles (and a non-practicing Jew into the bargain), as a German-speaker amongst Czech-speakers (though he was in fact fluent in Czech), as a writer amongst philistines, and so on. (Incidentally, all such labels would also fit Max Brod or Franz Werfel, and any number of other German-language Jewish writers in the city.) Indeed, as we have seen, the dividing-line between German-speaking Jews and non-Jews was so vague as to be effectively non-existent, and it was the norm among Prague Jews—Hermann Kafka was typical—to be lukewarm and superficial in the practice of their religion. Finally, there can have been few cities in Europe where the vocation and practice of writing were more highly esteemed than in Prague, though here admittedly Kafka senior was a boorish exception to the rule. It needs to be said that no character in Kafka's work is *identifiably* Jewish and that his novelistic vision is anything but the view from the ghetto, which in any case was no more than a memory as a distinctively *Jewish* quarter of the city as Kafka grew up on and around Old Town Square, geographically only a few hundred yards from Josefov, it is true, but a whole universe away in terms of values, attitudes and lifestyles.

Living with his parents until aged thirty-two, Kafka never moved far, in terms of the daily routine of his life, from the Old and New Towns. His work took him to the offices of the Assicurazioni Generali and, after 1908, the Arbeiter-Unfall-Versicherungsanstalt (Workers' Accident Insurance Company) on Wenceslas Square. From here it was

Kafka's House

a short walk to the various literary cafés that Kafka frequented: the Louvre, the Continental, the Arco, all of which were situated on or around the present Národní trída, known before 1918 as Ferdinandstrasse. One of Kafka's earliest texts, now lost, is entitled *The Child and the City*, and, if his childhood city was undoubtedly circumscribed, that of the adolescent and adult was far broader, and more varied, than the received image of his life would suggest. He obviously knew Malá Strana—it was there in a hotel that he lost his virginity in 1903, and he later rented an apartment in the Schönborn Palace, the present American Embassy, in 1917. He was also a regular visitor to his sister Ottla's tiny lodgings on Alchimistengässchen (Zlatá ulička) in the Hradčany complex.

But Kafka was also familiar with areas further afield, not least the "classic" working-class suburb of Žižkov where his brother-in-law Karl Hermann owned an asbestos factory in which Kafka had a financial—if no other—interest. He was nonetheless obliged to go there from time to time, and his diary contains fascinating descriptions of the factory, its (principally female) employees, the streets he went through, by tram, in order to get there, and of the "mixed feelings of fear, of being abandoned, of pity, of curiosity, of pride, of joy of travel, of manliness" that he experienced as he did so (*Diary*, November 18, 1911). It was, apparently, after one such visit that he noted a reaction not uncommon in a city where the verbal surname

Vyscočil ("he jumped out") is as familiar as Nevečeřel ("he didn't get any supper"): "Was reproached because of the factory the day before yesterday. Then spent an hour on the sofa thinking about jumping out of the window." (*Diary*, March 8, 1912).

Virtually nothing of this appears by name in any of his works. Only the early text *Description of a Struggle*, begun in 1904, contains precise topographical references, and then only of a schematic kind: Ferdinandstrasse, Laurenziberg (Petřín), Karlsgasse (Karlova) and, inevitably, Charles Bridge, where we can deduce from the words of one character how much Kafka admired the statue of St. Ludmilla, especially the hands of the angel to her left: "How delicate they are! Real angel's hands!" That Kafka had studied the statues with the attentive eye of a roving semiotician is shown by a letter of 1920 to his friend Minze Eisner in which he likens the artistic process to the relief on the base of the statues of Saints Vincent Ferrer and Procopius. This shows St. Procopius pushing a plough drawn by a devil, the point being, according to Kafka, that the artist must make use of the devil in himself if he is to cultivate and make fertile the soil of his genius. But otherwise there is only inference and guesswork to go by. Thus it is clear from the context that the "small stone quarry, deserted and bleak" where K. is put to death at the end of *The Trial* "corresponds" to the quarry on Strahov on the other side of Petřín where the Spartakiad Stadium was built in the 1930s to showcase the Sokol movement's massive gymnastics displays.

Similarly, Kafka's biography enables us to locate the bridge from which, in the story *The Judgment*, his alter ego George Bendemann throws himself in obedience to his father's sentence of death by drowning: not Charles Bridge, as the Nepomuk parallel might plausibly suggest, but the Čech Bridge further downriver that leads from Pařížská over to Letná. In June 1907, the Kafkas moved from Zeltnergasse (Celetná) to a flat at 36 Niklasstrasse (the future Pařížská) overlooking the bridge, and it was here, in a single sitting on the night of September 22-23, 1912, that Kafka famously wrote the story—namely *The Judgment*—that in many ways marked his breakthrough as a writer. Kafka called Niklasstrasse the "Run-up Street for Suicides," and it is along this street and to the bridge that Bendemann heads following his father's condemnation.

Out of the front door he rushed, across the roadway, driven towards the water. Already he was grasping at the railings as a starving man clutches food. He swung himself over, like the distinguished gymnast he had once been in his youth, to his parents' pride. With weakening grip he was still holding on when he spied between the railings a motor-bus coming which would easily cover the noise of his fall, called in a low voice: "Dear parents, I have always loved you, all the same," and let himself drop. At this moment an unending stream of traffic was just going over the bridge.

Dear parents, Dearest father...

It is impossible, even in a book such as this, to pass over Kafka's relationship with his father, not for reasons of individual psychology, but because, in his work, the totality of experience, historical and individual, collective and personal, is patterned according to the original father-son template. In his extraordinary *Letter to his Father* (November 1919)—extraordinary not least because Kafka partly refutes the accusations he makes, justifying his father as much as condemning him—we glimpse what Gilles Deleuze and Félix Guattari, two of Kafka's most stimulating critics, call a comprehensive "Oedipianization" of the universe. Father is to Son as God is to the world, as the Law is to mankind, as Name is to Thing and Power to its objects, as Gentiles are to Jews, Austria to Bohemia, and so vertiginously on, until the son can see nothing more than a "map of the world spread out flat and you stretched out diagonally across it." Like a gross provincial version of the Emperor Franz Josef on his throne in Vienna, "from your armchair you ruled the world." Of course, by the time Kafka came to write these undelivered words, both the Austro-Hungarian Empire and its aged emperor had been swept away by the cataclysm of 1918. The son and ex-imperial subject now knew, if he had not done so before, that the Father, like God, like the Law and the Austria and Franz Josef of old were as empty as Hradčany castle had been for three centuries, and that his (and their) "power" existed only by image, by its imprint on the mind of the subject and son. The father first appears to the son as both magician and Golem—spiritually all-powerful, physically vast—but gradually reveals himself to be no more than a bullying homunculus, a cliché-spouting puppet, no more powerful in reality than the "old dolls with no heads" that the young

Kafka, in another classic Prague image, imagines he sees when the doors of the Ark of the Covenant are opened on one of the rare visits he and his father make to the synagogue. The paternal Golem is powerful only because the son cannot bring himself to remove the parchment he has placed under his tongue or, varying the image, because every day he restores the *aleph*, or "E", to the letters incised on his head, himself transforming the truth (METH, he is dead) into the lie (EMETH, he is truth) that oppresses him. The father has power only to the extent that the son cannot, or will not, contest it, just as the authority of K.'s accusers resides solely in the authority he concedes them: "The Court makes no claims on you," the priest tells K. in the cathedral, "it receives you when you come and it relinquishes you when you go."

And it was the same thing, arguably, in the political sphere: Austria was able to rule Bohemia for so long only because, at some level, Bohemia permitted it to do so. Like K. before his illegitimate and in reality powerless judges, Bohemia stood before Austria as a self-accused defendant before an incompetent and toothless tribunal, the self-condemned victim of a still guiltier victimizer, both protesting against and accepting the sentence passed on it. How appropriate, incidentally, that Leopold von Sacher-Masoch (1835-95), author of *Venus in Furs* (1870), was the son of the Austrian chief of police in Prague after 1848. Even in 1914, most Czech nationalists did not envisage a total break with Vienna as either possible or desirable, remaining in thrall, like Kafka to his father, or the citizens of *The Great Wall of China* to the memory of their probably long since dead Emperor, to the image of the decrepit Franz Josef, physically absent but present in their homes, offices and pubs in countless mass-produced portraits, even if, like the one in *U kalicha*, they were spattered all over with fly-shit.

The Castle

Things had changed at least outwardly by the time—August-September 1920—that Kafka made the first sketches of *The Castle* (*Das Schloss*). Czechoslovakia was independent, and Hradčany, though in a state of considerable disrepair pending Plečnik's renovations, was at least formally a locus of power for the first time for three hundred years or more. But Kafka's castle is obviously not a transcription of the Hrad in any straightforward sense. It is, in the first place, located in the country and looks out not even over a town, let alone a major European city, but a village with a couple of inns, a schoolhouse, and various other buildings with which it co-exists in deeply problematic symbiosis. Most spiritually or metaphysically oriented interpretations of the novel set up a fairly clear-cut opposition between castle and village, making of the first the abode of divine law and grace into which K., the land surveyor (a modern version of the Comenian pilgrim), is trying to gain entrance, and of the second the domain of mere existence, the fallen world of eating, sleeping, copulation, from which he, again like Comenius' pilgrim, seeks deliverance. Yet closer reading of the novel deconstructs any such dualistic opposition of castle/spirit/essence versus village/matter/existence, showing them to be in alliance rather than antithesis with each other. *Schloss* in German means "lock" as well as "castle", and the castle is less the goal of K.'s "pilgrimage" than an obstacle to it. Indeed, the castle, or what can be seen of it, seems curiously village-like, "just a wretched-looking small town, a collection of rustic hovels", differentiated from the village only—or rather "possibly"—in that it appears to be made of stone: "It was neither an old-style knight's stronghold, nor a modern palace, but an extended complex consisting of a few two-storied but a great many lower buildings set close together; had you not known it was a castle, you might have taken it for a small town."

A small town: that at least bears more than a passing resemblance to Hradčany, just as its bizarre hierarchies recall those of the now vanished Austro-Hungarian empire. A "Count Westwest" is said to live there, but all K. ever encounters are the deputies of deputies, secretaries' secretaries, messengers without a message, women who are by no means the intermediaries to power they claim to be: "Nowhere before had K. seen officialdom and life as interwoven as they were here, so interwoven that it sometimes even looked as if officialdom and life had changed places." The paradox of *The Castle* is that the "action" of the novel—in reality, the whole of this non-pilgrimage is made up of one non-action after another—takes place principally in the Bridge and Count's inns, on which a hypothetical watcher from the castle "found no purchase and kept sliding away." Indeed, *The Castle* is scarcely less a pub novel than the first part of *The Good Soldier Švejk*, and turns the religious commonplace of life-a-way-without-an-inn comprehensively on its head: life here is an inn without a way. Not that K. is any more "at home" in either of the inns than anywhere else: "You're not from the castle, you're not from the village, you're nothing," K.'s landlady tells him. "Unfortunately there's one thing you are, though, namely a stranger, an outsider, someone who's superfluous to requirements and in everybody's way." Kafka would have written those words not long after the anti-German/anti-Jewish riots of November 1920 confronted him as never before with the ambivalence of his civic, let alone, his metaphysical identity. Both castle and village are suspended in a state of in-betweenness, and K. is suspended in between them, ironically "freer than ever before" and curiously invulnerable, and yet convinced at the same time that "there was nothing more futile, nothing more desperate than this freedom, this waiting, this invulnerability." In Kafka's world, there is no way in and no way out; the labyrinth of the world without is mirrored in the labyrinth of the world within, and there is no "paradise of the heart" outside the labyrinth, because the very opposition of inside/outside has been deconstructed like that of guilt and innocence, freedom and unfreedom, essence and existence, and any other such antithesis on which the structured universe is founded.

Švejk: Stupidity and Survival

To move from Kafka to Haček, and from K. to Švejk, is, on the one hand, to move from existential anguish to picaresque farce but, on the other, to confront the same set of issues, differently presented from a different point of view and with very different fictional results. For Švejk, like Kafka's land surveyor, is a version, comic not tragic, of the Comenian pilgrim in the *Labyrinth of the World*, and, like his seventeenth-century prototype, he does indeed discover—in fact he never leaves—an inner Paradise of contentment, in his case the paradise of an impregnable idiocy. In the course of his "odyssey" or "anabasis"—Hašek's own words—he does not so much discover as repeat himself in an endless variety of circumstances. With one "Humbly report, sir" after another, and with a "When I was in the 91st regiment" always ready on his lips, Švejk resembles nothing so much as a ventriloquist's dummy who is spoken through rather than speaks. He is a puppet out of whose mouth issue narratives so tortuous, extended and essentially meaningless as to confer upon him a total immunity. For Švejk is, or feigns to be, an idiot in the literal sense of the word: one so self-enclosed, so turned in on himself, that the world simply bounces off his impervious exterior, rebounding time after time from "the innocent, gentle, modest and tender warmth of his gaze". Švejk has the "god-like composure of an innocent child", the impenetrable radiance of the truly imbecilic: it is impossible for the powerful to gain any hold on one so manifestly and undividedly doltish.

Things are stupid, so I'll be stupid: such, to the extent that he reasons, is Švejk's response to the power of the Austro-Hungarian empire which, in the process, is revealed to be something like ninety percent illusion and ten percent real force, and Švejk has sense enough to realize that that ten percent is important. Power, to repeat, is the central theme of both Kafka and Hašek, but their characters' response to it could not be more different. K., at root, thinks that he is brighter, intellectually, than his accusers and that, ultimately, reason—*his* reason—will prevail. Švejk, on the other hand, accepts the illogic of the system and tailors his behavior accordingly. He survives by dint of his cloddishness, while K.'s constant ratiocination leads to his death. K. is led *up* to Strahov to be slain as some kind of sacrificial victim—but to what?—with a "long, thin, double-edged butcher's knife", such as Jakob Kafka, Hermann's father, wielded for a living; Švejk is led *down* from detention in Hradčany to continue his life in the city below. K. dies with the words "Like a dog!" on his lips; Švejk makes a living by catching and selling stray dogs, "ugly, mongrel monstrosities whose pedigrees he forged." Could ever a contrast be starker?

But, for all their differences, the worlds of Kafka and Hašek, and of K. and Švejk, are recognizably cognate. It is not just that Švejk, like

K., goes from office to office, and from one tribunal or court to another, caught up in the labyrinthine complexities of a decaying autocracy, nor even that he encounters a succession of sadists and fanatics far more terrifying than anything in *The Trial*. The works of both writers are pervaded by what Hašek calls "the spirit of alien authority"—political in *Švejk*, metaphysical in *The Trial*—and teem with all manner of spies, informers, proxies and agents. One of Švejk's co-accused has been arrested for the Kafkaesque offense of *not* being concerned in any way by the assassination of the Archduke Ferdinand at Sarajevo. Both Kafka and Hašek draw on the same corpus of typical Prague images; there are executions, martyrs and victims on practically every page of *Švejk*, from the "naked man with a halo and a body that was turning green, like the parson's nose of a goose which has begun to rot and is already stinking" on Father Katz's field altar to the picture that he has on the wall of his vestry of a martyr who stares open-mouthed and almost indifferent as his buttocks are sawn through by a band of Roman mercenaries, showing neither suffering nor joy, "as though he wanted to say: 'How on earth did this happen to me? What on earth are you doing to me, gentlemen?'" There are not too many puppets and dolls, other than the doll-like Švejk himself, repeated *seriatim* in Josef Lada's famous illustrations, but it is with a sigh of familiarity that we read of Švejk's charwoman threatening to throw herself out of a window or learn, from Hašek's biographer, that he himself once tried, or pretended, to commit suicide by—inevitably—throwing himself, Nepomuk-style, off Charles Bridge.

Perhaps the most obvious difference between their two worlds is that, with Hašek, we move a class down, from the sophistication of the Louvre and the Arco to the bonhomie and vitality of the *pivnice* and cabarets that were at once the blessing and bane of his life. These were the Montmartre on Řetězová, the Kopmanka on Templová, the Vales on Karolina Světlá, all these in the Old Town, and, in Vinohrady, U zlatého litru (The Golden Liter) on Balbinová and U kravína (The Cowshed) on Korunní. At the last of these establishments the Party of Moderate Progress within the Bounds of the Law was launched to contest the imperial parliamentary elections of June 1911: Hašek received thirty-five votes, seventeen invalid and eighteen spoiled. It was in places like these that Hašek boozed, boomed, stuffed himself with *knedlíky* and watched. Here, too, that he wrote, *slivovice* in hand, until, what with the food, the drink and the writing, he burned himself out. "Man proposes, the pub transposes," he memorably wrote: it is a typically double-edged summation of the man and his work.

K. and Švejk under Communism

The terms "Kafkaesque" and "Švejkism" (Švejkovina) came to have such currency in discussions of the Czech historical experience between 1948 and 1989 because they so suggestively evoke, in the first case, the most daunting characteristic of the country's Communist regime—all-encompassing but invisible, absent and present, the hyperlogic of its discourse concealing all manner of irrational obsessions—and, in the second, the way most Czechs, including those nominally in power, sought to deal with "the system", not by open resistance, which was clearly impossible, but by a combination of masquerade, maneuver and manipulation designed to preserve at least a modicum of inner freedom beneath a facade of external compliance. It was not, of course, *just* the Communist regime to which the two concepts, born of the Austro-Hungarian Empire, might be applied— for Czechs, neither oppression nor opposition began in 1948—but never before, not even under the Nazis, had a political system so dominated first public and then private space, creating what seemed to be an absolute disparity between the *total* power of the powerful and the *total* powerlessness of the excluded. It was not just that the political system dominated civil society but that there was, in effect, no civil society at all. But even the idea of the all-powerfulness of the powerful was an illusion, because, as Václav Havel argued in his great essay "The Power of the Powerless" (1979), surely one of the key political texts of the twentieth century, even the powerful are in thrall to an ideology that dominates them as much as the powerless. In this way the distinction between ruler and ruled becomes virtually meaningless, as "by pulling everyone into its power structure, the post-totalitarian system makes everyone an instrument of mutual totality, the auto-totality of society." Writes Havel, "everyone in his own way is both a victim and supporter of the system."

It was not until the early 1960s that Czechs began, *sotto voce*, to say "it's pure Kafka" when confronted with the labyrinthine absurdities of the Communist system. This was because the regime had until then effectively suppressed all discussion of Kafka or, when his name came to be mentioned, instantly labeled him and his work as the epitome of "capitalist" alienation, decadence, pessimism, intellectualism, idealism, negativism and whatever: the fact that he was Jewish and a German-speaker to boot was also explicitly leveled against him. Things began to change in November 1963 when, to celebrate the eightieth anniversary of Kafka's birth, a conference organized by the scholar Eduard Goldstücker (Jewish, German-speaking, former Terezín internee and a life-long Communist) took place at Liblice just outside of Prague. All the participants were Communists, but several came from outside the Soviet bloc, particularly the Austro-Marxist Ernst Fischer and the French Communist Roger Garaudy who made no secret of their admiration for Kafka. The conference lasted only two days, but is now widely seen as one of the earliest sources of the spirit of "Prague 68", notably in its defense of Kafka's blend of hyper-realism and surreality—so contrary to the morally and politically simplistic socialist realism of accredited party literature. Still more provocative was its insistence that the kind of "alienation" evoked in *The Trial* was not a monopoly of capitalist societies, but could equally exist under "socialism" as well. The papers themselves were suppressed, but from the attacks on the conference published in the widely read *Literární noviny* (see Chapter Six), Czechs were able to deduce what had been said. The defense of Kafka, or even a simple interest in his work, little of which was available in Czech translation, became a scarcely veiled attack on the regime's intellectual repression as a whole. In the 1970s, Kafka would virtually be blamed for causing Prague 68, and reading, and admiring his works once more became a necessarily private oppositional activity.

It was also after 1970 that Švejk and Švejkism came into their own. The situation of Czechoslovakia under "normalization" was very different from that, say, of Poland at the same time. In Poland, the existence of the Catholic Church *outside* of "the system" provided an ideological and institutional space from which Communism could be *resisted* and from which, in due course, a mass movement like Solidarity could be born. But in Czechoslovakia, the Catholic Church was effectively part of the system, for reasons that need briefly to be explained. Between 1948 and 1952, a bitter ideological and political war was fought between Church and newly implanted regime. Catholic schools, publishing houses and newspapers were closed and by April 1950, 2,000 monks had been interned in concentration camps; monasteries and convents dissolved and one priest, Father Josef Toufar, tortured to death. Not only this, but what remained of the Church had been split by the creation of an organization called Catholic Action (later Pax in Terra) under a Father Joseph Plojhar which was able to recruit enough priests and practicing Catholics to be able to pose, despite papal excommunication, as the "official" (i.e. pro-regime) Catholic Church in the land.

The "True Church" went underground but was never strong enough to act as a counter-force to the ideology and institutions in place. In the absence of any "unoccupied" territory outside of the system from which a coherent strategy of *resistance* might be mounted (as in Poland), Czechs were reduced to *opposing* the system from within. This involved the day-to-day tactics of role-playing, malingering, petty theft and corruption ("Anyone who does not steal from the state is robbing his family" was a common saying at the time), covert mockery and sarcasm and, most commonly, simply withdrawing from the public world into a privatized space populated only by self, family, friends, lovers and pets.

It was a time when educated Czechs spoke of an "internal emigration", embodied for those Praguers who could afford it by the so-called "*chata* culture", a *chata* being a country cottage—often no more than a shack—to which they would withdraw at every opportunity. By means such as these, hundreds of thousands of Czechs contrived to preserve some kind of inner freedom and to "get by" under a repressive regime which, for its part, was perfectly happy to accept their duplicity and passivity. Manipulating "the system" ultimately confirms it, and, by the 1970s, the "rulers" had long passed the stage when they required that the "ruled" actually believe in Communist ideology—not least because they had long ceased to believe in it themselves. "Rulers" and "ruled" entered into an unspoken compact of both saying one thing and believing and doing another. Both parties, in short, acted stupid, and both parties survived, at the price though of living a lie—certainly outside, but often inside as well—thus the cogency of Václav Havel's later exhortation that they, like him, try to "live in the truth."

"Normalization" was both the zenith and the nadir of Švejkism, as a whole nation acted stupid in order to survive. Philosophers and novelists spoke of "the power of the powerless" (Havel), the "solidarity of the shocked" (Jan Patočka) or the "community of the defeated" (Ivan Klíma) and looked back to Thomas Masaryk's idea of the *drobná prace* or "small-scale works" by which, little by little, a dominated people might remake itself. It was the tarnished golden age of the *MCC* or *malý český člověk* (little Czech man) in his daily struggle to outwit, without getting crushed, the Golem of an apparently impregnable system. Some Czechs came to pride themselves on the cleverness of their dumbness while others, more critically, spoke of a centuries-long "habit of surrender": 1620, 1938, 1948, 1968, as though, despite considerable evidence to the contrary, Czechs had never resisted either external occupiers or internal rulers but merely accommodated themselves, always complaining, to one form of domination after another. This one writer in the journal *Mladý svět* in 1990: "With us reigns the tradition of giving up: the years 1938, 1939, 1948, 1968—we have always given everything up without a fight; Švejk became the role model for the people."

In these circumstances, Švejk and Švejkism came to seem less admirable to some than they had in the past, less a role model to emulate but an embarrassing and superannuated national icon fit now for breaking. It was as though, some intellectuals complained, the Czechs were a nation of Sancho Panzas with no Don Quixote to redeem them. Even when the Communist system collapsed in November 1989, it did so—or so it was and is argued—not because of anything Czechs actually *did*, but under the pressure of its own inner contradictions and of the spectacle of other regimes disintegrating around it.

Historically, Czechs have put themselves forwards as victims but are they, as some critics say, collaborators in their own victimization? Do they so venerate their "national martyrs" because, as a people, they have, allegedly, been so very reluctant to martyrize themselves? We shall return to these, and similar, questions in our concluding chapters. In the meantime, it may be considered a sign of national maturity and of the acquisition, since 1989, of a genuine freedom that the cult of Švejk and Švejkism seems more and more limited to (mainly German-speaking) tourists at *U kalicha* who, for the most part, fail to see that the joke, not to mention the inflated price of the *pivo*, is on them. But, then, Švejk always did have a knack of getting the last laugh.

CHAPTER FOUR

Theater, Music, Nation

On May 16, 1868 there took place in Prague what has been described as "the greatest national celebration of Czechs" prior to actual independence half a century later, in 1918. A three-day extravaganza of parades, pageants, regattas and firework displays culminated with the laying of a foundation stone at the corner where Ferdinandstrasse (Národní třída) met the Vltava embankment, on a site where the communal salt house had formerly stood. The foundation stone came from Mount Rip, the mountain from which the nation's Abraham-figure Čech first sighted the Promised Land of Bohemia. Additional stones had been brought from Blaník, Práchen and Trocnov, associated with Wenceslas, Jan Hus and Žižka respectively; a further stone had been sent by Czech émigrés in Chicago, and there was even a casket said to contain stones from the prison cell in Constance in which Hus waited and prepared for his execution. Many towns and regions were represented by stones of their own: clearly this was to be a *national* building before all else.

It was not, however, a national palace or parliament that was being inaugurated—in Vienna-dominated Prague these were out of the question—but the closest possible equivalent, a National Theater to which, in the absence of full sovereignty, the task of enshrining Bohemian-ness was being entrusted. It was as though a temple to the Czech language, to Czech art, to the quintessence of Czechness was being erected in the heart of the "occupied" city that was a capital only in name. In the constitution of 1867 that had created the dual monarchy of Austria and Hungary, Emperor Franz Josef II had refused to recognize Bohemia as a third equal partner, hence his conspicuous absence at the ceremony. No matter: the theater would be the embryonic nation made stone, both a substitute—for a time—for the authentic nationhood that was being denied and a pledge that, with Vienna or against it, such nationhood would one day be achieved.

The foundation stone was jointly laid by the proto-nation's greatest historian František Palacký and her greatest composer Bedřich Smetana. It was a combination both ironic, for neither spoke Czech as his first language, and eloquent in that, for the Czech *buditelé* or awakeners, the history of the Czech lands was encapsulated in its music, and Czech music was the very incarnation of the whole Czech experience, whether sung or played by peasants in their villages, intoned in churches and chapels or performed in the few theaters and concert halls that accepted works written in Czech. That this was so was stressed by the personification of Czech music, Smetana himself, when, trowel and mallet in hand, he helped tap the foundation stone into position: "In music is the life of the Czechs." Theater, music, nation: probably no other European nation has defined itself as much in terms of its performing arts as did the Czech portion of the future Czechoslovakia. Czech art, it could be said, did not so much express the nation as create it. Culture preceded politics, and made politics possible; fiction, in the best as well as, sometimes, in the worst sense of the word, had priority over fact, as did conception and image over reality.

The Estates Theater

The problem was that, in 1868, Czech art had scarcely more substance than had Czech nationality, not least because there was no physical institution in which Czech-language works, either music or theater or, above all, the operatic combination of the two, could be performed and showcased on an equal standing with works written in German. There were, of course, individual plays, even individual operas, by Czech artists written in Czech. Václav Tham (1765-1816) is usually credited with having written the first play in Czech to be performed by professional Czech actors (*Břetislav and Jitka*, 1786), and the first Czech opera *The Tinker* (*Dráteník*), music by František Škroup, libretto by Chmelesný, was performed at the famous Estates Theater in February 1826.

Situated in the middle of the present Ovocný trh, formerly the Obstmarkt or Fruit Market, the Estates Theater (Stavovské Divadlo in Czech, Ständetheater in German) had begun life in 1783 as the Count

Nostitz Theater, after the name of its principal benefactor František Antonín Nostitz (1725-94), a German-speaking nobleman committed to the artistic enhancement of his native Bohemia, whence the dedication of the theater *Patriae et Musis*: to the *homeland* (not the *nation*) and the muses. Significantly, the original plans for a building in the Baroque style were rejected, and the present neoclassical structure stands as an early architectural expression of Bohemian autonomism.

Nonetheless, its repertoire consisted almost exclusively of works in German or Italian, with Czech-language works, such as Tham's pioneering play, being irregularly performed as Sunday afternoon matinées. Works in Czech, incidentally, were also performed at the Bouda ("The Shack") theater on Wenceslas Square before it was burned down in 1789, and then, for a few years, at the Divadlo U Hybernů, close to the still-existing Powder Tower on Na Příkopé.

The Nostitz Theater is renowned above all for having staged the first performance of *Don Giovanni*, conducted by the composer himself, in October 1787, a few months after its staging of *The Marriage of Figaro*, as popular with Prague audiences as it was detested in Vienna. The Nostitz was renamed the Estates Theater in 1797 and became an exclusively German-language theater after 1862, pending its "liberation" by a Czech nationalist mob in November 1920 (see Chapter Two). During the Communist regime, the Estates Theater was given the "democratic" name of the Tyl Theater, after the dramatist Josef Kajetán Tyl (1808-56) who is best remembered as the composer of the words of the Czech national anthem *Kde domov můj?* (Where is my home?), taken from what is often described as the first opera in Czech. This work, *The Shoemakers' Guild Festival* (*Fidlovačka*, libretto by Tyl, music by František Škroup) was first performed at the Estates Theater in 1834. The Tyl Theater became the Estates Theater once more in 1989. Despite its central position, the theater is now somewhat peripheral to Prague's artistic life, and a minatory statue of the Commendatore squats at one of its corners.

The Committee to Build the National Theater had been set up in 1850, in the wake of the revolutionary year of 1848 which, in Bohemia, had brought no constitutional or structural change beyond the suppression of the *robota*, or forced labor, to which peasants were subject. Centralization, Germanization and Catholicization were re-imposed with a vengeance, and, throughout the 1850s, in a kind of reprise of the "dark time" that followed White Mountain, the Czech lands "groaned" beneath what one contemporary called "a standing army of soldiers, sitting army of officials, a kneeling army of priests, and a creeping army of denunciators." Denied any possible political outlet, the movement for national rebirth focused even more intently on cultural action, and the building of a national theater became both a step towards, and a substitute for, the building of a national state. The radicalism of the Committee should not be overrated. Its two leading figures, Palacký and Reiger, had no plan, at this or any stage, for political independence from Vienna, and, as the Committee's manifesto of March 1851 makes clear, thought entirely in terms of constructing a national cultural identity within the existing political arrangements: "We are still lacking something without which Europe will hardly regard us as an educated and cultured nation. We mean an independent *national theater* which will testify to the world of our national culture."

The National Theater: Dalibor and the Shrine of Nationhood

Culture first, politics later. Even so, the "moderates" on the Committee, who would before long be known as "Old Czechs", soon came under pressure from a more radical group, forerunners of the "Young Czechs", who viewed the construction of the theater in much more oppositional terms. It was the leader of this group, Karel Havlíček (1821-56), a radical spokesman in 1848 and traditionally regarded as "the founder of Czech journalism", who made the crucial proposal that the theater should be financed as far as possible by voluntary contributions by the Czech people themselves, rather than by taxes or government grants, and who, in 1851, launched the first of several appeals to the public for funds. The response was considerable and cut significantly across class with all groups from what remained of the old Bohemian aristocracy to the newly freed peasantry contributing their share, with, not surprisingly, the rising Prague bourgeoisie very much in the van.

The initial appeal allowed the Committee to acquire a site, but it was not until 1862 that a temporary or provisional theater (*Prozatimní divadlo*) able to accommodate a mere nine hundred spectators was opened on its southern edge, pending the construction of a permanent building. Things began seriously to languish and, under renewed pressure from the radicals, a fresh appeal to the public was launched in 1865. The whole of civil society was mobilized in a truly national campaign, and fund-raising became an occasion of intense socialization as all manner of voluntary associations—amateur theater groups, choral and gymnastics societies, rifle clubs and the like—rallied to the cause with card evenings, skittle competitions, raffles and auctions, and so permitted the Committee, finally, to commission the architect Josef Zítek, after a public competition, to design the theater itself. The inauguration ceremony was neither specifically anti-Austrian nor anti-Catholic—indeed, the date, May 16, had been deliberately selected as the feast of St. John Nepomuk—but it was striking that no member of the imperial family was present and that the Archbishop of Prague pointedly declined to participate in the occasion. The inauguration of the National Theater was a secular celebration in which, so to speak, the embryonic Czech nation became its own creator and, through the ritual of inauguration, crowned itself king.

After the inauguration, the dignitaries repaired to the Novoměstské (New Town) Theater to attend the premiere of Smetana's new opera *Dalibor* which, completed in December 1867, had been offered by the composer to the National Theater Committee to mark the occasion. We have already encountered the story of Dalibor in connection with Hradčany (see Chapter One) and, if we return to it here, it is because Smetana's opera offers a prototype for so much subsequent Czech theater and music, with respect both to content and to expressive style. According to legend, Dalibor (to repeat) was condemned to prison, and subsequently death, for having killed a tyrannical nobleman, usually said to be the Burgrave of Ploškovice, in the course of defending his peasants' rights against him; the fact that the king who passed sentence upon him was a "foreigner", the Polish-born Vladislav II, was grist to the myth-making mill of nineteenth-century Czech nationalists. The legend further recounted that, while imprisoned in the tower on Hradčany that was named after him after his death, Dalibor learned to play the violin, and so beautifully that crowds would gather at the foot of the tower to hear the exquisite sounds issuing from it. Tyranny, rebellion, imprisonment, death, music: how could any Czech composer resist such a combination of themes?

The reality was both more humdrum and macabre. In 1496 Dalibor led an uprising for the recognition of peasant brewing rights (Smetana, incidentally, was the son of a brewer), had killed the Burgrave (or another nobleman) in the course of a brawl and confessed to the crime only after being subjected to torture. The torture instrument in question was a kind of rack known in Czech as a *skřipek* from a verb meaning "to scrape", the word also being used for a type of peasant stringed instrument. In other words, Dalibor was stretched out on the "violin" like a string and, when "scraped", like the proverbial canary he sang. *Mistr Nouze naučil Dalibora housti*, said knowing folk to each other; Master Necessity taught Dalibor to play the violin, giving rise, over time, to the myth that Dalibor had actually learned to play the violin while in prison, and that the "music" coming from the tower was not the screams of a man under torture, but the freedom song of a national martyr.

In the nineteenth century, a number of German or German-speaking writers used the story of Dalibor as a romantic myth of redemption by music, in which form it passed with ease into the nationalist repertoire. Smetana's libretto was the work of one Josef Wenzig (1807-76); the fact that his text had to be translated from German into Czech by a third party is, as we now know, typical of the paradoxes of Czech nationalism in its formative phase. To the familiar legend, Wenzig added significant new elements, some borrowed, some invented by himself, particularly the figure of Dalibor's bosom friend Zdeněk, a violin-playing virtuoso, whom the evil Burgrave has murdered, thus prompting Dalibor to kill him in revenge. Smetana's opera begins—how could it be otherwise in this seminal Czech work—

precisely with the *trial* at which Dalibor confesses to the killing. The Burgrave's sister Milada entreats the King to pronounce the death sentence but, as she does so, falls in love with Dalibor's noble demeanor and striking good looks. When he is imprisoned (the death sentence comes later), she vows to release him. The echoes of *Fidelio* are obvious as she tricks her way into prison, bringing him tools to escape with concealed in a violin. Dalibor has a dream of Zdeněk who appears on stage playing his fiddle, whereupon Dalibor is miraculously able to play the instrument himself: first *Fidelio*, now *The Magic Flute*.

But, as befits a Czech opera of the mid-nineteenth century, the prison and underworld of *Dalibor* remain closed. Milada-Fidelio descends once more to the prison, but is unable to rescue her Bohemian Florestan. They die in each others' arms, she thinking of him, he rather more of Zdeněk—recent productions of the opera have rather clumsily underlined its supposed homoerotic subtext—and the briefly threatened regime of the foreign King Vladislav and his Czech collaborator Budivoj comes out on top.

As a fable of the weaknesses of Czech nationalism in the late 1860s, *Dalibor* could hardly be bettered, which is why, rather than its alleged "Wagnerian" character, the opera was not widely appreciated until considerably later. But the symbolism is clear. Whatever happens to Zdenek, Dalibor and Milada, the violin's music, that alchemical union of all that is Czech, will penetrate any prison-wall and overcome in the end.

"These Hallowed Walls"

The construction of the theater took, in all, thirteen years, and the sluggish progress often set "Old" and "Young" Czechs at each others' throats. When at last the building was approaching completion, the moderates wanted its opening to coincide with the wedding of Crown Prince Rudolf and Princess Stephanie of Belgium that was due to be celebrated in Vienna on May 10, 1881; their intention, as ever, was to underline the *partnership* between Prague and the imperial capital. To the radicals, this subordination of the *national* theater project to a dynastic occasion was utterly unacceptable, and eventually a compromise was worked out whereby the Prince and his bride would attend a special inaugural performance at the theater after their wedding; the theater would then close and reopen for its official "consecration" some time later. Rudolf and Stephanie duly made the journey to Prague and, on June 11, Rudolf alone attended a one-off performance of Smetana's patriotic opera-cantata *Libuše* which the composer had completed as early as 1872 but had voluntarily held back so that it could be premiered in the new theater.

In the interim, Smetana had gone deaf, and his name was for some reason omitted from the list of those officially invited. When he arrived at the theater, he had the greatest difficulty in obtaining entrance and, having at last done so, could hear neither the opera nor the Crown Prince's congratulations. His duty done, Rudolf left during Act II and so, deliberately or not, was absent for Libuše's vision of the future glories of Prague that were presented as *tableaux vivants* at the opera's climax. Rudolf and Stephanie went back to Vienna and, give or take some last-minute touches to the building, everything was ready for its formal inauguration, a Czech-only occasion scheduled for September 28, the feast of St. Wenceslas.

Then, on the night of August 12, thanks to a freak lightning storm, some building materials on the roof of the theater caught fire, and the whole edifice burned down within hours. In desperation, a new appeal to the nation was launched, and within two weeks 500,000 florins had been donated, 69 percent of it by private individuals, and only 35 percent by residents of Prague: truly the reconstructed theater would be national in more than just name. The role of women in raising funds was noted and commented upon, as were the contributions made by other Slav nations and communities. Many more peasants and urban workers contributed to the 1881 appeal than had to its predecessors of 1851 and 1865, and the men of the village of Odřepsa characteristically vowed not to smoke until the theater was rebuilt and to donate the money saved to the fund (in a nation of chain-smokers, this was sacrifice indeed). Having taken thirteen years to construct, the theater was reconstructed in just over two, and on November 18, 1883 the new building was consecrated—the term is wholly appropriate, for it truly was a shrine—by a fresh performance of *Libuše*. This, for Czechs then and since, was the real inauguration of the theater, a truly *national* occasion, made more so by the absence of any validating imperial dignitary.

Zítek's theater—its rebuilding was superintended by his student Josef Schulz—is an impressive rather than aesthetically pleasing construction, and its interior is markedly superior to its hulking neo-Renaissance shell. Only Czech materials and Czech labor were employed in its construction, and, as with the later Obecní dům (see Chapter Five), an effort was made to involve every Czech-speaking artist of note. The decorations are principally the work of Mikoláš Aleš and František Ženíšek, and many of the sculptures of Czech composers and dramatists that line its foyers and galleries are, inevitably, the work of Josef Václav Myslbek. The Committee insisted that the auditorium be "democratic" in lay-out, and although there was a royal (but no imperial) box—which would remain permanently empty since Emperor Franz Josef, unlike his predecessors, disdained to be crowned King of Bohemia—the few other boxes were deliberately open in structure. In no other theater in the world, said Rieger, could people in the least expensive seats enjoy such a good view of the stage.

But the theater's most striking feature, then and now, is the motto displayed above the proscenium: *Národ sobě*, the Nation to Itself, meaning this is the nation's gift to itself, this is the truly foundational act whereby a mere people created, or recreated, itself as a fully-fledged *národ*. In few other European capitals is a secular building more laden with sacred meanings and values, and, as Rieger said in his inaugural address, all who go there, performers and spectators alike, should act "as priests and priestesses within these hallowed walls which testify to the sacrifices of poor widows, workers and patriots, who may never see the monument their contribution helped erect." And banks and insurance companies, but let us let that pass: in no other major city, with the exception of Sydney, does going to the opera have the quasi-sacramental character that it still has in Prague.

The Bartered Bride

If there is one opera that Czechs, and Praguers, prefer to all others, it is not the tragic *Dalibor* or the declamatory *Libuše*, but Smetana's delightful comic opera *The Bartered Bride* (Prodaná nevěsta) which, begun in 1864 and first performed in a two-act version with spoken dialogue in May 1866, underwent several major revisions before it reached the definitive form that was premiered at the Provisional

Theater in September 1870. It quickly established itself as the quintessential Czech opera, notching up a hundred performances by May 1882, and no fewer than 2,881 between then and 1983 at the National Theater alone, an average of 29 performances a year. Above all other theatrical works it was beloved by the Communist regime, and when Czech-speaking rioters "liberated" the Estates Theater in November 1920, it was inevitable that their "triumph" would be consecrated by a performance of *Prodaná nevěsta* that very night. *The Bartered Bride* does for Czech music what Josef Mánes (see Chapter Five) and Božena Němcová were already doing for Czech painting and Czech fiction respectively: it presents an image of Bohemian rural life sufficiently sentimental and lyrical but also sufficiently "real" to delight the opera-going bourgeoisie of Prague while feeding its desire to feel authentically Czech. Apparently simplicity and spontaneity itself, *The Bartered Bride* is in reality a carefully contrived work, as its numerous rewritings reveal, and presents a number of curiosities to which, living in a climate of suspicion and duplicity more severe than anything Smetana had to endure, several Czech writers addressed themselves during "normalization".

There was first the fact, alluded to above, that Smetana had needed a German crib of the libretto in order to be able to compose the opera at all. No real problem here—it is the kind of paradox found in much early "anti-colonialist" writing in the twentieth century—but things get more complicated when we learn that the libretto of this masterpiece of Bohemian folksiness was by a Czech working as an informer and spy for the Austrian police, whose name, when his unsavory second job was revealed, was for many years removed from the score and from playbills advertising the opera. A prolific writer of Dumas-style historical romances, Karel Sabina (1813-77) was a proletarian of the pen who, like many of his kind throughout Europe, fought on the insurgent side in Prague's brief version of the 1848 Revolution (see Chapter Six). Like Havlíček and other radical intellectuals, he was imprisoned for his pains, but, on his discharge in 1856, turned, or was turned, into a police spy, operating under the direction of the Police Chief of Prague who was none other than Leopold von Sacher Masoch, father of the author of *Venus in Furs*. (To add further piquancy to the tale, his code name was "Roman", or "novel").

In a *samizdat* article of 1977, Jiří Grusa, a signatory to the recently issued Charter, uses the strange career of Karel/Roman Sabina as an example of the "philosophy of the humiliated" to which intellectuals and writers are so often driven in repressive states ("it is a philosophy that does not distinguish between high and low, serious and profane"). He sees the librettist's double life—a defender of Czech nationhood in his work, its betrayer in his second occupation—as "an archetype of the tortured Czech lands, a sad comedy without any relief." Grusa then goes on, not entirely convincingly, to read the masks, double identities and barterings of the opera as an allegory both of Sabina's duplicity and of the double-dealing surrounding the Czech national soul, figured, inevitably, by Mařenka, the bride of the title. The final image is of the great and the good of the Communist regime, including a large number of artists, gathering at the "Golden Chapel"—that is, the National Theater—to sign a counter to Charter 77 "provided by a latter-day Super Sacher Masoch", namely the architect of normalization himself, President Husák. The suspect national masterpiece, the Janus-faced writer, the search for encrypted and allegorical meanings, the projection of Sabina as an image of "our inner shadow" which believes that "it *is* possible to wait it out and that one can win one's cause even by a trick": only in normalized Czechoslovakia would such readings be made.

Theater Capital of Europe

Czech national operas may have provided the core of the National Theater's repertoire, but the theater has never become the ossified "official" institution that its name might suggest. Most of the major Czech directors of the last hundred years have spent greater or lesser parts of their career at the National, and, since, as we shall see, Czech theater is much more a theater of directors than of playwrights, their names are worth recording as they bulk rather larger in (ex-) Czechoslovakia than their equivalents do in Britain or France: Jaroslav Kvapil (1868-1950), Karel Hynek Hilar (1885-1935), Jindřich Honzl (1894-1953), Alfred Radok (1914-76) and Otomar Krejča (born 1921). On the other hand, when Kenneth Tynan wrote in a *New Yorker* article in 1967 that "Prague has a strong claim to be regarded as the theater capital of Europe", he was not thinking so much of the National

Theater as of the considerable number of "little", "underground" or "peripheral" theaters that exist in creative osmosis with it. If the National Theater has been the institutional pivot of Prague's theatrical life, the creative energies have tended to come more from the circumference than from the center. It is not possible in a book of this kind to cover more than a handful of Prague's "alternative" theaters— and it should be remembered that provincial cities, particularly Brno, also have a distinctive theatrical tradition of their own—but they have much in common, as the following discussion of the principal companies, personalities and locales sets out to show.

Pride of place in any history of "alternative theater" in Prague must belong to the Liberated Theater (Osvobozené divadlo) of the 1920s and 1930s. The Liberated Theater is inseparable from the whole Dada/modernist/surrealist complex in inter-war Prague, with particularly strong links to the so-called Devětsil group (see Chapter Five). Much of its self-consciously anti-realist style was defined by its early stagings of French avant-garde plays such as Apollinaire's *Les Mamelles de Tirésias* and Cocteau's *Les Mariés de la Tour Eiffel*, and its name also pays homage to the example of André Antoine's innovative Théâtre Libre (1887-94). Its actual founder was Jiří Frejka (1904-52), but its history is dominated by two names we have already encountered, Jiří Voskovec (1905-81) and Jan Werich (1905-80), the celebrated "V + W", who were not only its star performers but its leading writers as well. To them must be added, above all, Jaroslav Ježek (1906-42), whose music, blending Stravinský and *Les Six*, Tin Pan Alley and jazz, did not so much accompany performances as belong integrally to them, the designers František Zelenka and the surrealist painter and photographer Jindřich Štýrský (see Chapter Five), and the choreographers Saša Machov and Joe Jenčik, whose company, Les Jenčik Girls, provided a zany and acrobatic chorus-line to many a performance. Jindřich Honzl was the principal director responsible for coordinating the generalized mayhem. Merely to list these participants gives some idea of the Liberated Theater style: not text-bound dramas, but total spectacles incorporating song, dance and slapstick comedy, closer to music hall than orthodox theater, and countering the artistic and ideological portentousness of the National Theater with the values and mentalities of *Majáles*, the annual student carnival in Prague.

Probably nowhere in Europe was the spirit of Dada more successfully translated to the stage.

The Liberated Theater had a number of venues, first at the premises of the Umělcká Beseda (Society of Artists) in Malá Strana, where its two most celebrated shows *Vest Pocket Revue* (1927) and *Smoking Revue* (1928) were performed, then in the imposingly modernist Palác Adria on the corner of Jungmannova and Národní and, finally, throughout the 1930s, at U Nováků, one of the finest Art Nouveau buildings in Prague, on Vodičkova in Nové Město. As already indicated, the Liberated Theater dealt not so much in fixed texts as in semi-improvised sketches around one or more themes, and specialized in debunking received national myths. Thus the eponymous hero of *Don Juan a Comp* (*Don Juan and Co*, 1931) is too timid and tongue-tied to make even one conquest let alone the canonical *mille e tre*, while the Golem, in the theater's Rudolfine extravaganza of that title (also 1931), is a harmless hulk who falls in love with a "materialized moonbeam" named Sirael, the unfortunately frigid magnum opus of the alchemist Břeněk. Towering over everything was the joint genius of V + W who, from their recorded songs and their films, may seem no more than a Czech version of Flanagan and Allan, but whose performances— particularly their improvised routines in front of the curtain—were of sufficient intellectual substance, and the role of the one so sharply demarcated from that of the other, for the noted linguists Román Jakobson and Jan Mukařovský, founders of the celebrated Prague School of Linguistics (see Chapter Five), to analyze their dialogues and exchanges in the classic structuralist terms of the interplay of binary opposites.

From the early 1930s onwards, the Liberated Theater became increasingly political. *Caesar* (1932) and *Osel a stín* (*Ass and Shadow*, 1933) tackled fascism head-on while *Kat a blázen* (*Executioner and Fool*, 1934) was broken up by fascist demonstrators from the National League after depicting Hitler as a donkey. *Rub a líc* (*Two Sides of the Coin*, 1936) showed an attempted fascist coup being foiled by "the people", and was made into a successful film entitled *Svět patří nám* (*The World Belongs to Us*, 1937), a presumably intentional echo of Jean Renoir's Popular Front classic *Le Monde est a nous* (1936). The Liberated Theater was closed down in November 1938 by a Ministry of the Interior fearful of its anti-fascist stance in the aftermath of Munich and, foreseeing the worst, V + W left for France, and then the United States, before the Nazi invasion the following March. Their last show *Pěst na oko* (*A Fist in the Eye*, March 1938) ends, typically, with an explicit allusion to Hus' *Pravda vítězí*: "To defend our truth and to judge by truth/Depends entirely on us/Not to fear truth but to believe in truth/To struggle for truth/To conquer with truth/Depends entirely on us." Voskovec and Werich returned to Prague after 1945 and resumed their act, but Voskovec left permanently for the US after February 1948, leaving Werich to continue as a solo actor-entertainer.

Following German occupation, when Czech theater—except, ironically, at Terezín— was effectively neutered, and the Communist take-over of February 1948, the experimental, subversive tradition embodied by the Liberated Theater truly did "go underground". It resurfaced only in the late 1950s as censorship was gradually relaxed; the suicide of the Liberated Theater's founder, Jiří Frejka, in 1952 was all too telling a symbol of the fate of "free theater" in Stalinist Prague. Within the limits of ideological orthodoxy, however, committed Communist directors like Jindřich Honzl and E.F. Burian (1904-59), founder of the pre-war Brechtian "D" theater, were able to create powerful and original versions of plays approved by the regime, though Burian who, as director of the Army Art Theater, routinely wore the uniform of a full army colonel, was regarded even by convinced Communists in the theater world to have overstepped the limits of what nobody yet called political correctness. The "D" in Burian's establishment stood for Divadlo (theater) and was followed by the date of the year (D34, D35, etc.) to underline its contemporaneity.

Yet under this Procrustean surface, reflection, discussion and experiment continued, much of it outside even the broadest definition of the theatrical milieu. Thus at the still thriving Reduta Jazz Club on Národní, the young bass-player and poet Jiří Suchý (born 1931) teamed up with Ivan Vyskočil (born 1929), a writer and performer in the V + W tradition, to create what they called "text-appeals"—spoken monologues and dialogues with musical accompaniment. Out of this experimentation grew, in 1958, the first and most famous of Prague's alternative theaters, the Divadlo Na zábradlí (Theater on the Balustrade) based in a former warehouse on the banks of the Vltava near the Convent of St. Agnes in the Old Town. Leaving Vyskočil in charge of the Balustrade, where the talented Jan Grossman (1925-93) was appointed principal director in 1962, Suchý then launched the Semafor theater in conjunction with the composer Jiří Šlitr (1924-69). This then sparked off a series of similar ventures of which the Divadlo Za bránou (Theater Beyond the Gate), founded in 1965 by the well-known National Theater director Otomar Krejča, was to prove the most influential. These theaters and others—the Drama club, the Rokoko—both captured and amplified the "wind of change" of the early 1960s and have been credited, more than any other cultural movement, with articulating the whole complex phenomenon known simplistically as Prague Spring. It was not so much that these theaters put on "subversive" plays, in the sense of plays with an explicitly counter-regime message (even in the comparatively relaxed climate of the mid 1960s, this would be to invite instantaneous closure), but that the very experience of producing plays as a collective endeavor involving not only directors and actors, but designers, musicians, dancers, technicians and even stage-hands created the kind of democracy in action that was so conspicuously absent in society at large. Significantly, Václav Havel began his theatrical career as a stage-hand at the Balustrade, from which he advanced to the post of "dramaturge", or dramatic consultant and play-reader, under Jan Grossman.

To think imaginatively was in itself to challenge the ossification of neo-Stalinist society, and to offer the fruit of that reflection to an imagination-starved public, no matter how socially and numerically restricted, was to engage in the kind of two-way exchange that Prague had been denied for close to a quarter of a century. As one well-known critic, Karel Kraus (born 1920), wrote at the time, the Balustrade's productions "do not draw the viewer into the play but provoke him to take a stand, do not suggest a solution but count instead on his intellectual revolt. The center of gravity shifts from the stage to the space between stage and audience."

Clearly, such an experience of living democracy could not easily survive under the post-1970 "normalization process", and the closing of the Theater Beyond the Gate in March 1972 inaugurated a decade-long suppression of the free theater tradition. When the tradition resurfaced in the early 1980s, it was more from Brno, in the form of the celebrated Theater on a String (Divadlo na Provázku), than from Prague that the initiative came, though the Studio Ypsilon, originally from Liberec in North Bohemia, moved to Prague in 1984 where, under its founder Jan Schmid (born 1936), it successfully revived the cabaret plus social comment mode of Voskovec and Werich. As in the late 1950s and 1960s, these tiny, packed theaters became what Petr Oslzlý (born 1945), the pivotal figure of the Theater on a String, called "sacred circles" within a pervasive culture of unfreedom, a kind of conspiracy between performers and audience in which the former transmitted coded political messages and the latter stretched allegorical readings to the limit to pick up sub-textual references to contemporary Czechoslovakia in plays devoid of ostensible political content.

Unfortunately, the authorities also honed their interpretative skills and became as adept as audiences at decoding political meanings. One particular object of their attentions was a play by Daniela Fischerová (born 1948) entitled *The Hour between the Dog and the Wolf* (*Hodina mezi psem a vlkem*) performed at the Realist Theater in Prague in 1979 and based on the trial—always the trial—of the fifteenth-century French poet François Villon who, four decades earlier, had inspired V + W's *Balada z hadrů* (*The Ballad of the Rags*, 1935). As a metaphor of the conflict between artist and society, the play was too obvious and was closed down by the Prague City Council after just four performances. It was safer to take a figure like Jan Hus that the Communists themselves had co-opted and turn his trial and execution to the dissident cause, as Oldřich Daněc successfully did in *You Are Jan* (*Vy jste Jan*, 1987), one of the first plays to be performed at the ultra-modern Nová scéna next door to (and under the aegis of) the National Theater. All such performances, no matter how cautiously over-coded, kept alive the Masaryckian ideal of *drobná práce*, or small acts, and permitted performers and audience, within limits, to "live in the truth", pending the explosion of November 1989 in which, as we shall see, the central role played by the theater, and the fact that the leading figure to emerge from it was a man of the theater, could be seen as the fulfillment of the Czech theater's historical vocation as foreseen by the founders of the National Theater a century before.

Puppets

There are two forms of Czech theater, neither of them specific to Prague, that require separate discussion, not least because, relying on spectacle rather than the word, they will be of particular interest to non-Czech-speaking visitors. The tradition of puppet theater—originally common to the whole of Mitteleuropa—enjoys a particular vitality in the Czech lands into which it was introduced, in the sixteenth century or earlier, by itinerant puppeteers from Germany and Italy. The

first recorded puppet show in Prague dates from 1563, entitled—and this is suggestive, given our later discussion of the parallels between marionettes and martyrs—"The Play of the Suffering of our Lord Christ" and performed by one Heinrich Wirre from Zürich. Passion and Nativity plays continued to be the staple of puppet shows well into the eighteenth century, and it is interesting that puppets were made as a lucrative sideline by wood-carvers whose main employment was the making of church statues. Rooted in the Baroque sensibility with its love of mimicry, mirrors and mechanics, the puppet is in many ways a scaled-down, secularized and animated version of the holy men and women who populate the churches of Bohemia and Moravia in such prodigious numbers.

Secular puppet plays begin to be recorded from the mid-seventeenth century—one performed in Prague in 1651 was on the theme of "The Arch Magician Doctor Faustus" and had allegedly strong local connections. According to Prague lore and legend, the "original" of Doctor Faustus was a Bohemian student named Jan Šťastný (meaning "lucky" in Czech, or "faustus" in Latin) who reputedly made a pact with the Devil in a house, the present Faustův dům (Faust House) on Charles Square, which was frequented by Edward Kelley and other would-be magicians and alchemists. Another, rather later, puppet play was entitled "Don Juan"—and, by the late eighteenth century, puppetry had established itself as an autonomous dramatic tradition, preserving the scenic trickery of the Baroque just as it was going out of fashion on the orthodox stage.

The art of puppetry ran in families, and there were several generations of Meissners, Kočkas, Malečeks, Dubskýs and Kludskýs. The most famous "dynasty", however, was founded by Jan Kopecký (first mentioned in 1779) who passed on his skills and materials to his son Matěj (1775-1847), traditionally regarded as the greatest of all Czech puppeteers. He, in his turn, passed them on to his sons Jan (1804-52), Josef (1807-56), Václav (1815-71) and Antonín (1821-85); Václav's daughter Arnošta Kopecká was still performing in Prague on the eve of the First World War. Until the mid-nineteenth century, puppet theaters were officially banned within the then city limits of Prague, suggesting some subversive political potential, and enthusiasts had to go out to Smíchov and Nusle, still separate towns, to enjoy the art of Matěj Kopecký and his sons.

A leading puppeteer of the next generation, Jan Nepomuk Lašt`ovka (1824-77), started to mount shows based on the lives of Bohemian heroes such as George of Poděbrady and Jan Žižka, and by the time puppets were exhibited at the great national Ethnographic Exhibition in 1895, the whole tradition had been recruited into the nationalist cause, with Matěj Kopecký, whose puppets were again displayed at a separate exhibition in 1905, hailed as having done for Czech puppetry what Němcová had done for Czech literature and Smetana for Czech music. (In 1862 Smetana wrote an overture to Kopecký's puppet version of *Doctor Faust* and followed it in 1863 with an overture to the same performer's *Oldřich and Božena*.) But puppetry went well beyond professional theaters and performers, and shops, schools, taverns, not to mention private households, all put on shows. Amateur puppet societies were grouped together as a branch of the nationwide Sokol gymnastics federation, and in 1912 the world's first specialist puppet magazine, *Český loutkář* (*Czech Puppeteer*), was founded by Jindřich Veselý. Together, puppeteering, gymnastics and choral societies (see below) were the great, if somewhat improbable, mobilizing forces of Czech nationalism between 1880 and 1914.

Puppeteering reached out to, and drew upon, other forms of expression. Well-known authors like Eliška Krásnohorská (1847-1926), the founder in 1891 of the famous Minerva school for girls on Vodičkova, wrote plays specifically for puppet theaters, and scenery was designed by artists of the stature of Ladislav Šaloun and František Kysela. The architect Vladimír Zákrejs (1880-1948) produced puppet versions of *Hamlet, Macbeth,* and *The Merchant of Venice* in 1917 alone, and independence saw the formation, or development, of more and more ambitious puppeteering projects: the Puppet Theater of Art Education (founded 1914), the Art Puppet Theater (founded in 1918 by the great National Theater diva Liběna Odstřeilova, 1890-1948), and the Realm of Puppets (1920), the joint project of the husband and wife puppeteering team of Vojtěch Sucharda (1884-1968) and Anna Suchardová (1883-1944). They were joined in 1922 by the Sokol Puppet Theater of Prague, whose version of Sophocles's *Oedipus* (1933) directed by Jan Malík (1904-80) is regarded as one of the summits of Czech puppetry, and in 1936 by Jiří Trnka's Wooden Theater. Just as the Liberated Theater became more political after 1930, so too did sections of the Prague puppet world, notably Josef Skupa (1892-1957) who satirized Hitler in the autocratic figure of Paní Drbálková (Mrs. Gossip) in his *Merry-go-round with Three Floors* that was still being performed after March 1939. Skupa continued to delight his audiences with barely coded shows such as *Long Live Tomorrow* (1941) and *Miracles Today and Tomorrow* (1942) until he was arrested by the Gestapo in 1944 and his company disbanded.

Since its heyday between the two wars, the Prague puppet theater appears to have lost some of its creativity through a combination of restrictions imposed under Communism and commercial pressures, which have led most of the surviving companies to gear their performances primarily towards tourists. The famous duo of Špejbl and Hurvínek created by Skupa in the 1920s, the former a balding, big-eared father-figure with bulging eyes and ill-fitting clothes, the latter a mischievous falsetto-voiced street-urchin, continue to draw audiences to their own special theater in the suburb of Dejvice, but choice in the city center is largely restricted to rival productions of *Don Giovanni*. The only complete version—and by all accounts the best—is that offered by the Umělecká scéna říše loutek (The World of Puppets) on Žatecká in Staré Město, which, appropriately for an opera premiered in Prague, draws on local mythology to create a climax infinitely more terrifying than most orthodox stage productions of the work. As tension mounts, and the music becomes progressively more menacing, the Don is revealed by the presence of the puppet strings and the fact that, all along, the hands of the operators are visible to the audience, as the plaything of higher or lower external forces that he is: the arch-manipulator is unmasked as a creature manipulated by fate. Then, on the scaled-down stage, the Commendatore finally makes his promised appearance, not as the conventional statue suddenly come to life, but, precisely, as *the Golem*, played not by a puppet but by a full-size human actor, dressed in a vast shapeless gray costume, who bursts through the paper scenery like the force of destiny itself. It is a defining "Prague moment": puppet, statue and Golem brought together at the culmination of what is both tragedy and farce and dramatically highlighting the links between the three figures that are discussed more fully in Chapter Seven. Immense, formless Golem versus diminutive humanoid puppets: it is the Czech experience of history contained in a nutshell.

Black Light Theater

The puppet theater almost certainly had an influence on another highly popular form of non-verbal theater known as *černé divadlo*, or "black light theater", that appears to be peculiar to the Czech Republic. Its immediate origins lie in mime, such as that practiced most recently by Ladislav Fialka (1931-91), and in its "classical" form involved actors dressed entirely in black performing against a background of alternating black screens and mirrors arranged in such a way as to disrupt entirely the audience's perception of what is "reality" and what is "image". In the 1930s, E.F. Burian's Theatergraph complicated things still further by adding slide projections of the performers to the already disorienting interplay of reality and appearance, creating a truly Comenian labyrinth of illusion whose links to the whole Baroque sensibility, as expressed, for example, in the Mirrored Chapel (*Zrcadlová kaple*) in the Klementinum need hardly to be stressed. The Klementium, formerly the Jesuit College and German-speaking rival to

Charles University, is situated between Karlova and Platnérska streets in the Old Town. It now houses the National Library, and the Mirrored Chapel is a regular venue for concerts.

It was a mixed-media spectacle of this kind that was performed to huge international acclaim under the title *Laterna Magika* as part of the Czechoslovak contribution to the Brussels Expo 58. The show was the joint creation of the National Theater's Alfred Radok and the exceptionally gifted scenographer Josef Svoboda (born 1920) whose revolutionary and resolutely anti-realist sets, based, *inter alia*, on an extensive use of projected film images, had been enriching the major Prague theaters since the end of the war. *Laterna Magika* was so successful, and opened up so many scenographic possibilities, that a permanent theater of that name was established, initially under Radok's direction, in a former cinema located in the basement of the famous Palác Adria on Národní třída where the Liberated Theater had once had its home—a highly appropriate venue in that, almost alone, *Laterna Magika* sought to revive the spirit of Dada and surrealist Prague in an otherwise inimical cultural climate. For a decade or more, it performed to mainly Czech audiences but, under "normalization", became more and more geared towards the growing tourist market, and as Svoboda, director since 1973, developed his so-called Polyekran system of multi-screen projections, spectacular effect increasingly predominated over its original intellectual and theatrical substance, until its transfer to the Nová scéna complex next to the National Theater effectively destroyed it as anything other than a money-spinning visual extravaganza attended now only by tourists. Nonetheless, it was appropriate that, in the *dénouement* of November 1989, it was from the *Laterna Magika* then still at its (and the Liberated Theater's) old headquarters at the Palác Adria, that the actors' and theater workers' strike which, as much as anything, brought the Communist regime to its knees was coordinated. Guided, one would like to think, by the spirit of Voskovec and Werich, the Prague Theater, with more than a little help from its counterpart in Brno (see Chapter Eight), finally achieved some kind of historical apotheosis, toppling one regime and installing another—with, moreover, a man of the theater as its symbol and president.

Not the least remarkable thing about Czech theater is that its world-class reputation was established without the country actually producing a playwright of the absolute first rank. Karel Čapek (1890-1938) was at one time greatly respected, and widely performed, as an enemy of the totalitarianisms of both left and right, but even his greatest admirers would not place him on the same level as contemporaries or near-contemporaries such as Anouilh, Brecht, Lorca, or Pirandello. Similarly, if not unkindly, one might say of Václav Havel that, if his standing as a dissident originally depended on his prowess as a dramatist, the current reputation of his plays depends more on his aura of the dissident-who-became-president than on their own intrinsic qualities: good, certainly, but too redolent of Ionesco and Beckett to count internationally as the formally innovative works that they seemed to Czech audiences in the mid-1960s.

From Dvořák to Rock

If Czech theater is a great theater without great national dramatists, it is quite otherwise in the case of Czech classical music. The Czech lands (Bohemia and Moravia) have, since the mid-nineteenth century, produced three composers of unquestionable greatness (Smetana, Dvořák, Janáček), and one, Bohuslav Martinů (1890-1958), whose frequent prolixity should not detract from his very finest compositions: *Double Concerto for Two String Orchestras, Piano and Timpani* (1938), *The Epic of Gilgamesh* (1954-5), and *The Greek Passion* (1955-8). Three others, less well known outside their homeland, are considerably more than the run-of-the-mill nationalist composers they were once treated as: Dvořák's son-in-law Josef Suk (1874-1935) whose great *Asrael Symphony* (1907) has already been referred to; Zdeněk Fibich (1850-1900); and Vítězslav Novák (1870-1935). To these may be added a dozen or more composers of enormous quality and interest, making Czech music one of the great national schools of the nineteenth and twentieth centuries.

Of twentieth-century Czech conductors, three, Václav Talich (1883-1961), Karel Ančerl (1908-73), the conductor of Terezín (see Chapter Two) and Rafael Kubelík (1914-1996), whose name will always be associated with his performance of *Má vlast* on his return from exile after the Velvet Revolution, can rightly be counted amongst the greatest anywhere of their times. The violinists Jan Kubelík (1880-1949), father of Rafael, and Josef Suk (born 1929) grandson of the composer of that name and thus great-grandson of Dvořák, would be similarly rated, as would the pianist Rudolf Firkušný (1912-1994), known above all for his interpretation of the keyboard music of fellow Moravian Leoš Janáček. The heritage of the great Ema Destinová (1878-1930) is continued today by the soprano Eva Urbanová who, remarkably, began her career as a pop singer after failing to be admitted to the Prague Conservatory, and the vocal "sensation" of the moment, the mezzo-soprano Magdalena Kožená (born 1973) whose prize-winning recital of love songs by Dvořák, Janáček and Martinů is the best possible introduction to the glories of Czech solo vocal music.

In addition to its principal concert hall at the Obecní dům (see Chapter Five), Prague's prodigious number of churches provide cheap and accessible venues for classical music, though the tourist demand for non-stop Vivaldi is pushing even the best known Czech music, other than *Má vlast* and the *New World Symphony*, to one side. The five o'clock concert is one of Prague's most agreeable institutions and contributes greatly to the city's reputation as a leading European musical center.

But classical music constitutes only the uppermost stratum of Czech musical culture and depends for its vitality on the multiple strata below: the medieval Saint Wenceslas Chorale which so many modern Czech composers have incorporated into their works, the hymnody stemming from the Hussites and Community of Brethren, and the traditional vocal and instrumental music of both Bohemia and Moravia which, as Milan Kundera says in an incisive analysis of Czech music in his novel *The Joke* (1967), came to be seen by Czech nationalists and, later, by Communists as "the only narrow footbridge across the two-hundred-year gap" opened up by the defeat of White Mountain and the "normalization process" that followed. The folk music tradition, Kundera continues, is "a tunnel beneath history, a tunnel that preserves much of what wars, revolutions, civilization have long since destroyed aboveground." After more than two centuries of domination by the Baroque, this subterranean channel came to the surface in the mid-nineteenth century, not only in the work of the first nationalist composers, who avidly tapped into it, but, just as significantly, in the thousands of choral societies, above all the famous Hlahol whose Art Nouveau concert hall is on Masarykovo embankment, that sprang up throughout the Czech lands and which were grouped together as the union of Czech Choral Societies in 1894. Smetana and Janáček, among many other composers, wrote pieces especially for choral societies, and the whole phenomenon may be regarded as the musical counterpart of the nation-wide Sokol gymnastics organization, drawing the same social groups for its membership and diffusing the same nationalist-populist ideology.

To the closely connected folk and art music traditions must be added, after 1920, one of the most vigorous jazz scenes in continental Europe, one which was challenged by both Nazi occupiers and, after 1948, by the Communist regime which sought to counter the appeal of trumpet and saxophone with traditional instruments like the iconic cimbalom. Neither, predictably, had the slightest success and, as we shall see, jazz was throughout the four decades of Communist control a focus of opposition as significant as the theater with which the jazz milieu frequently overlapped. From the 1960s onwards, rock music—listened to clandestinely, like jazz, on the Voice of America and other western stations—joined the earlier music as a rallying point for a somewhat younger generation and, as again we shall see, was to play a quite critical role in the eventual toppling of the regime in 1989.

Music and Resistance

From the outset, Czech music had had a didactic intent, and this tradition of *musique engageé* was continued, in very different ways, by the folk-singer (in the western, Bob Dylan sense) Karel Kryl (1944-94) who, in 1968 and again in the 1980s, really did become the Voice of Czechoslovakia and by the Plastic People of the Universe, Prague's somewhat more intellectual version of the Pogues. Thus if nineteenth-century England was famously described as a land without music, Bohemia and Moravia have, since the 1850s, possessed music in superabundance. Musical production indeed often became a substitute for political action—Czechoslovakia is often said to have a poor record of resistance to Nazism, but between 1939 and 1945 no fewer than twenty new operas, thirty new cantatas and thirty new symphonies were reputedly performed in the country—but could, in the right circumstances, also provoke and lead into concrete resistance. Whoever said that late November 1989 was not a revolution but a week-long street concert was not criticizing, but paying tribute to, the Czech musical tradition.

Czech music, it goes without saying, has closely reflected the fluctuations and discontinuities of the country's historical experience. Between 1620 and 1800, Bohemia and Moravia produced an abundance of highly talented musicians who, in the absence of a court based in Prague, had to go elsewhere in search of patronage and employment. Thus the greatest Czech Baroque composer, the magnificent Jan Dismas Zelenka (1679-1745) spent almost all of his creative life in Dresden, while the scarcely less gifted Heinrich Biber (1644-1704), composer of the extraordinary *Rosary Sonatas* (1681), a sequence of fifteen pieces each depicting one of the mysteries of the rosary, was in the employ of the Prince-Archbishop of Salzburg. Other fine eighteenth-century composers—Josef Mysliveček (1737-81), Jan Vanhal (1739-1813) and any number of interrelated Bendas (František, Friedrich, Jiří, Karel)—joined the drove of musicians employed at the imperial court in Vienna. All composed in the international style of the times, but with various individual innovations, like Biber's use of *scordatura*, or deliberate mistuning of instruments, that suggest a definite Bohemian quirkiness; Zelenka's "Hypochondria" sinfonia, a mordant evocation of the groaning and grousing of a self-pitying valetudinarian, seems positively Arcimboldesque in its astringency and wit.

However, it was not until Jan Jakub Ryba (1765-1815), composer of the perennially popular *Czech Christmas Mass* (*Česká mše vánoční*, 1796), that an attempt was made to incorporate Czech folk themes, using the Czech language, into elite music. The unfortunate Ryba committed suicide, inaugurating another baleful Czech tradition (see Chapter Five), and a play about him, entitled *The Czech Christmas Mass*, by Milan Calábek (born 1940) was the first play by a Czech writer to be premiered after the Soviet invasion in December 1968: "Even one second of freedom makes it all worthwhile," declares Ryba when—inevitably—he is accused of staging his nativity play illegally.

But even Ryba's example found few emulators over the next fifty years; the fine symphony and influential piano impromptus of Jan Voříšek (1791-1825) owe more to the contemporary Viennese style, and particularly to his friendship with Beethoven, than they do to any underground Bohemian musical tradition. Thus the habitual description of Smetana as the "founder of Czech music" is true to the extent that, prior to him, no major Czech-born composer had made his career almost exclusively in the land of his birth or made it his intention to develop a specifically national musical style in the service, loosely but explicitly, of the national cause. Moreover, though he was born in the small town of Litomyšl eighty-five miles southeast of the capital, Smetana clearly thought of himself as a Prague composer before all else. Despite its rural setting and theme, *The Bartered Bride* was composed beside the Vltava in Prague, and it was without hesitation that he dedicated *Má vlast* (My Homeland) to the city since it was there that "I received my musical education, where for many years I performed officially and where I was smitten with deafness."

A six-part cycle of symphonic poems begun in 1872 and first performed as a whole at the National Theater in November 1882, *Má vlast* is the seminal work of Czech music in more than a casual sense since it has seeded the public and artistic imagination of the country for well over a century and shows no sign of losing its potency. Three of its six movements (*Vyšehrad*, *Vltava* and *Šárka*) allude specifically to Prague or to myths associated with the city, and two others evoke the myth of Blaník mountain and the story of the Hussite stronghold of Tábor; the fourth movement, *From Bohemia's Fields and Groves*, sets everything, in true town-dweller style, amidst the idealized continuum of Czech rural life. It was only comparatively late on that Smetana added "Má" to the original title of *Vlast*, immediately personalizing the work and inaugurating a tradition of autobiography plus evocation of history, geography and myth that has proved astonishingly long-lasting and fertile in Czech musical production. It also introduces the practice of musical citation—above all of the Hussite hymn "Ye Who Are God's Warriors"—to which virtually every Czech composer has had recourse at some time, almost always in order to make some national or political point. Finally, the Czech countryside is co-opted into the urban-led nationalist cause, unleashing a flood of "Moravian Rhapsodies" or "Bohemian Serenades" that are as much a staple of Czech music as "Somerset Suites" or "Norfolk Overtures" were of the English equivalent at the time. But, in the Czech case, this was not the "cow-pat music" of city-dwellers nostalgic for the imagined simplicities of the countryside, but a deliberate enlistment of *vlast* in the cause of *národ*, so that nothing could be more symbolically appropriate than the fact that Czech independence was declared not, as might be anticipated, in the National Theater but, precisely, in the concert hall named after Smetana in the Obecní dům (see Chapter Five) where, ever since, even under German occupation, the annual Prague Spring Festival (*Pražské jaro*) has been inaugurated every May by a performance of *Má vlast* in the presence of the national president.

"In song alone, in song alone/We found sweet relief": thus Bohuš and Julie in Dvořák's opera *The Jacobin* (1889) describe how, when far from their native land, they consoled themselves by singing a Czech song, "and the gloom disappeared from the soul." Given this virtual identification of *národ, vlast* and song, every loss and recovery of freedom in the Czech lands has been celebrated by an outpouring of music, beginning in 1918 when Josef Suk's choral symphony *Ripening* (*Zrání*) was given its premiere; continuing his earlier *Asrael Symphony* (1907), inspired by the death of his wife, it typically equated national and personal rebirth. Yet the best Czech music of the 1920s, like the best Czech theater, self-consciously reacted against the portentousness of the nationalist tradition, and, influenced in equal proportions by modernism and jazz, produced sparkling, irreverent work that is the equivalent in sound of the poems and paintings of the contemporaneous poetist and artificialist movements (see Chapter Five). This was music such as Martinů's delightful *Revue de cuisine* (1927) and his jazz ballet *Checkmating the King* (1930), Jaroslav Ježek's innovative score for the ballet *Nerves* (1928) and Erwin Schulhoff's equally acerbic *Rag Music* (1922), *Cinq études de jazz* (1926), and *Hot Sonata* for saxophone and piano (1930). But, again in tandem with the Liberated Theater, the same composers became more and more attuned to the global economic, social and political crisis of the 1930s, producing increasingly anxious and pessimistic music as the decade wore on. Ježek's *Symphonic Poem* (1936), his self-styled exercise in musical surrealism, combines fireworks and foreboding in an inimitable way, while Schulhoff, a member of the Czech Communist Party since 1933 and its delegate at the International Congress of Revolutionary Musicians in Moscow that year, wrote symphonies inspired by hunger riots in Slovakia in 1935 and by the Spanish Civil War (1936-37) in which many Czech Communists fought for the republican cause. Munich prompted a further outpouring of musical anger and angst— Schulhoff's *Fifth Symphony*, Martinů's biting *Double Concerto for Two String Orchestras, Piano and Timpani* (1938)—and was followed by, as we have seen, a spate of works composed immediately before and after the eventual Nazi invasion, with Ladislav Vycpálek's *Czech Requiem* (1940) outstanding among them.

By now Martinů and Ježek were in exile in the United States and Schulhoff in the Soviet Union where he was taken prisoner in 1941 and sent to concentration camp and death in Bavaria. Most touchingly of all, Martinů's star pupil and *inamorata*, Vítězslava Kaprálová (1915-40), fled to France and early death after composing the exquisite song "Waving Farewell" ("Sbohem a šáteček") to a text by the surrealist poet Vítězslav Nezval dedicated "to that most beautiful city—Prague." The massacre of Lidice (see p.3) inspired one of Martinů's finest orchestral scores (1943), and the elderly Vítězslav Novák composed an impressive *De profundis* dedicated to the suffering of the Czech nation, that was given its first performance in Brno in November 1941 on the very day that the regional president, a Dr. Mezník, jumped, or was pushed, out of a window: clearly Prague did not have a monopoly on voluntary and involuntary defenestration.

Liberation was greeted by yet another deluge of patriotic music, with Novák dedicating his *May Symphony* (*Májová Sinfonie*), premiered in Prague in December 1945, to none other than Stalin himself, whose views on modern music had been made clear when, in 1934, he famously condemned Shostakovitch's great opera *Lady Macbeth of the Mtsensk District* as "muddle, not music." Sure enough, when the Communists came to power in 1948, music immediately felt the impress of Zhdanovist orthodoxy. Rafael Kubelík, a composer as well as a conductor, left Czechoslovakia forthwith to be followed in 1954 by one of the more adventurous younger composers, Karel Husa (born 1921). Even the most timidly innovative music became susceptible to the blanket accusation of "formalism", and Oldřich Korte (born 1926) was forced radically to revise his *Song of the Flutes* (1949-51) on the grounds that the two flutes (that is, supposedly, "the artist") and the orchestra (meaning "society") were presented in the composition as "antagonistic forces".

Composers, like playwrights and theater directors, were left with the usual Švejkian tactic of saying one thing and implying another, knowing that their audience could be relied upon to pick up and elaborate any sub-textual allusion and, if need be, create one where none was intended. Did Vladimír Sommer's *Antigona* (1957), like the Sophoclean tragedy to which it was composed as an overture, comment indirectly on the relationship between individual and state? And what political meanings might be intended by his *Vocal Symphony* (1958, revised 1963—a good half of Czech compositions of this period seem to have been subsequently "revised") which, very daringly, set to music texts by the still stigmatized Kafka (the early prose poem "At Night"), the dangerously subversive Dostoyevsky (Raskolnikov's nightmare in *Crime and Punishment*) and the uncategorizable—and suicidal—Cesare Pavese (the poem "Death will come and he will have your eyes")? No Czech-based composer could make a *direct* comment on the Soviet invasion—that was left to the folk singer Karel Kryl (see Chapter Six) and the exiled Karel Husa, now professor of music at Cornell University. But perhaps Petr Eben's massive organ cycle *Faust* (1979-80) could be read as a critique of the Prometheanism of the whole socialist project, and his *Job* (1987), also for organ, as an evocation of the unjust sufferings of the Czech people and nation, underlined by its clinching quotation from the Bohemian Brethren hymn "Kristus, příklad pokory" (Christ, the model of humility). Eben (born 1929) is probably the finest living Czech composer. A former prisoner in Buchenwald and later professor of music theory at Charles University, he has written mainly religious music for organ and chorus, his most important post-1989 work being a setting for organ of readings from *The Labyrinth of the World and the Paradise of the Heart*. The full Czech premier took place in 1996, although parts had earlier been performed at the surviving Bohemian Brethren church on Sovkenická in the Old Town.

There was no mistaking, however, the meaning of works produced in the wake of November 1989, like Eben's own *Prague Te Deum 1989* (*Pražské Te Deum 1989*) and Othmar Mácha's *Patria Bohemorum* (1990), a work as conservative in conception and theme as it was in musical idiom. Perhaps the most striking feature of Czech music—a source both of strength and weakness—is the extraordinary permanence of its subjects and style since the path-breaking example of Smetana.

Kings of Swing

If the solemnity which, for all too understandable historical reasons, hangs over much Czech classical music briefly lifted in the 1920s, it was in large part under the influence of jazz which composers like Martinů and Schulhoff first heard live in Paris and Berlin respectively but which, by the mid 1920s, was firmly implanted in Czechoslovakia itself. The 1930s saw an explosion of local swing bands inspired by the likes of the Chick Webb, Jimmy Lunceford and Tommy Dorsey orchestras, with many professionals graduating from the Charles University Gramophone Club orchestra established in 1935. Drawing large crowds to theaters and dance-halls on and around Wenceslas Square, above all to the Lucerna Hall in the famous modernist *pasáž* (arcade) of that name (see Chapter Six), the bandleaders Harry Harden (alias David Stoljarovič), Harry Oslen (Siegried Grzyb), and Rudolf Dvorský vied for the title of the Czech King of Swing. Prague had its blond-banged would-be Ella Fitzgeralds in Zdenka Vincíková and Fany Koudelová, while the Allanovy Sestry made a pleasantly rotund Bohemian version of the Andrews Sisters on whom they modeled their style. To these must be added the ubiquitous Jaroslav Ježek, composer, in his jazz incarnation, of "David and Goliath" in 1937, possibly the only explicitly anti-fascist swing hit anywhere in the world: no Czech jitter-bugger would need to have the Biblical allusion explained.

Surprisingly, these and similar bands continued to perform after March 1939, but German losses on the eastern front in 1941-42 caused swing music and dancing officially to be banned, and the Nazi propaganda machine weighed in against a music that it denounced for its "Negroid excesses" and "Jewish-Masonic howl". But, according to Josef Škvorecký (born 1924), whose preface to his novel *The Bass Saxophone* (1978) is the best discussion of jazz in Czechoslovakia, fans continued to listen to jazz on Radio Stockholm, the only non-German foreign station the Nazis did not jam. Bands continued to perform semi-clandestinely, if need be disguising the "Saint Louis Blues" as "The song of Rešetova Lhota" or the like ("Goin' to Rešetova Lhota/Goin' to see my Aryan gal…") and, above all, young Czechs continued to jive and jitterbug like crazy in whatever venues they could find. Between 1941 and 1945, Škvorecký writes, jazz was "the sacrament that verily knows no frontier", and the Prague-based *O.K.* magazine (*Okružní Korespondence*, or "circulating correspondence") produced a carbon-copied jazz newsletter that was distributed to crypto jazz fans by "lovely *krystýnky* on bicycles, the bobby soxers of those perished times." This truly was "the swell season"—the title of another collection of jazz stories by Škvorecký—for the Bohemian jazz fan.

What had been played, listened and danced to semi-secretly under Nazi occupation briefly exploded into full publicity between 1945 and 1948, with Karel Vlach and Bobek Bryen now the Kings of the Lucerna, only to be driven back underground following the Communist take-over. According to Škvorecký, the new dictatorship's strictures against jazz reproduced almost verbatim those of the Nazis—"decadent", "perverted", "lying", "degenerate", with additional references to a concerted capitalist plot to "deafen the ears of the Marshallized world by means of epileptic, loud-mouthed compositions." When attempts to counter the saxophone with the cimbalom predictably failed, the regime promoted the then Communist fellow-traveler Paul Robeson as the "authentic voice" of oppressed black America, and Škvorecký records his disgust when Robeson gave an open-air concert in Prague at the very time that Milada Horáková (1901-50), the only woman to be purged during the Stalinist trials, was awaiting execution. Karel Vlach and his sidemen were dispatched to the provinces to play in a touring circus orchestra, and the regime created its own Prague City Stompers and Czechoslovak Washboard Beaters in an effort to deflect recalcitrant jazz fans from "decadent" swing music—be-bop seems not to have reached Prague until the late 1950s—to the ideologically safer and allegedly more "authentic" Dixieland style. When this failed in its turn, and facing a new and more potent enemy in the form of rock music, the musical apparatchiks declared jazz to be "safe" (within limits) and, during the cultural thaw of the early 1960s, it was possible to hear the Modern Jazz Quartet and even Don Cherry in live performance in Prague. As we have seen, the jazz and theater milieu moved closer together, and the Reduta and Agharta jazz clubs were as much the seedbed of the spirit of Prague '68 as the Gate and Balustrade theaters.

"Normalization" hit jazz as hard as the theater, though it was not until 1984 that the Jazz Section of the Musicians' Union was formally abolished, following the trial and conviction for dissident activities of two of its members Karel Srp and Joska Skalník who, in the wartime tradition of *O.K.* magazine, produced and distributed a jazz newsletter which, this time, contained articles on broader cultural issues as well. Driven underground, the Jazz Section network would again play its part in November 1989.

The most distinctively Czech jazz musician of the moment is the multi-instrumentalist Jiří Stivín (born Prague 1942) whose work is a truly alchemical marriage—see the combination of jazz, vocal and classical string quartets on his 1995 album *Alchymia Musicae*—of disparate musical elements including, most recently, Bohemian and Moravian folk music: the old antagonism of saxophone and cimbalom has at last been laid to rest. Stivín's music is both avant-garde and deeply traditional: the spirit of Arcimboldo and Zelenka relives in the two extended compositions of his 1977 album *Zodiac*, "The Elements" ("Fire", "Water", "Air", "Earth") and "Moods" ("The Phlegmatics", "The Sanguinics", "The Melancholics", "The Cholerics").

Plastic People: Prague's Rockers

By the mid-1970s, the "jazz threat" had been largely neutralized by a combination of repression, co-option and edulcoration. Meanwhile, a new, and potentially far more dangerous, form of musical opposition had emerged in the shape of rock music, either foreign groups listened to clandestinely on smuggled or pirated cassettes, or, more menacing still, created by local groups that sometimes changed their names by the month to avoid detection. The regime responded by outlawing "hard rock" in 1973, mere possession of banned tapes became an offence, gigs were broken up by the police, causing Smetana's beloved Bohemian fields and groves to echo with the sounds of electric guitars as fans staged mini-Woodstocks in remote country areas.

Two groups that refused to change or disguise their names and so attracted especial police attention were D6 307 and above all Plastic People of the Universe. This nine-man group, headed by the guitarist and vocalist Milan Hlavsa, included in its line-up flute, clarinet and fiddle as well as guitar, saxophone and synthesizer: a typically Czech appropriation and indigenization of a foreign musical idiom. The group's spiritual mentor and artistic director was the somewhat older dissident intellectual Ivan Jirous who, in a *samizdat* article of 1975, wrote of the emerging musical underground as "a community of mutual support of people who want to live differently", "a culture not dependent on official channels of communication, or on the hierarchy of values of the establishment." It was a clear foretaste of the slightly later Charter 77-inspired notion of dissidence as a "parallel polis" operating outside, and implicitly against, the established structures of the game, and it was enough to bring Jirous and several members of the Plastics and other groups to trial in September 1976.

The trial was held at a court on Karmelitská Street in Malá Strana, and, surprisingly, the regime permitted Václav Havel to attend as an observer. His subsequent article—inevitably entitled "The Trial" (October 1976)—denounced "an inflated, narrow-minded power, persecuting everything that does not fit into its sterile notions of life, everything unusual, risky, self-taught, and unbribable", everything that, in the words of one defendant, Pavel Zajíček, sprang from a "deeper level of being" than official party ideology. The trial, said Havel, was in reality "an impassioned debate about the meaning of human existence, an urgent questioning of what one should expect from life," questions embodied first in the music of the Plastics and similar groups and then posed by the support groups that came into being as the trial proceeded, "a very special, improvised community," said Havel, "a community of people who were not only more considerate, communicative, and trusting toward each other, they were in a strange way democratic." Jirous, not for the first or last time, was sentenced to several months' imprisonment, the importance of the trial being, first, that it crystallized the alienation of tens of thousands of young people, previously "apolitical", from the regime and, second, that it was the seedbed of Charter 77 that emerged early the next year. All the Chartists agree: it was the trial of Jirous and the Plastics that was the catalyst, and the support groups formed in September 1976 that mutated into Charter 77 in January 1977.

Under more or less continuous government pressure, the Plastics and similar *alternativní kapely* (alternative groups)—Stehlik, Extempore, Elektra—continued to perform and record in conditions of greater or less secrecy. Listening to their music and sporting the insignia of musical dissidence—jeans, T-shirts, long hair, no hair—were theorized by Jirous and others as forms of "counter-socialization", a means of nullifying ideological indoctrination by the regime. Drink and, when available, drugs also formed part of a potent oppositional culture, creating a musical version of the "parallel polis" imagined by the Chartist philosopher Václav Benda. The outstanding musical monument of the Czech counter-culture is the Plastics' album *Hovězí porážka* (Cattle Slaughter) recorded clandestinely in several stages in 1983-84, first at the home of the parents of one of the group's members Jan Brabec, the final version being put together at the flat belonging to the keyboard player Josef Janíček on Podskalská Street (Nové Město).

With Havel acting as a kind of literary consultant, the group put together a sequence of nine numbers all more or less on the slaughter of animals, a theme close, if not dear, to the heart of the lead vocalist Milan Hlavsa who had actually worked for a time as a slaughter man. "Prasinec" (Piggery) "celebrates" the killing, dissection and processing of a pig, while "Kanárek" (The Little Canary), by the late Petr Lampl (died 1978), founder-member of the latter-day Dadaist "Order of Crusaders for Pure Humor without Banter" recasts the crucifixion of Christ as the snuffing out of a canary. Most graphically, "Bleskem do hlavy" (Lightning in the Head) by the group's clarinetist Petr Placák appears to liken the whole of existence to a single massive abattoir into which stupid lumbering animals, not sheep but cattle, troop to meet an anonymous, mechanized death:

Which one shall we take
This big one
Hush lazy beast
Thunder in the head

Upside down
Something leaking
Lazy ox
Lightning in the head

Cut the meat with that axe
Chop the bones the remains will be ground

We'll eat quickly
No talking
Don't even like it
What next

Stand over there
Stupid beast
Lightning in the head
Lightning in the head

Cut the meat with that axe
Chop the bone remains will be ground
(translation by Šárka Dalton)

The whole album works a series of obscene scatological variations on the classic Bohemian theme of sacrificial death, delivered in a dirge-like monotone in which the curious mixture of instruments combines in some malignant alchemy of grunge and traditional folk music. As Havel says, it is "upsetting and powerful music", but not, in his view, nihilistic: "I feel something deeply liberating, purifying, uplifting and an element of salvation in the fact that the pain of life is screamed out in this way; it appears to me that if a person is able to play and sing in such a way, not everything can yet be lost."

In 1983 the regime launched an all-out attack on rock music for "spreading amongst youth opinions unacceptable to our ideology, a philosophy of nihilism and despair, a cynical approach to life and all its values." In response, the Jazz Section of the Musicians' Union issued a defense of rock music entitled *Rock na levém křídle* (Rock on the Left Wing) and, through its newsletter *43/10/88* (its telephone number), provided the diffuse counter-culture with a regular focus and forum. On December 8, 1985, the fifth anniversary of the murder of John Lennon, groups of rock fans gathered on Velkopřevorské náměstí in Malá Strana, a square close to Charles Bridge leading to Kampa Island. It was here that a wall of the Priory of the Knights of Malta had for some years been transformed into an impromptu shrine to the author of "Imagine". Covered in graffiti and festooned with flowers every December 8, it was, as it were, the musical counterpart to the unofficial shrine to Jan Palach on Wenceslas Square (see Chapter Six). In 1985 demonstrators arrived carrying placards asking "when will there be peace, John?", placed flowers and lit candles at the foot of the wall and then, numbering about 600, marched back across Charles Bridge to Old Town Square chanting "Flowers, not weapons" and "Abolish the army". It was small stuff compared to the huge demonstrations of 1968 and of those of November-December 1989 still to come, but a clear sign of rock's mobilizing potential amidst even the most discouraging conditions.

While it was Charter 77 that attracted international attention, the influence of the musical counter-culture reached far beyond the intellectual and professional elite. Through its inept efforts to control the lifestyles and musical tastes of the post-1968 generation, the regime created the crowds—overwhelmingly aged under 30—who would sweep it from power in November 1989 (see Chapter Nine). That month's "revolution" was velvet not just because it was essentially non-violent but because—or so Czechs insist—it was made as much in the name of Velvet Underground as of Václav Havel. The Velvet Revolution was probably the only revolution in history that was in large part made by, with and for music and, as such, represents the culmination of the Czech association of music and freedom made by Smetana, Dvořák and Janáček who, it is pleasant to conjecture, would have recognized in the Plastics' doom-laden droning some distant echo of the Bohemian and Moravian folk music they loved.

CHAPTER FIVE

Prague Modern, 1900–1948

For many first-time visitors to Prague, the experience of the city's Gothic and Baroque architecture is so utterly compelling that they fail simply to register that Prague is also one of Europe's greatest centers of the Art Nouveau and modernist styles. There are good reasons for this omission. Whereas the principal Gothic and Baroque buildings are concentrated along the Hradčany-Malá Strana-Staré Město axis, their twentieth-century counterparts are scattered throughout the city, often far from the center at Vyšehrad, Dejvice or Vinohrady. Some, like Adolf Loos' Müller Haus (1930) in the suburb of Strešovice to the west of Hradčany, are privately owned and effectively unvisitable, and many more are in a poor state of conservation.

Even the most accessible modernist masterpiece, Otakar Novotny's Mánes Museum (1930), which spans the narrow channel of water between Žofín Island and the "mainland" and which brilliantly incorporates part of the old water-mill into its ultra-rectilinear design, badly needs not so much restoration as a good coat of paint. On the other hand, there are enough "secessionist" (as Art Nouveau was known in the Austro-Hungarian Empire, taken over in Czech as *secesní*) buildings in the center of Prague to place it alongside Glasgow and Brussels, but well behind Barcelona, as one of the Art Nouveau capitals of Europe. And Prague (along with Brno) also contains a small number of properly cubist buildings that, as Karel Teige (1900-51), the great theorist and publicist of Czech modernism in all of its forms, rightly described as "unlike anything else in Europe".

Like everything else in Prague, secessionist architecture had a political dimension, though this time less as an assertion of national distinctiveness than as a conscious attempt to "rejoin Europe" after the architectural introversion and isolationism of neo-Gothic and neo-Renaissance eclecticism. To the extent that Prague derived the secessionist style in the first instance from Vienna, it was the familiar Czech paradox of protesting in German against the threat of Germanization. On the other hand, Art Nouveau seems most to have thrived in marginalized political and cultural entities (Scotland, Catalonia, Belgium, and Bohemia/Moravia) and may be seen as a protest against provincialization by a dominant metropolis (London, Madrid, Paris and Vienna respectively) formulated in an international rather than a national style. It is thus doubly appropriate that Czech independence should have been declared in the concert hall of the city's finest secessionist building, the Obecní dům, or Municipal House, on Náměstí Republiky, for on October 28, 1918 it both *seceded* from the Austro-Hungarian Empire and *acceded* to full membership of the European comity of nations. Czech secessionism, wrote Teige in 1947, was essentially an "intermediate style" corresponding to an intermediate stage in the nation's development: "It started out with a powerful denunciation of the eclecticism of the architecture of the dying century, yet it was not consistent enough to carry secession right to its conclusion by leaving the old world and crossing over to the frontier of the new." As an overall judgment, this is undoubtedly true, for secession did indeed, as Teige said, "define architecture as an essentially decorative art", which was why it could so readily incorporate, and be

Obecní dům

incorporated by, the traditional themes and motifs of Czech nationalist ideology. The vigor of the secessionist style in Prague is, however, undeniable, as is the quality of at least half a dozen buildings whose architects, though no rivals to Charles Rennie Mackintosh or Antonio Gaudí, deserve rescuing from their anonymity outside the former Czechoslovakia.

Obecní dům: Art Nouveau

Czech Art Nouveau is, in general, more restrained than its Scottish or Catalan equivalents, as though a combination of nationalism and Puritanism prevented Czech architects from indulging in the kind of flamboyance they associated with the "foreign" style of the Baroque. With few exceptions, like the Obecní dům, the buildings are not set apart and, with the help of decades of Prague grime and institutional neglect, they can all too easily merge with the undistinguished structures around them. There is no missing, however, the Grand Hotel Europa (1906) and its next-door neighbor, the Hotel Meran, on Wenceslas Square, built as a pair by Alois Dryák and Bedřich Bendelmayer. Both were graduates of the School of Decorative Arts in Prague where they had been taught by the Ukrainian-born Bedřich Ohmann who, along with his successor, Jan Kotěra, is usually credited with having pioneered the secessionist style in the city. Purchasing the Europa in 1924, Karel Šroubek coined its famous publicity slogan "U Šroubků (At the Šroubeks') in life, in heaven after death", and there are some to whom the hotel's sumptuous interiors—including its inevitable, and quintessentially Czech, Mirrored Hall—will seem like some exquisitely ornate paradise on earth.

More interesting architecturally, particularly on the outside, is the U Nováků building (1902-3) on Vodičkova, built as a department store by the greatest Czech secessionist Osvald Polívka (1859-1931). It is famous above all for its bucolic murals by Jan Preisler allegorizing the virtues of Obchod (Commerce) and Průmysl (Industry); a sculptured frog reminiscent of Gaudi clambers up to one of the windows, a scarlet sash tied round its waist. Polívka also designed the impressive pair of buildings on Národní třída (1907-8), one as the headquarters of the Prague Savings Bank, the other of the one-time Topič Publishing House before it was taken over by the state as the Československý spisovatel or Czechoslovak Writers' House. Many visitors will also encounter as a matter of course the Main Station (Hlavní nádraží) on Wilsonova, designed by Josef Fanta and inaugurated in 1909 as the Franz-Josefs Bahnhof, virtually the last public building in Prague to invoke the imperial Methuselah and his equally decrepit "Dual Monarchy".

Even as the station was being declared officially open, another building a few hundred yards away, stylistically similar but utterly different in ideological intention, was nearing completion on the present Náměstí Republicky. The decision to create a Czech-speaking equivalent, and counter, to the German Kasino (see Chapter Two) on nearby An Graben (Na příkopě) was taken by the Prague City Council in 1901. After an inconclusive competition between architects, the project was entrusted to Osrvald Polívka and Antonín Balšanek; construction began in 1904, and the completed complex was officially opened in November 1912. Obecní dům was above all a collective undertaking, and virtually every contemporary Czech-speaking painter, sculptor and designer of note made his contribution to the whole. To the already familiar names of Ladislav Šaloun, Max Švabinský, Josef Myslbek and Alfons Mucha must be added those, among many others, of Mikoláš Aleš (1852-1913), the doyen of traditionalist Czech painting and Karel Spillar, the designer of the mosaic *The Apotheosis of Prague* above the main entrance which declares, with pardonable bombast, "Success to you, Prague! Defy time, defy malice! May you withstand every tumult!" (Perhaps it was indeed "malice" that prompted the Germans to make Obecní dům their headquarters in Prague during the "tumult" of 1939-45.)

The Obecní dům consists of three levels and covers a rhombus-shaped site of 45,000 square feet. The basement contains a beer hall, an American bar, a Pilsen restaurant (i.e. a restaurant serving Czech food), a succession of games rooms and what must be the most palatial cloakroom anywhere in Europe. On the ground floor are a French restaurant and a magnificent many-mirrored café, almost a *Laterna Magika* in itself, but it is the first floor that concentrates more Art Nouveau marvels than any single building in Europe, outside of Barcelona. The centerpiece, in every sense, is the Smetana Hall where independence was declared in 1918 and where, as we have seen, the

famous Prague Spring Festival begins every year with a ritualistic rendering of *Má vlast*. This is, in a sense, the Holy of Holy of Czech nationalism, the place at which, mediated through music, *vlast* at long last became truly *národ*, and, lest the symbolism of the whole thing escape some benighted concert-goer, a huge statue entitled *Má vlast* by the inescapable Ladislav Šaloun looms out from a wall over the auditorium.

Around the concert hall is grouped a series of inter-connecting rooms, some of which, principally those facing on to Náměstí Republiky, are included in the guided tour of the building. Each room is a masterpiece of refinement, intricacy and sumptuousness, and each combines glorification of the nation, and specifically of Prague, with the fulfillment of some practical purpose: debating (the Grégr Room on the corner of Náměstí Republiky and Celetná), lectures (the Sladovský Room on the opposite corner), talking and smoking, once a civilized activity requiring an appropriate setting (the Slavic Salon) and chess and card-games (the Serbian or Oriental Room). There are rooms dedicated to the "founding fathers" of Czech history, Palacký and Rieger, and one to the "founding mother" of Czech literature, Božena Němcová. The Rieger Room contains group portraits, by Švabinský, of the "greats" of Czech music and painting (Smetana, Dvořak, Mánes, Aleš and Myslbek) and literature (Němcová, Svatopluk Čech, Jan Neruda, Julius Zeyer and Jaroslav Vrchlický). It was a mixture of genius, talent and nonentity that looked down as, amidst a décor suitably dominated by blue velvet, Václav Havel and Mikhail Gorbachev sat down for their first meeting after November 1989.

The finest of the rooms is undoubtedly the Mayor's Room directly over the entrance, and it is here, much more than at the museum devoted to him on Panská, that the art of Alfons Mucha (1860-1939) can be seen at its best. Born in the southern Moravian town of Ivančice, Mucha voluntarily expatriated himself in his mid twenties and developed the light-hearted, free-flowing, gently erotic painterly style for which he is renowned (and which made him very wealthy) in Paris and elsewhere and in the process—or so Czech nationalist critics maintained both then and since—effectively "de-Slaved" himself in the name of pan-European and transatlantic success. But in 1900 Mucha visited the Balkans and underwent a personalized version of the *národní obrození* (national awakening) from which he emerged determined, as he put it, that "the remainder of my life would be filled exclusively with work for the nation." He returned to Bohemia in 1910, and the Mayor's Room was the first important "national" commission he received on home soil. He duly confounded his critics by producing one of the great icons of Czech national rebirth, from the ceiling fresco representing a vision of "Slavic Concorde" to the eight pendentives in which this or that human virtue is personified by a character from Czech history. It is the usual cast of national characters—Comenius (Faithfulness), Hus (Justice), Žižka (Militancy), George of Poděbrady (Independence), and so on—but painted with such flair and inventiveness as to transcend the limitations of an increasingly conventional visual lexicon.

After 1918, it was Mucha who principally designed the currency of the newly independent nation, and he spent the 1920s completing his massive *Slav Epic*, a cycle of huge paintings for which he had received a commission from an American admirer of Masaryk. The works were exhibited at the Klementinum in 1928 for what has proved to be the one and only time. The cycle's twenty paintings depict scenes from Croatian, Serbian, Bulgarian and Russian as well as Czech history and, were they to be brought together and exhibited as a totality in Prague, as Mucha intended, not only would Mucha's reputation as an artist, rather than as an illustrator of genius, be enhanced, but Prague and its visitors would be able to appreciate at its full value what is clearly one of the masterpieces of twentieth-century historical painting. A late convert to Czech nationalism, Mucha did not escape the almost predestined fate of the Czech nationalist artist: arrested, aged almost 80, by the Gestapo in 1939 and interrogated, he died very shortly afterwards and, for reasons of security, was denied the public funeral that his standing as an artist deserved.

One of the most pleasing murals in the Mayor's Room is entitled "Dreaming of Freedom" and depicts a stereotypical Czech maiden, all blond pigtails and traditional head-dress, staring doe-eyed into the mid-distance, with the cathedral and castle of Hradčany silhouetted behind her. The mural was first seen by the public in 1911, and seven years later, far more rapidly than anyone had imagined, dream had become reality, and already secession was a style of the past.

Architectural Modernism and Cubism

In point of fact, the reaction against secession had begun well before 1918, indeed even while the Obecní dům was being constructed. Czech architectural modernism has its origins in the work of Jan Kotěra (1871-1923), head of the Prague School of Architecture from 1898 to 1910, who as well as pioneering the secessionist style, also initiated the reaction against it with a series of much more rigorous and uncluttered buildings such as the Mozarteum, otherwise known as Urbánek House, built on Jungmannova in 1911. Even this, however, seems tame beside the small number of buildings that were constructed under the influence of the Czech cubist movement and which represent Prague's most innovative contribution to twentieth-century European architecture.

Of the several buildings concerned, the most radical are those designed by Josef Chochol (1880-1956) just north of Vyšehrad, particularly his wedge-shaped apartment block on the corner of Neklanova Street and, more striking still, the Vila Kovařovicova on Libušina Street a short step away. This remarkable building (1911-13) eschews curves completely, and is built up, like a cubist painting, of

Vila Kovařovicova on Libušina Street

rhomboids and lozenges interlocking with each other to produce a fractured and discontinuous façade of remarkable power. Even the flower beds, steps, gates and fences consist of repeated geometrical shapes, all angles no curves, that mimic in brick, concrete and iron the constructivist logic of painters like Kubišta and Filla (see below). This is linearity and structure with a vengeance, and the other great cubist building in Prague, the House of the Black Mother of the Lord (Dům u černé matky Boží), on the corner of Celetná and Ovocný trh draws back somewhat from this extremism and, blending well with the surrounding Baroque buildings, even manages to incorporate a statuette of the Black Madonna without detracting from the purity of its lines. Built as a department store in 1911-12 by Josef Gočar (1880-1945), perhaps the greatest Czech architect of the century, the building now houses on its upper floors a museum of Czech cubism containing, in addition to paintings and sculptures, highly original pieces of furniture—chairs, tables, sideboards, sofas, all entirely rectilinear in structure that testify to the movement's determination, in Prague, to be functional as well as aesthetic and to transform daily living in a radical way. The most striking instance of this project—though its state of disrepair is a scandal—is the single standing "cubist lamppost" variously attributed to Vlastislav Hofman or Emil Králíček that stands, barely visible unless you are looking for it, in a corner of Jungmannovo Square: a kind of utilitarian Brancusi column, whose abandonment symbolizes the impasse into which the out-and-out cubist style ultimately led.

Only for a very brief period, in the so-called "national style" of the early 1920s, did Czech architecture achieve some kind of synthesis between its "classical" and "Baroque" elements. Of the dozen or so buildings built in this style, two very definitely merit visiting: the already mentioned Palác Adria, one-time home of both the Liberated Theater and Laterna Magika, on the corner of Jungmannova and Národní, built to a design by Pavel Janák and Josef Zasche between 1923 and 1925, and, above all, Josef Gočar's masterpiece, the former Czech Legionnaires' Bank (1921-23) on Na poříčí. Both buildings combine alternating rectangles and circles— whence the name "rondocubism" sometimes given to the style—and make extensive use of sculptures to introduce further variations into the faćade: the bronze allegory of "Seafaring", by Jan Štursa, that draws the straight lines of the Palác Adria into focus is particularly striking.

Still more successful is the extraordinarily sinewy and energetic

Palác Adria

façade of the Czech Legionnaires' Bank. Curved and straight lines, red stone and white, are set dramatically against each other, and Otto Gutfreund's frieze depicting aspects of Czech Legionnaire life further strengthens the impression of national endeavor and purpose. Whether fighting, working, embracing or playing, a whole people, men, women and children alike, are shown acting together in pursuit of full nationhood, in the absence, be it noted, of the usual cast of national heroes. Here every man, every woman and every child is a hero, in a strikingly democratic vision of national self-making. The sense of meaningful, collective activity is sustained within the atrium itself, though here the means used are entirely non-representational: the whole central area is bound into a powerful unity by the repetition of the circle-within-a-square motif found on the façade, interspersed with other geometrical forms based on an amalgam of straight lines and curves. A fountain plays gently in the center, and the delicately rounded green glazed roofs provide both the security and openness of a grotto. Heroism plus industry without, hedonism plus economy within. It is difficult, with the possible exception of Osvald Polívka's somewhat earlier (1892-4) Živnostenská Bank at 20 Na příkopě a few blocks away—in which neo-Renaissance and secessionist elements combine to suggest both power and elegance—to think of a more beautiful commercial building in Europe.

Having squared the circle and produced its architectural philosophers' stone, the rondocubist style could go no further, and by the end of the 1920s, Czech architects, Gočar and Janák amongst them, were moving away from complexity to the uncluttered lines and surfaces of the functionalist style, and, with it, Prague ceded its architectural primacy to Brno. This discussion of architectural modernism in Prague may conclude with three remarkable churches, all within a few hundred yards of each other in the Vinohrady district. Gočar's St. Wenceslas Church (1928-33) on Svatopluk Čech Square is almost unrecognizable as the work of the architect of the Czech Legionnaires' Bank: all ornamentation has gone, and curves have been eliminated entirely in favor of straight lines epitomized by the 250-foot-high tower that rises up above its distinctive stepped roof. Built in the early 1930s, Pavel Janák's Hussite Church a few blocks to the north on Dykova moves beyond even functionalism into something like minimalism. The heavy decoration of the same architect's Palác Adria has disappeared completely, leaving only a slender open-work tower, standing apart from the entirely rectilinear church building itself, to thrust a giant copper chalice up towards heaven. This is "Protestant", anti-Baroque architecture in the extreme, dramatic but, like Gočar's St. Wenceslas, soulless in its determination to eliminate all extraneous matter.

It is with some relief that one moves once more to the north to Náměstí Jiřího z Poděbrad where, in the middle of a grassy expanse, stands one of the most remarkable buildings in Prague, the church of the Most Sacred Heart of Our Lord (Nejsvětější Srdce Páně), built in

1930 by the Slovenian-born architect Josip Plečnik. The church is an extraordinary combination of styles—Byzantine, classical, secessionist and modernist all blended together—and, if it lacks grace, it imposes by its sheer audacity and scale. The lower two-thirds of the walls are built of vitrified gray brick and are unbroken by either windows or decoration; the top third is of white ashlar into which are set windows each surmounted by an inverted half moon. The same proportions, materials and patterns are repeated in the huge oblong tower, as broad as the church itself, at its eastern end, in the center of which a massive transparent clock is installed. The effect is extraordinary, and rich in architectural and religious allusions. On the one hand, the Cyclopean clock-face echoes the neo-Gothic rose window at St. Vitus Cathedral; on the other, it suggests a communion wafer set in its monstrance. And, though there is no question, presumably, of direct rondocubist influence, the tower strikingly combines circle and square and so permits the whole building to transcend its eclecticism and become an amalgam of the country's contending architectural styles: Gothic and Baroque, neo-Renaissance and secessionist, rondocubist and constructivist, a truly national synthesis created, ironically, by a non-national.

The church appears to be almost totally unknown outside of the Czech Republic and is, for that matter, virtually ignored by a Tourist Board so obsessed with marketing the Baroque that it fails even to register the city's modernist masterpieces. Were Sacred Heart located in France, it would be recognized for what it is, one of Europe's greatest twentieth-century churches, bearing comparison with Le Corbusier's at Ronchamp, though it could not be further from the latter's architectural ideal.

Veletržní Palác

When Le Corbusier himself visited Prague in 1929 (he had previously come in 1911 as mere Charles-Edouard Jeanneret), there was one building he admired before all others,

The Czech Legionnaires' Bank

namely the Veletržní Palác (Trade Fair Palace) in Holešovice on the north bank of the Vltava. Completed in 1928 to house commercial exhibitions, the eight-story Palác is the joint work of Oldřich Tyl and Plečnik's star pupil Josef Fuchs (1898-1979) who, rejecting his teacher's love of complexity, created a functionalist masterpiece of streamlined simplicity, all rectilinearity without and airy vastness within, that make it the ideal home for the National Gallery's nineteenth- and twentieth-century collections.

The exhibition begins on the seventh floor with room after room of nineteenth-century Bohemian landscapes, portraits and historical scenes, of which the best one can say is that there is little to detain even the most committed gallery-goer. The national awakening signally failed to produce any painterly equivalent of Smetana and Dvořák, and neither the historical painter Mikoláš Aleš (1852-1913), beloved of both the nationalist bourgeoisie of the late nineteenth century and of the Communist regime of the second half of the twentieth, nor Josef Mánes (1820-71), as conservative a painter of landscapes as the building named after him is radical, is able to transcend the ideological and stylistic constraints of his epoch. The impressionist revolution seems to have had little effect on the dark Bohemian palette, and it is only with the symbolist and early secessionist painters that the visitor is likely to feel some stirring of interest. But, even here, the influence of Redon, Moreau and Rops is oppressive, making the impact of the wood carvings of František Bílek (1872-1941) all the more intense: here, for the first time, one confronts a truly original Czech artist.

There are only a handful of works by Bílek in the Veletržní Palác. Many more will be found in the Vila Bílková, the secessionist-cum-modernist house in Hradčany that he had built to his own design in 1911 as both a family home and "cathedral of art". More still can be seen at his country home in his native village of Chynov near Tábor, which similarly was designed by himself. Bílek studied in Paris in 1891-92, and his monumental style owes something to Rodin and Bourdelle, but infinitely more to the autochthonous traditions of medieval wood-carving and Baroque statuary, whose tormented intensity he carries through into the twentieth century. Bílek's subjects are never merely nationalist, like those of Aleš, but dramatize a highly personal eclectic philosophy that draws equally on Catholicism, Nietzsche, spiritualism and eastern mysticism. His human figures are eight- to ten-foot-high giants, their heads are characteristically thrown back in various poses of anguish and ecstasy, their backs arch with suffering or effort, and many strain upwards and forwards in quest of some impossible vision of bliss; blindness and illumination are Bílek's recurring obsession.

Some of Bílek's best known works, like the statue of Comenius in front of his villa, breathe real passion and energy into the most hackneyed themes of the national awakening, and his strikingly original—and, at times, sacrilegious—variations on Christ's Passion will be discussed in due course (see Chapter Seven). All of Bílek's writings insist on what he calls "the building of the future temple within us", and on the evidence of works like his "Allegory of the Czechs' Great Fall" (1898), in which a naked female figure sprawls at the feet of a giant cut off at mid calf, or his plaster relief "Oppressed by the Body, the World and the Spheres" (1909), in the Vila Bílková, that temple is at once political, spiritual and sexual. It is evident from any one sculpture by Bílek—and still more from the assembled figures of the Vila Bílková—that something is seething within the Czech psyche. This sense of ferment and energy is confirmed when, at the Veletržni Palác, one moves down to the two floors devoted to Czech art from 1900 to 1950.

Foreign Influences

It is out of the question, in a book of this kind, to give a chronological account of Czech modernism even as it affects only Prague: there are simply too many fine painters, too many groups, manifestos, exhibitions and reviews, too many movements, theories and "isms", to make for either comprehension or completeness. Far better, in the circumstances, to focus on the forces and conditions that have shaped modern painting and related art forms in the city, and then single out just two or three artists for individual discussion. There is first the question of foreign, and specifically French, influence. It is indisputable that, in its general progression from Art Nouveau and symbolism, through cubism and expressionism, to surrealism, Czech art in the first half of the twentieth century closely mirrored that of France (with a significant German in-put as well), and that, without the example and inspiration of Paris, Prague's modernist movement may not even have extended, let alone transcended, the limits of provincialism to the degree that it did. Almost every twentieth-century Czech artist of note visited Paris at some time or another, and several, out of choice or constraint, made permanent or semi-permanent homes in the city: Mucha (from 1889 to 1904), František Kupka (from 1895 to his death in 1957), Josef Šima (from 1921 to 1971) and the remarkable Marie Čermínová, alias Toyen, who lived in Paris with her partner the painter and photographer Jindřich Štyrský from 1925 to 1929 and again, after Štyrský's death, from 1947 to her own death in 1980. The art of others was stimulated or renewed by visits to Paris— Josef Čapek (1910-11), Emil Filla (1910) and Bohumil Kubišta (1909-10) among many others—and numerous were the poets and theorists who made one or more pilgrimages to what they clearly saw as the source: Karel Teige (1922), Jaroslav Seifert (1923) and, above all, Vitězslav Nezval whose long poem *Akrobat* of 1927 established him as a poet of Paris as much as *Praha s prsty deště* (Rainy-fingered Prague, 1936) later did of the Czech capital.

Visitors from Paris were no less important, whether it be Rodin and Apollinaire in 1902, Le Corbusier in 1911 and 1929, or Breton and Eluard in 1935: all had a galvanizing effect on the local artistic scene. A crucial role, too, was played by exhibitions of the work of foreign artists, the most important being the Exhibition of Contemporary French Arts in 1902 (Monet, Pissarro, Renoir, Bonnard, Degas), the Munch Exhibition of 1905, the Modern Art Exhibition of 1914 (Picasso, Braque, Derain, Delaunay, Archipenko), and the *Poesie 1932* Exhibition that gave Czechs their first direct experience of surrealist art (Dalí, Arp, Giacometti, Ernst, Di Chirico, Miró, Klee). Almost all of these exhibitions were organized by the Mánes Union of Fine Arts (S.V.U. Mánes) that was founded in 1887 in honor of Josef Mánes, and held first at the Rudolfinum and, after 1930, in Otakar Novotný's dynamic functionalist gallery built across the former mill-stream between Žofín Island and the embankment. In the geography of modernism, Prague lies well behind Paris, Barcelona, Berlin and Vienna, but continuous osmosis with the first of those cities placed it firmly in the second rank with Brussels and Munich and well ahead of London, which it might otherwise have resembled.

Czech modernists took over from the broader European avant-garde an obsession with groups, movements and "isms" with their accompanying manifestos, secessions and exclusions. The groups include, in roughly chronological order, Osma (The Eight, 1907-8), the Group of Fine Artists (Skupina výtvarných umělců, 1911-16), Sursum (1910), Tvrdošíjní (The Stubborn Ones, 1918-c. 1920), Devětsil (1920-31), Levá fronta (Left Front, 1929-32), the Czech Surrealist Group (1934-8), Skupina 42 (Group 42, 1942-4) and Skupina Ra (1945-6): not even occupation could thwart the inveterate urge of Prague artists to associate, collaborate and argue with each other. Prague had its version of more or less every French "ism" of the first half of the century, plus several original creations of its own: cubo-expressionism, rondocubism, social civilism, poetism and artificialism. Of these, social civilism is associated principally with the name of the sculptor Otto Gutfreund (1889-1927) and is represented in the Veletržní Palác by a dozen or so extraordinarily life-like painted terra-cotta figurines. These seem to have no parallels in twentieth-century European sculpture but immediately evoke the painted statues and carvings of Bohemian tradition and the dolls and puppets linked to it. Few works in the gallery

Otto Gutfreund, Self-portrait

give as much sheer pleasure as Karel Dvořák's double sculpture *Girl Friends* (1924) and Bedřich Stefan's *Girl with Absinthe* (1924).

Many artists moved from group to group and from "ism" to "ism", and there is a remarkable stability in the personnel of Czech radical art movements between 1900 and 1920, on the one hand, and 1920 and 1940 on the other. Similarly, though there are clear differences between Devětsil and the earlier groups, what distinguishes, say, poetism from artificialism, and artificialism from surrealism, may not be immediately obvious to outsiders.

Most groups published manifestos setting out their artistic and ideological wares, but again there is more continuity than discontinuity between František Xavier Šalda's early modernist tract *Fight for Tomorrow* (*Boje o zítřek*, 1905), Nezval and Teige's *Manifesto of Poetism* (1928) and Nezval's *Surrealism in the Czechoslovak Republic*, published in *Doba* (*The Epoch*), the review Teige was then editing, in 1934. As in Paris, artists foregathered at particular times at particular cafés—the Corso for cubists, the Union for Devětsil and, later, the Slavia for surrealists—and there was a proliferation of small-circulation periodicals, some of them remarkably durable, others folding after two or three numbers. Founded in 1894, *Moderní revue* sustained the secessionist cause throughout its duration, and the S.V.U. Mánes house journal *Volné směry* (*Free Directions*, established 1896) was an enduring focus for the whole modernist movement. Devětsil produced one review after another—*Revoluční sborník* (1922), *Disk* (1923-5) and *ReD* (1927-31)—and, as the group fragmented, spawned a host of even littler little magazines: Štyrský's *Eroticka revue*, Seifert's *Nová scéna* and Nezval's *Zvěrokruh* (*Zodiac*), most of which came and went in 1930 alone. Devětsil had its own publishing house, Odeon, founded in 1923, and Štyrský set up the aptly entitled Edice 69 to publish his own erotic works and the Marquis de Sade. Outside Paris and Berlin, the Prague modernist movement may have had the strongest infrastructure in Europe.

The two most substantial groups were undoubtedly the Group of Fine Artists (1911-16) and Devětsil (1920-31). Growing out of Osma, the former brought together an exceptionally gifted collection of painters, sculptors and architects committed to pursuing the cubist revolution in their respective fields: the painters Emil Filla (1882-1953) and Josef Čapek (1887-1945), brother of the novelist and dramatist Karel, the sculptor Otto Gutfreund (1889-1927) and the already mentioned architects Gočár, Janák and Chochol. The Group organized important exhibitions in 1912 and 1913 to which the most talented Czech cubist, the presciently named Bohumil Kubišta (1884-1918) also contributed, though not formally affiliated to the group. Both Filla and Kubišta began as disciples of Munch whose 1905 exhibition, said Filla, exploded on them "like a grenade"; Filla's *Reader of Dostoyevsky* (1907) and *Night of Love* (1908) are particularly fine examples of the expressionist style. Following visits to Paris, Filla and Kubišta then, as it were, married Munch to Braque to create a characteristically Czech fusion of styles to which the name cubo-expressionism came to be given. Kubišta's self-portraits as *The Smoker* (1910) and *Saint Sebastian* (1912), both in the Veletržní Palác, stand as monuments to the style, a typically Czech appropriation and adaptation of an international style which, like rondocubism in architecture, produced a handful of masterpieces and then disappeared.

Cubo-expressionism's main figures also, for the most part, faded away quickly. After serving in the Austrian army during the First World War, Kubišta fell victim to the global flu epidemic in 1918. Gutfreund fought with the Czech Legion in France but spent much of the war in detention for insubordination; he drowned in a swimming accident in the Vltava in 1927. Filla spent the years 1914-9 in the Netherlands but, a vocal anti-fascist, was arrested by the Gestapo in 1939; he nonetheless survived both Terezín and Buchenwald. Joseph Čapek died in Bergen-Belsen in 1945.

Devětsil: Poetry of the Present

Devětsil, founded on October 5, 1920 at the Café Union, was much more than the loose association that the Group of Fine Artists had been. Its members were, on average, ten years younger than those of the earlier group, they were on the political left and, in the manner of the French Dadaists with whom they had otherwise little in common, sought to precipitate a revolution that would, in the apocalyptic language of the time, embrace the totality of existence. They did not, like the Dadaists, thirst for a nihilistic, anti-rational revolution but, precisely, a constructive, even constructivist, transformation of art, architecture, internal design, typography, sexuality, and politics in the name of what came to be known as poetism. Four years in advance of the Parisian surrealist group (founded 1924), the Prague avant-garde sought to constitute itself, under the informal leadership of the then twenty-year-old Karel Teige (1900-51), as a cohesive force for artistic, social and political change. The name Devětsil—it is not known who had the inspirational idea—means, on the one hand, "nine forces" (*devět + sil*, conceivably a reference to the traditional nine muses) and, on the other, the plant *petasites vulgaris*, butterbur in English, a flower notoriously hard to uproot and, according to the flora, "a boon to beekeepers, for its numerous flowers are rich in nectar."

It was a singularly well-chosen name. Not only did Devětsil survive much longer than comparable vanguardist groups, influencing Czech art, literature, architecture, photography and design well after its formal demise in 1931, but its "flowers" were numerous and varied indeed: about sixty in all over the eleven years of its existence, including poets such as Nezval, Seifert, František Halas (1901-49), and Konstantin Biebl (1898-1951). There were painters like Toyen (1902-80), Jindřich Štyrský (1899-1942), Šíma (1891-1971), the group's "ambassador" in Paris, architects such as Bedřich Feuerstein (1892-1936), Jaromír Krejcar (1902-90), and Chochol, musicians (Erwin Schulhoff, 1894-1942, Ježek), photographers (Jaroslav Rössler, 1902-90), theater directors (E.F. Burian), typographers, journalists and film-makers, plus three names familiar to us from the Liberated Theater: Honzl and V + W themselves. Devětsil also named Charlie Chaplin and Douglas Fairbanks as honorary members, but whether word reached Hollywood is to be doubted.

The cross-fertilization of talents and disciplines was fundamental to Devětsil's overall achievement, for its most enduring creations are not its poems and paintings as conventionally understood, but what

Teige called "pictorial poems", "the fusion of poem and image in a single unity". To which end he, Nezval, Biebl and Štyrský, among others, crafted assemblages of words, photographs and images cut out of magazines, stamps, bus tickets, postcards and other ephemera, with the emphasis always on deliberate construction rather than, as with the surrealists' *objets trouvés*, random juxtaposition and collision. It was a kind of twentieth-century version of the artfully composed visual puns of Arcimboldo's fantastical   heads: a poem, Teige averred, should be "read like a modern picture, a modern picture like a poem." Seifert (*On the Waves of the Telegraph*, 1925) and Nezval (*Poems for Picture Postcards*, 1926) both dabbled in what would later be called concrete poetry before reverting to more conventional forms, and Toyen and Štyrský turned book cover design into something more than a minor art form.

Although poetism's emphasis on structure placed it in many ways at the antipodes of the Baroque, it shares with that style a desire to aestheticize—or, as Toyen and Štyrský would put it, to artificialize—everything. The poetists' insistence on construction, system and reason is also what marks them out most clearly from the French surrealists. Poetry, said Nezval, the most surrealistically inclined among them, is a "systematization of confusion", while Teige insisted in 1924 that "life needs as much reason as poetry": neither proposition would have found much sympathy in Paris at the time. The poetists had no time for *écriture automatique* and stressed the autonomous, constructed character of every work of art. In all this, it is possible to discern clear parallels with the Prague Linguistic Circle which, formed in October 1926 and revolving around the exceptional talents of the Russian-born Roman Jakobson (1896-1982) and the Czech Jan Mukařovský (1891-1975), is generally held to have originated the term structuralism. "Poetism is the crown of life," wrote Teige in 1924, "constructivism is its basis"; it was not a literary or artistic movement as conventionally understood but rather "the art of living in the most beautiful sense of the word, a modern Epicureanism." Poetists did not merely "write poetry" but sought to transform life into a "magnificent entertainment, an eccentric carnival, a harlequinade of feeling and imagination, an intoxicating film track, a marvelous kaleidoscope." Poetism "relieves depression, worries, irritations, it offers cleansing and moral health." It seeks to make permanent and available to all "the poetry of Sunday afternoons, picnics, luminous cafés, intoxicating cocktails, lively boulevards, spa promenades, but also the poetry of silence, night, quiet, and peace."

"The heroism of modern life" (Baudelaire), "be absolutely modern" (Rimbaud): Poetism and, after it, Czech surrealism pushed this cult of the modern to the limits, it being Teige's conviction that "the modern global creed" alone guarantees authenticity. To this end, poetists, both during and after the formal existence of Devětsil, took the city—in practice Prague and/or Paris—as their subject and set out to celebrate not its heroic past in the manner of the old-style nationalists but its still more heroic present, especially those of its aspects where the contemporary was most intoxicatingly alive; its cafés, circuses and theaters (as evidenced in Nezval's early titles, *Pantomima*, 1924, *Karneval*, 1926 and *Akrobat*, 1927), its *pasáže* and flea-market, its brothels and night-life (Nezval, *Sexuální nokturno* (1931) with erotic collages by Štyrský). Not that the traditional sites were neglected. In 1928 Nezval and Štyrský collaborated on *The Jewish Cemetery*, and Seifert would go on to celebrate virtually every major *lieu de mémoire* in Prague: Charles Bridge, the Belvedere, the Loretta, Old Town Square, Petřín, as well as such notable events as Mozart's visit to the city.

Though it avoided the overt nationalism of earlier art movement—poetism has no place even for the likes of Hus and Žižka—it remained intensely national even as it identified with international modernism. Its cult of the modern led it into revolutionary politics—according to the Devětsil writer Vladislav Vančura (1891-1942), a future victim of Nazism, "outside Communism there can be nothing modern"—and thence into the kind of internal and external conflicts that bedeviled the French surrealist movement. Seifert began as a populist revolutionary poet with *City of Tears* (1921) in the manner of Jiří Wolker (1900-24) whose early death from tuberculosis made him the Communist martyr-poet par excellence. By 1922, however, whilst still calling themselves revolutionaries, Teige and Seifert denounced the straightforward "proletarian poetry" favored by the Czech Communist Party which Seifert, but not Teige, had joined, and, with the slogan "ENOUGH OF

WOLKER", they abandoned a poetry of sentiment and exhortation in favor of the complexities of poetism.

A visit to the USSR in 1925 brought a distinct cooling off in Seifert's revolutionary ardor reflected in his collection of the following year, *The Nightingale Cannot Sing*, and in 1929 he left the Communist Party for good and joined the Social Democrats from whom the Communists had split in 1921: had he joined a party of the right, it would have been a lesser crime in Communist eyes both then and later. It was around this time that the hard-line Stalinist Klement Gottwald (1896-1953) seized control of "the party" from the old-style Austro-Marxists and delivered a speech to parliament that does not lose its power to chill:

> *We are the Party of the Czechoslav proletariat and our supreme revolutionary headquarters are in Moscow. And we go to Moscow to learn to do you know what? We go there to learn from the Russian Bolsheviks how to wring your necks. And as you know, the Russian Bolsheviks are masters at that.*

A party with this kind of ideology and leader was unlikely to indulge Devětsil's pursuit of the "new beauty" at the expense of explicit political commitments, and the problem became more acute with the setting up of the Czech surrealist group in 1934. With Teige unaffiliated to any party, Nezval moved progressively closer to the orthodox Communists who were not best pleased when Teige attacked the early Stalinist show trials in 1936. Things came to a head in March 1938 when, at a fiery gathering at a *pivnice* called U Locha (now the café-theater Viola) on Národní, Nezval unilaterally wound up the surrealist group and proclaimed his adhesion to the party's position on all matters political, ideological and artistic. A surrealist "rump" was reconstituted around Teige, Biebl, Toyen and Štyrský, and a bitter polemic ensued that Teige is generally thought to have won. Nezval would get his revenge after February 1948.

Karel Teige: A Truly Modern Man

Karel Teige, it should now be clear, is the intellectual pivot around which Prague modernism revolved for thirty years. Born in Prague in 1900, Teige had published his first article ("New Times in the Creative

Arts"), set up his first journal and held his first exhibition by the age of sixteen, and was already a veteran of the Prague avant-garde when, aged twenty, he was the key figure in setting up Devětsil. Over the next three decades he would address himself to virtually every aspect of modernism and modernity—painting, photography, poetry, interior design, typography, sexuality and politics—and has been compared, with some exaggeration, for his writings never really had a European resonance, to Breton, Gramsci and Walter Benjamin. His own pictorial poems and collages, of which he made over 350 between 1935 and 1951, have dated like so much surrealist art. Their juxtaposition of disparate images now seems more predictable than shocking, and his fondness for dismembering and reassembling the naked female body, substituting eyes for nipples and nipples for eyes, marks him out for ritual feminist immolation.

Teige's importance is not just that he theorized Czech modernism with a vigor and perception achieved by no other intellectual, but that he sought, and was seen to, embody modernity in every aspect of his life. "Only a truly modern man is a whole man," he proclaimed, and his determination to live modernity to the full and to achieve that wholeness which the present arrangements of society, he believed, set out to thwart is expressed most vividly in the attention he brought to his domestic environment. At the age of eighteen, Teige met Josefina (Jožka) Nevařilová who would remain his companion for the rest of his life. They never married, and in 1927-8 Teige had his family house on Černá just off Charles Square transformed both inside and out by the Devětsil architect Jaromír Krejcar. The fifth floor, where Teige and Nevařilová lived, was converted into two separate flats with no shared accommodation: this was a "modern" association of two separate equals, not a "bourgeois" marriage of the hierarchical kind. In 1937-8 Teige had a new house constructed by the functionalist architect Jan Gillar (1904-67) on Šalamounky on the fringes of the working-class suburb of Smíchov, and it was there that he installed his new *inamorata* Eva Ebertová along with Nevařilová in 1941. Defying bourgeois conventionality, the three lived, each in his or her separate "module", as an apparently successful *koldům*, or collective household, throughout the occupation as Teige worked on his massive *Phenomenology of Modern Art*. At the end of the war, Teige was required to submit an auto-critique of his activities to the Agitprop division of the Czech Communist Party, which duly found its way to the desk of the newly appointed Minister of Culture Václav Kopecký. Teige's anti-Stalinism, which may have saved him from Terezín and worse, now came back to haunt him, with what consequences we shall see in the chapter that follows.

Štyrský and Toyen: Phantom World

Two figures stand out as individuals from the vigorous Prague art scene of the 1920s and 1930s and, along with Teige and Nezval, encapsulate in their work its leading aims and themes. Jindřich Štyrský and Marie Čerminová, invariably known as Toyen, met on holiday in Yugoslavia in 1922 and remained companions in life and art until Štyrský's death in 1942, joining Devětsil together in 1923 and jointly signing the first manifesto of the Czech surrealist group in March 1934. While living in Paris in 1925-27, they launched their own "ism", artificialism, which they promoted as a bridge "between abstraction and surrealism." Štyrský engaged in manifold activities—painting, book design, pictorial poems, biography (lives of Rimbaud,1928, and of the Marquis de Sade,1931) and publishing (*Erotická revue*, (1930-33) and *Edice 69*). Both *Erotická revue* and *Edice 69* were published for subscribers only, with the result that the erotic art of Štyrský and Toyen is almost entirely privately owned. Štyrský's sequence of erotic collages *Emilie Comes to me in a Dream* (1933) is believed to have been inspired by his half-sister Marie Křivohlávková who died at the age of 21 in 1905 when Štyrský was five.

It is Štyrský's photographic work that has best survived, principally on account of its striking images of Prague. This is not, however, the Prague of the great monuments and vistas so memorably photographed by Josef Sudek (1896-1976), but the Prague of fairgrounds, circuses, shop-windows and *pasáže*, as celebrated by Nezval, with whose poetry Štyrský's photographs co-exist in illuminating symbiosis:

> *For a long time I didn't understand what shop windows meant to me*
> *For a long time I didn't understand their charm*
> *And yet I'm grateful to them for the magic of my walks*
> (Nezval, "Shop Windows", in *Woman in the Plural,* 1935)

Štyrský presented a selection of his photographs at the first exhibition of Czech surrealist art held at the Mánes Gallery in 1935, dividing them into two cycles entitled *Man with Blinkers* and *Frog-Man* which, together, constitute a visual anthology of recurring Prague obsessions: tailors' dummies, wig-stands, anatomical models, masks, mirrors, artificial limbs (severed hands and heads a specialty), dissected corpses, coffins, statues, crucifixes, fairground freaks (the frog-man of the second sequence), plus the inevitable puppets, dolls and assorted automata, as in Nezval's poem "The Talking Dummy" of 1933. Everything is suspended between the animate and inanimate; as in Eugène Atget's photographs of Paris that so influenced Štyrský, there is scarcely a fully living human being to be seen. Instead we view only images, effigies and replicas that haunt some limbo-world between life and death which, as so often, seems to constitute the predestined habitat of so much of the art of Prague.

Teige described Štyrský's world as a "phantom which transfixes, reveals and fascinates." The world of Toyen is much less somber than her companion's—she is arguably the finest colorist of twentieth-century Czech art as well as indisputably its finest draughtsman—but is populated by much the same eerie intermediate beings: skeletons, scarecrows, owls, lemurs, creatures once more in the frontier-zone between the living and the dead.

The origins of her adopted (and gender-less) name are not known. One theory derives from the French word *citoyen* (citizen), with its implications of political radicalism, another from the Czech *to je on*, meaning "it is he." This latter is often interpreted as a reference to what Seifert called the painter's "male autostylization": she is almost always photographed wearing overalls and a black beret, and is said by Nezval always to have used the masculine verbal form *já byl* (I was) rather than the feminine *já byla*. The partnership of Štyrský and Toyen recalls that of Teige and Jožka Nevařilová: not a marriage or even a couple, but a very modernist association of two equals. During her long creative life, Toyen's work oscillated between the abstract and the figurative, with abstraction predominating during the two artists' "artificialist" phase in Paris in the 1920s and again in the 1950s when, now a permanent resident rather than a sojourner, she was once more in Paris. In the 1930s and 1940s, and again after 1960, her work combined hyper-realism and hallucinatory juxtapositions of de-familiarized objects in a manner obviously reminiscent of Dali, Delvaux and Magritte, products, like her, of "marginal" artistic cultures (Catalonia, Belgium). As in alchemy (one of Štyrský's continual points of reference), opposites or unlikes meet to create a disturbing but intoxicating surreality of the kind announced by Štyrský in a lecture given to the Prague Linguistics Circle in 1938:

> *It will be a time of the gradual blending of air, water, earth and fire, a time of that long-desired synthesis of three-dimensional and lyrical beauty. Creatures will cross-breed and, without the supervision of biologists, we will see the dawn of new unicorns and beetle-mammals, fabulous wethers and creatures fashioned from swords, needles and daggers, animals of cotton wool, snake-skins, feathered trees, bestial amalgams of immortal poetic works and flower pots and many other prurient monstrosities.*

In fact, the "monstrosities" to which 1938 gave birth were hardly those so exhilaratingly prophesied by Štyrský and inspired Toyen to create two remarkable series of drawings, *The Shooting Gallery* (1939-40) and *Hide, War!* (1944), in which, said Teige, "the world of childhood confronted the world of war." Meanwhile, Toyen had collaborated with the poet Jindřich Heisler on the egregiously entitled *Only Kestrels Calmly Piss on the Ten Commandments* (1939) and *From the Casemates of Sleep* (1941), the latter one of the most successful examples of the fusion of text and image that remains Prague's most distinctive contribution to European modernism. More and more, birds and animals dominated her paintings and drawings, cockerels, eagles, wolves, rabbits, often associated with the figure of a prepubescent girl, and her wartime output culminated with the remarkable *Field Scarecrow* of 1945 in which the central figure resembles a pregnant woman clad in a ragged uniform and mounted on a pole, her head a seething nest of hornets.

In 1945 Toyen collaborated with Jindřich Honzl on a production of Vladislav Vančura's play *The Teacher and the Pupil* at the National Theater where, anticipating Josef Svoboda, she projected on to the backdrop huge enlargements of animals, flowers and cosmic nebulae with the express purpose of reducing the actors to puppet-like proportions. In 1947 the Czech phase of her career came to an end when she and Heisler decided to stay on in Paris after organizing an exhibition of her work and both joining the greatly diminished Paris surrealist group. She is arguably the greatest Czech painter of her century, and it is a tragedy that the galleries of her native city contain so few examples of her work, much of which, like Štyrský's, is privately owned or in galleries abroad.

Socialist Art

For reasons best known to its curators, the Veletržní Palác exhibits only a meager number of Czech art works produced between 1948 and 1989, and what it does show seems designed to present so-called "socialist realism" in the worst possible light. Thus Alena Čermáková's wooden *We Produce More, We Live Better* of the early 1950s depicts a young working-class couple with two children, surrounded by a cornucopia of bread, eggs, apples, grapes, sausages and tinned sardines. Lest any viewer fail to recognize the source of these riches, a copy of Volume I of the complete works of Klement Gottwald stands on the bookshelf. Renato Guttoso (1912-87) gives his version, after many others, of Julius Fučík (1903-43), the Communist militant and poet killed by the Nazis whose prison writings, the carefully doctored *Report from the Gallows*, were a sacred text of the Stalinist regime and whose mass-produced portrait, based on an original by the aged Max Švabinský, adorned public buildings throughout Communist Czechoslovakia with what Kundera calls "the radiant expression of a young girl in love." There are the expected pictures of female "pioneers" and squads of Stakhanovite workers and some small attempt, it is true, to recognize the tenacity of the continuing, if greatly domesticated, Czech surrealist movement which continued, under great pressure, to produce after 1948: Mikuláš Medek (1926-74), Václav Tikal (1906-65) and Jiří Kolář (1914-2002), a man as fated by name to produce collages as Bohumil Kubišta was to follow Picasso and Braque.

A native of Potrivín in south Bohemia, Kolář held his first exhibition of collages in Prague in 1937, was a member of Skupina 42 and, following a nine months' prison sentence in 1953, was banned from publishing or exhibiting until 1964. Originally a poet, he has developed an extraordinary number of collage-related techniques, to which he has given such names as "chiasmages" (a multitude of torn paper fragments containing text are glued to a support, such as an apple), "prollages" (two reproductions of a painting, e.g. a Mondrian and a Caravaggio, are cut into strips of varying width and the strips are reassembled to create a new combinatory image), as well as "crazygrams", "kinetic collages", "zipper collages" and "crumplages". Blending image and text, his work is an elaboration of the collages of Teige and Štytrský, and the analogy with Arcimboldo is invoked by Kolář himself. Other artists who continued to paint well, if not to exhibit, under Communism are, for whatever reason, simply not represented. It is as though the National Gallery seeks to demonstrate that nothing was possible under Communism, or that what was produced is unworthy of serious attention. Forty years of Czech painting have simply been erased in keeping with what seems an almost universal desire to expunge the memory of Communism entirely.

History ended in 1948 and, after a hiatus of four decades, began again in 1989: if only the gallery's post-1989 collection showed signs of some great renewal. But, alas, there is as little to detain the visitor on the second floor as on the sixth, as the new Czech Republic's Damian Hirstský's and Tracy Eminová's rework the dreariest clichés of international "concept art", with no evidence of any individual appropriation or national inflection, as in earlier Czech versions of international styles. The present writer first came to Prague in search of the Baroque, found it, marveled at it and then grew tired of (most of) it before discovering, in compensation, the small glories of Czech modernism. On the evidence of the works in the Veletržní Palác, post-1989 Czech art stands to Kubišta, Filla, Toyen and Štyrský as Frank Gehry's *Tančící dům* (1995), the Dancing House (known to Czechs as "Fred and Ginger" after the swaying couple it supposedly resembles), on the corner of Resslova and Rašinovo nábřeží stands to Otakar Novotný's Mánes Gallery a block further down river from it: mere cleverness and virtuosity against clarity, simplicity and intensity of purpose. In the past, Czech artists, like the Czech people, specialized in finding fissures within the systems that oppressed them in which to express themselves, if necessarily by indirection or allusion, or even in making a creative friction out of constraint itself. But lack of constraint brings problems of its own, both for artists and societies, as we shall see in the concluding chapter of this book.

The Dancing House

CHAPTER SIX

In Durance: Prague Under Communism, 1948–1989

Wenceslas Square

And so to the last and possibly the most potent of Prague's "sacred spaces", the focus of every political protest and celebration in the city for almost a century and a half (1848, 1918, 1939, 1948, 1969, 1989), and familiar the world over from newsreels, films and photographs: Václavské náměstí, Wenceslas Square. The one-time Horse Market

(Koňský trh) received its present name only in the wake of the revolutionary year of 1848 when it served as a rallying-point for Prague's small radical movement—mainly students and middle-class professionals, with a smattering of workers—during its confrontation with the Austrian state in the form, latterly, of Alfred Prince Windischgrätz and the ten thousand troops at his command. The final show-down between the two ill-matched adversaries began on June 12, 1848
when, in a fusion of politics and religiosity typical of that year throughout the whole of Europe, an open-air mass was celebrated on Koňský trh, at the conclusion of which the participants fanned down to Windischgrätz's headquarters on Zeltnergasse (Celetná) to protest against the militarization of the city. Shots were fired, barricades went up, and for the next two days there was intermittent fighting throughout the Old Town, with the playwright Jan Kajetán Tyl, author of the future nation's anthem, inaugurating Prague's tradition of

theatrical activism by leading the insurgents on Bethlehem Square. Windischgrätz withdrew his troops and, more important, his cannons over to Malá Strana where, over the following days, he proceeded to bombard the Old and New Towns into submission. A total of forty-six people lost their lives, including Windischgrätz's own wife Eleanor, killed by a ricocheting bullet whilst standing at that fatal place, a window, at her husband's headquarters on Zeltnergasse.

The renaming of Koňský trh was proposed by the well-known radical journalist Karel Havlíček whom we have already encountered in connection with the National Theater movement and who has been rightly described as "the first Czech intellectual in the modern sense" in that his literary and political projects formed a single whole. Inaugurating another, and this time unhappy, Czech tradition, Havlíček suffered imprisonment and exile for his beliefs and writings, which contributed to his early death in 1856. Fittingly, then, it was one scholar-martyr who proposed that Koňský trh be named after another some nine centuries earlier, and in the half century following Havlíček's death Wenceslas Square would become as central to Czech national consciousness as the murdered prince who gave it its name.

A massively broad, and now virtually traffic-free, boulevard rather than a square, Václavské náměstí was constructed more or less *ex nihilo* between 1880 and 1920. It is an entirely Czech creation, with not a single example of Baroque architecture amongst its serried ranks of multi-story secessionist, modernist and functionalist buildings. In addition to the Hotels Europe and Meran, discussed in Chapter Five, the most noteworthy buildings are the Peterkův dům at no. 12 by Jan Kotěra (1899), the Palác Koruna on the corner of Wenceslas Square and Na příkopě (Antonín Pfeiffer, 1911), and the Bat`a Shoe Store at no. 6 (Ludvík Kysela, 1927-9), early examples of, respectively, the secessioniat, modernist, and functionalist styles. Throughout its length, and along the numerous *pasáže* that run off it, above all the Palác Lucerna built by Václav Havel's grandfather (also Václav) between 1912 and 1916, stand monuments to Czech business acumen, Czech sense of style and, not least, Czech love of pleasure and distraction. At its southern end, however, it becomes suddenly more serious, and the emphasis switches from the present to the past in the glowering neo-Renaissance form of the National Museum, completed in 1890 and, since the 1950s, cut off from the square by a six-lane highway now named Wilsonova, after the American president who, more even than Masaryk, was the real founder of modern Czechoslovakia. Until 1989, the highway was known as Vítězného února (Victorious February) in memory of the 1948 coup that brought the Communists to power. It remains the principal—and presumably permanent—memorial to Communist "planning" in the center of the city.

Like the inauguration of the National Theater in 1883, the opening of the National Museum was the climax of a movement going back to the early 1800s, the pivotal figure being, as so often, the historiographer František Palacký. Its interest today is largely restricted to its façade (damaged by shelling by Soviet tanks in 1968, but subsequently restored), to its endless cases of fossils, stuffed animals, butterflies, beetles and pickled fetuses that testify to a properly Rudolfine quest for totality and to its Pantheon of forty-eight national worthies commemorated by statue and bust at the top of the main staircase. In front of the museum, and on the Wenceslas Square side of the highway, stands a typically grandiloquent mountain of statuary by Jan Václav Myslbek and others, the centerpiece being a colossal equestrian statue of Wenceslas, on which Myslbek worked from 1887 until its unveiling in 1913, flanked on both sides by a quartet of lesser national patrons, Saints Ludmila, Prokopius, Adalbert (Vojtěch) and Agnes, the last named canonized on November 12, 1989, just days before the Velvet Revolution. St. John Nepomuk is conspicuously absent.

The vast square and its statue provided a natural focus for independence celebrations in 1918, and were also the setting for one of the First Republic's great civic occasions, the funeral in March 1930 of the historical novelist Alois Jirásek (1851-1930) who, by romancing Palacký, diffused the nationalist version of Czech history to several generations. Nine years later, on October 28, 1939, demonstrators, many of them wearing the peaked cap made famous by Masaryk, gathered on Wenceslas Square to protest against German occupation. In the struggle that followed, a medical student named Jan Opletal was shot and died in hospital on November 11. Three days later his fellow students held a wake in his honor at U Fleků off Charles Square, home of the world famous black beer that is brewed on the premises. Fired, one imagines, by this most potent (13%) of potions, the mourners attended his funeral the following day and marked the occasion by tearing down the re-imposed German-language street signs that, more than anything else at this early stage, symbolized the humiliation of Nazi domination. Retaliation came with quite lethal rapidity. On November 17, nine student leaders were arrested and shot without trial, and a further 1,200 students were taken from their halls of residence and sent to Oranienburg concentration camp as hostages for future Czech conduct. The memory of this sacrifice runs deep in the Prague student community, and, as we shall see, the demonstration that precipitated the Velvet Revolution was called to commemorate the fiftieth anniversary, give or take a few days, of the deaths of Jan Opletal and his comrades.

Site of Martyrdom

Wenceslas Square, then, symbolizes not just national protest, but specifically protest by those—students, writers, intellectuals—who embody the qualities that Czechs are said most to value themselves for, namely critical intelligence, creativity, knowledge. Both Wenceslas and Hus are esteemed as scholars no less than as martyrs or, rather, it was their commitment to "truth", both intellectual and moral, that led to their martyrdom at the hands of essentially false and ignorant enemies. It was, therefore, with a keen sense of Prague's symbolic geography that, thirty years after the death of Jan Opletal, another student—a student of, precisely, *philosophy*—chose Wenceslas Square as the site of his martyrdom. On January 16, 1969, twenty-one-year-old Jan Palach, in full consciousness, one assumes, of the Hussite precedent and model, poured petrol over himself and, with a match, transformed himself into a human pyre in front of the fountain below the National Museum. His death three days later was followed by, in Josef Škvorecký's words, the "ominous, dark pathos" of a silent funeral procession numbering many hundreds of thousands and moving interminably through the Prague streets in the tradition of the funerals of Havlíček (1856), Jirásek (1930), Karel Čapek (1938), Opletal (1939) and the reburial of the remains of Karel Hynek Mácha (also 1939), but charged with still greater emotion in that Palach had voluntarily transformed martyrdom into an act. His stated demands were, in a

sense, almost disproportionately mild (freedom of the press and a ban
on the distribution of the Soviet propaganda news-sheet *Zprávy*), but
everyone knew that it was the Soviet occupation itself that was the
target of his action. His final letter promised that "other torches will be
ablaze", suggesting to some that he was part of a clandestine
movement committed to periodic self-immolation, and on February
25, 1969—pointedly the twenty-first anniversary of the Communist
take-over—another student, Jan Zajíc, did indeed set fire to himself,
and die, on the same spot as Palach.

As they presumably anticipated, the site of the two students'
voluntary martyrdom soon became an unofficial, and indeed illegal,
national shrine at which, throughout the remaining years of
Communist domination, the police did their utmost—but it was rarely
enough—to prevent flowers being placed there on the anniversary of
the deaths. Havel's final spell in prison (January-May 1989) was the
result, precisely, of his placing flowers on the spot on the day of the
anniversary.

Palach's grave in the Olšanske cemetery also became a place of
pilgrimage, so much so that, in 1973, the authorities had his body
exhumed and cremated and the ashes re-buried in the student's home
town of Všetaty fifteen miles out of Prague, thus creating two shrines
where formerly there had been only one, for flowers continued to be
placed each year on the original grave which now contained the remains
of an otherwise obscure woman; Palach's ashes were returned to the
cemetery after the Velvet Revolution. More than the square officially
named after him, it is an almost self-effacing monument—just a
wooden cross, with barbed wire twined around it like a twentieth-
century crown of thorns—located on a triangle of grass just north of
the statue of Wenceslas that best preserves the memory of Jan Palach
and of the countless other *obětěm komunismu*, or victims of
Communism, to whom, with its candle-stubs and wilting bunches of
flowers, the shrine is dedicated.

Victorious February

Palach and Zajíc were budding intellectuals, and it was intellectuals,
along with priests, "Zionists" (Jews), "Trotskyists" (anyone who had
criticized Stalin at any time) and "cosmopolitans" (Czechs who had

spent the war years in Britain rather than the Soviet Union), who were the principal early victims of "Victorious February", the Communist takeover in 1948. Sometimes, of course, the categories overlapped, as in the case of Jan Masaryk (1886-1948), intellectual-politician son of an intellectual-politician father, who, as Foreign Minister, was the only non-Communist to be included in Gottwald's first cabinet. Just ten days after the coup, he threw himself (or, according to tenacious and widespread belief, was thrown) out of an upper-floor bathroom window at the Foreign Ministry, the Černínský Palác, opposite the Loretta on Hradčany hill. Two years later, in June 1950, on the same day that Milada Horáková was hanged at Pankrác prison while Paul Robeson gave an open-air concert at Letná (see Chapter Four), the former Communist journalist and Surrealist sympathizer Záviš Kalandra was executed for the catch-all crime of "Trotskyism" which he had committed when, in 1936, he joined Teige, Seifert and Halas in signing a manifesto against the Moscow show trials. The Kalandra "case" caused particular outrage abroad, with André Breton publicly urging Paul Eluard, by now a card-carrying member of the French Communist Party, to use his influence with the Czech party hierarchy to obtain a reprieve, or at least a stay of execution, for a one-time mutual friend they had met during their visit to Prague in 1935. In Prague as part of the same Communist arts festival as Robeson, Eluard refused to intervene, and a lacerating chapter in Kundera's *Book of Laughter and Forgetting* (1979) shows him wooing his huge audiences with lines like "A man possessed by dreams never stops smiling" or "We shall fashion days and seasons/To the measure of our dreams" even as his Surrealist friend of yore went to his death.

Clearly the net was tightening around what remained of the Czech surrealist group, and it is difficult to avoid the conclusion that its former leader, Vítězslav Nezval, since 1938 an out-and-out Stalinist, was no innocent bystander in what shortly took place. As we saw in the previous chapter, Toyen and her new partner Jindřich Heisler elected to remain in Paris in March 1947, and František Halas (1901-49), whose 1936 poem "Old Women" had once been a sacred text of the Czech left, was denounced after his premature death as a "corrupter of youth"; his works, like so many others' to come, promptly disappeared from libraries and bookshops.

Even before "Victorious February", Karel Teige found himself the butt of Communist invective and, after the coup, was required to make a public statement of self-criticism in order to find work at all. In January 1950, an orchestrated campaign was launched against Teige, Devětsil and surrealism, and Teige was attacked in person by his erstwhile friend and co-surrealist Nezval at a meeting of the Federation of Czech Writers on January 22. The Federation was not, as its name might suggest, an autonomous organization run by the writers themselves, but a government controlled "trade union" for writers which, for most of the next four decades, would exercise almost total control over who, and what, could be officially published and read in Czechoslovakia. Teige's house in Smíchov was kept under constant surveillance, and his physical and mental state began to deteriorate under the pressure. It was by now virtually impossible for him to find paid employment, and on October 1, 1951 he died of a heart attack—not, as André Breton claimed in his monograph on Toyen, by self-administered poison after being arrested. His common-law wife Jožka Nevařilová burned Teige's letters to her and then committed suicide, by gas rather than, as again Breton says, by self-defenestration. Ten days later, the third member of the unorthodox household, Eva Ebertová, also gassed herself, and all of Teige's books, along with five hundred packets of manuscripts, papers and press-cuttings were carted off by the police.

Teige received not an obituary but a three-part denunciation in the Communist art review *Tvorba* ("Creativity") entitled "Teigeism (*Teigovština*)-a Trotskyist Agency in Our Culture." Around the same time, another surviving member of Devětsil and surrealism, Konstantin Biebl, committed suicide by the now "classic" method of self-defenestration. Finally, Seifert was banned from publishing on the grounds that "he does not see the joy of our working man, his heroism, his optimism, the marvelous new qualities germinating in our people, nor the grand and happy prospect for the morrow"—a rich list of charges seeing that Seifert's roots were in Prague's working-class (and Communist) heartland, Žižkov. Within three years of coming to power, the Communists had succeeded in doing what the Nazi occupiers had not even attempted: silencing, killing off or driving into exile virtually the entire Devětsil generation, barring those who, Communists of long date, were happy or willing to conform to the new dispensation (Nezval, Neumann, Burian, Honzl).

"Compulsory Jubilation"

In all, 300,000 people were "removed" from public life in Czechoslovakia in the wake of February 1948, with teachers, lecturers, doctors and other "engineers of human souls" (Stalin's term for writers and intellectuals—see Josef Škvorecký's ironically entitled novel of that name, 1977) being disproportionately likely to find themselves laboring in uranium mines or re-deployed as boiler-men, window-cleaners and garbage-collectors. Many of the victims were, of course, long-time members of the Czech Communist Party. It should always be recalled that Czechoslovakia, unlike other future Communist states in Central Europe and the Balkans, had a substantial and legal communist party before 1939 and that, in the elections of 1946, the party had obtained 40 percent of the vote in Bohemia and Moravia and 30 percent in Slovakia. Although trickery and force were involved in February 1948, the Czech Communist regime was not imposed by Soviet troops and for many years enjoyed a substantial base of support among workers and many intellectuals.

Yet, as Milan Kundera (born 1929) has repeatedly stressed (and he should know for he too was then a "believer"), there was a huge difference between the fervor that the Communist regime inspired in its numerous supporters in the late 1940s and early 1950s and the cynicism with which, in the 1970s and 1980s, it was regarded even by the diminishing numbers who, for whatever reason, continued to call themselves "Communists". At the top of the party hierarchy, it may have been a time of bitter in-fighting, show trials and murder, but among the lower ranks of the party faithful, and particularly amongst the tens of thousands of young or working-class replacements for those removed from their posts, there reigned, according to Kundera, "something of the spirit of the great religious movements." With the purging of non-Communist faculty, the Communist student unions virtually ran higher education for a time, so much so that "it was actually the examiner rather than the examined who was being subjected to an examination," and students as a body were possessed by "an altogether idealistic illusion that we were inaugurating a human era in which man (all men) would be neither *outside* history, nor *under the heel of history*, but would create and direct it." What Kundera finds disturbing about the Czechoslovak "case" is that its "criminal regime" was made "not by criminals but by enthusiasts convinced they had discovered the only road to paradise." In a climate of "compulsory jubilation" such as reigned in Czechoslovakia in the early 1950s, any expression of doubt, hesitation or irony called for instant "re-education", and if there is one lesson to be learned from *The Joke* (1967), Kundera's dissection of this early period and, in the view of many, his best single novel, it is this: when surrounded by idealists and believers, *never* send your girlfriend a postcard reading "Optimism is the opium of the people."

Thus, Kundera writes in *Life is Elsewhere* (1973), the early 1950s were "not only a time of horror but also a time of lyricism", a time when "the poet reigned along with the hangman", when, with no sense of inner contradiction, the Pauls Robeson and Eluard sang and recited even as Horáková and Kalandra went to their deaths. Nor, Kundera stresses, was the poetry of the period necessarily bad. Jaromil the young Communist poet of *Life is Elsewhere*, does not lack talent, even genuine inspiration, any more, for that matter, than did Kundera himself who, in his twenties, was as happy as any of his contemporaries to serenade the memory of the very Julius Fučík he would later revile. While novelists and film-makers were confined to historical epics (the regime adored novels and films about Žižka and Hus) or "Socialist Realist" presentations of working-class life, the lyric poet used language to celebrate not denote, and so long as he, or more rarely she, celebrated "the people", "the oppressed", "freedom" and "peace", obstacles were not so much placed in their way as lifted before them and, like Jaromil, they could rise without trace to prominence and power.

Similarly, music, so long as it remained broadly traditional in style, was actively promoted and, as we have seen, not every symphony or oratorio written in Czechoslovakia in the 1950s merits derision. With technically brilliant productions of uncontroversial plays, the National Theater under Radok and Krejča enjoyed one of its greatest decades, though any hint of irony and adventure in the visual arts—witness the ten-year ban on Jiří Kolář (1953-64)—was ruthlessly proscribed. When the young Václav Havel and his friends formed the "Thirty-Sixers" group, named after the year of their birth, in 1952, they had the greatest difficulty in locating and contacting the remaining members of Skupina 42. At a time when Mánes and Aleš were enshrined as the *nec plus ultra* of Czech art, any painter linked in any way with "the modern" was keeping his or her nose well to the ground.

Prose, Poetry, and Censorship

The real problem for the regime was prose writing, and specifically the novel. In the course of the 1950s, no fewer than 150,000 books out of a collection of 600,000 were removed from the Prague City Library in accordance with a set of "Instructions for screening of book collections in libraries of all kinds" issued in 1953. The complete works of TGM were only the most obvious casualty. But it was not just the books that were confiscated and impounded that made the Czech literary scene of the 1950s so unspeakably repressive, at least where fiction was concerned, but the books that never got written or were mutilated by "self-censorship", the books which, when written, went straight into the author's drawer in the hope of better times to come, the books which failed to make it past the censors or, if they did, were impounded and pulped down as soon as they appeared. At the risk of maligning some forgotten masterpiece, one can confidently say that no Czech fiction of value was published between 1950 and the early 1960s without, in the rare cases when such a book made it through the net, being instantly banned and seized by the police. As Haňťa, the narrator of Bohumil Hrabal's novelette *Too Loud a Solitude* (1976), soon discovers, it is possible to make a decent living pulping down banned books. Having failed to get *The End of the Nylon Age* past the censor in 1956, Josef Škvorecký was more successful with *The Cowards* (written in 1948) two years later, only for the novel to be seized by the police as soon as it appeared in the bookshops. Otherwise, none of the novelists who emerged in the 1960s—Klíma, Kohout, Vaculík, Lustig, even Hrabal, who would later be indulged by the regime to deflect and neutralize criticism—published a single work of prose fiction throughout the decade.

Why this disparity between poetry and prose? The answer, suggests Kundera in *Life is Elsewhere*, is that the language of poetry is acceptable to dictatorships because it does not "refer", because "rhyme and rhythm possess magical power: the formless world enclosed in regular verse all at once becomes limpid, orderly, clear, and beautiful." But the language of the novel breaks down, criticizes and complicates and is, by its very nature, anti-authoritarian and democratic. Poetry reconciles man to himself, to the world, to society, while the novel, through its analytical, deconstructive bent, makes any such atonement impossible. Dictatorships, says Kundera, love poets and poetry, but cannot but view novels and novelists with the gravest suspicion.

This certainly explains the absence of good fiction in 1950s Czechoslovakia, but cannot account for the banning of Seifert or for the fact that the greatest single poem of the decade by—many would argue—the greatest Czech poet of the century remained unpublished until 1964. Born in Prague and a perennial loner, Vladimír Holan (1905-80) was one of the few Czech modernists not to be involved at any stage with Devětsil. He published several slim volumes of verse in the 1920s and 1930s and first came to public attention with his *Reply to France*, a sequence of poems, all apparently written on September 30, 1938 itself, denouncing French (but not, for some reason, British) treachery at Munich with such violence that they were promptly banned by the newly installed government. Holan saluted the end of Nazi occupation with a resounding *Thanks to the Soviet Union* (1945), joined the Communist Party in 1946 and, publishing *Red Soldiers* in 1947, seemed poised to become the Poet Laureate, along with Nezval, of "Victorious February".

But no sooner had the party he supported come to power than Holan made a move whose symbolic meaning was and still is much debated. Having lived for many years in the suburb of Strašnice, Holan moved with his wife to a place which, geographically, was at the very core of the city but which, in other respects, could not have been further removed from the center of events. Kampa is the largest of the islands in the Vltava, separated from Malá Strana by a narrow strip of water called Čertovka (Devil's Stream) and traversed at its northern tip by Charles Bridge itself. It is Prague's urban village, somewhat like the Ile Saint-Louis in Paris, though with considerably more greenery, the one-time city wash-house (the church at its southernmost point is charmingly called Saint John the Baptist at the Cleaners, sv Jan Křtitel Na Prádle), and still with a couple of watermills to evoke its *rus in urbe* past. It was in a house next to one of these mills, Sovovský mlýn (Owl's Mill), the one-time home of Josef Dobrovský, author of the pioneering *History of Czech Language and Literature* (1792) which launched the whole movement of national (re) awakening, that Holan took up residence in 1948, he and his wife occupying a first-floor apartment with none other than Jan Werich living above them. In April 1949 his wife gave birth to their daughter Katerina who turned out to be severely mentally handicapped and, as the political climate worsened, Holan became increasingly reclusive, reputedly emerging from the house only at dawn and at dusk. He did, however, receive visitors: Seifert, the teenaged Václav Havel and, on one occasion, Dylan Thomas on a rapid liquid visit to Prague.

It was at Kampa, a human island on an island in the center of Prague, that on September 28, 1949, the Feast of St. Wenceslas, Holan wrote the poem that marked his break with the regime and effectively rendered him unpublishable for the next decade and a half. "To the Enemy" is, literally, a diatribe. "To be is not easy," it tells the party powerful, "Shitting is easy…," and shitting is all they can do for, hating themselves, they can only hate others. As for himself, Holan says,

> *If I haven't killed myself*
> *It is only that my life is not my own*
> *And I still love someone because I love myself*

Having broken with both party and city, Holan moved deeper and deeper into the labyrinth of his island fortress, writing poems such as "Ubi nullus ordo, sed perpetuus horror" which, almost alone, testify to the unparalleled bleakness of early 1950s Prague:

> *To live is terrible since you have to stay*
> *With the appalling reality of these years.*
> *Only the suicide thinks he can leave by the door*
> *That is merely painted on the wall.*
> *There is not the slightest sign that the Comforter will come.*
> *In me the heart of poetry bleeds.*

Between 1949 and 1956, and again in 1962, Holan worked on his greatest poem *A Night with Hamlet* (*Noc s Hamletem*), essentially an extended dialogue between melancholy poet and the ghost of the prince, which some critics regard as comparable with the great long poems of twentieth-century modernism, *The Waste Land*, *La Jeune Parque*, the *Duineser Elegien*. If it ultimately lacks the transcendent order of such masterpieces, *A Night with Hamlet* can still overwhelm the reader with its shifts between fury and tenderness, its blend of irony and lyricism, the tautness of its aphorisms ("The greater the poem, the greater the poet/*and not the contrary!*") alternating with images more surreal than anything to be found in the hit-and-miss poetry of Nezval (thus Hamlet speaks "frying the seed of the Word on the melted/bacon of his tongue"), and sexual disgust ("a fifth thumb between a pair of thighs", "sperm, sperm from nones to vespers") giving way to passages of amorous rhapsody, as in the wonderful duet between Orpheus and Eurydice. The poem paints a picture of man "caught between himself and himself", "face to face with the holy spirit of music" yet forced "to live for the takings of a whore/or the price of a dog", while "evil always rises/up humanity's spine, spattered with blood/like a dentist's staircase." Yet, over and above all this, the poem declares that "the everyday is the miraculous", that "it is precisely the real/that is metaphysical" and that before all else—this is the poem's last line—"a poem is a gift", even when, as in the case of *A Night with Hamlet*, there is no-one to receive it. Holan was a man full of contradictions, but as he magnificently says: "Have you no contradictions? Then you have no possibilities." *A Night with Hamlet* utters not a word about politics in the conventional sense, but it remains an intensely political poem: the testimony of a mind pushed to the limit by total excommunication yet still able to declare that "freedom, you know, is always kin/to voluntary poverty." Arguably the greatest single work written in Communist Prague and a living refutation of Kundera's argument that poetry is necessarily more acceptable to dictatorships than prose.

A Night with Hamlet was first made public on November 19, 1963 in a recitation given by actors at the Viola café-theater (which still flourishes) on Národní more or less opposite the National Theater itself. That such a gathering was possible at all is one sign among many of a loosening of the cultural vice brought about not so much by any liberalization of the regime—the party, led by Antonín Novotný since 1955, had largely disregarded the anti-Stalinist noises emanating from the Soviet Union—as by a general diminution of the ideological unity and fervor of the early 1950s. The young recruits who had flocked to the party in the wake of "victorious February" were now entering, or nearing, their forties, and the generation that followed them was conspicuously distancing itself from active involvement in politics. By 1966 only nine percent of party members were aged under 26, and membership of the Czech Union of Youth dropped from one and a half million to one million between 1963 and 1966 alone. Those who remained—still about half of the eligible population—did so principally for reasons of educational and professional advancement. There had been protests at the annual students' *majáles* in 1956, which were then promptly banned, and, when they were once more permitted in 1965, the students outraged the authorities by electing Allen Ginsberg, who happened to be in Prague at the time, as their carnival king. He was quickly escorted out of the country.

Throughout higher education, and particularly at Charles University itself, there were signs of restlessness and renewal. In philosophy departments, hitherto devoted to the inculcation of Marxism in its most dogmatic, deterministic form, there was a surge of interest in phenomenology (Edmund Husserl was, after all, Czech-born) largely inspired by the teaching and writing of Jan Patočka (1907-77). Even convinced Marxists like Karel Kosík, author of the hugely influential *Dialectics of the Concrete* (1963), began to stress the humanism and voluntarism of the young Marx at the expense of the ossified doctrine officially taught in universities and schools. The growing interest in Kafka (see Chapter Three) was a further sign of the changing intellectual climate, as was the passion for jazz and, closely related to it, the burgeoning theatrical scene. Even *Literární noviny*, the hitherto conformist review of the official Writers' Union, felt sufficiently free to criticize both censorship and "socialist realism", and a number of new literary reviews—*Květen* (May), *Tvář* (The Face)—were able, for a time, to operate outside of effective party control. *Tvář* was eventually closed down in December 1965 after a protracted struggle in which Václav Havel came to the public's (and the government's) attention for the first time.

What, simplistically, is known as "Prague Spring" was not born suddenly out of nowhere in February and March 1968, but was prepared by a long incubatory period beginning in the late 1950s in which intellectuals, in the broadest sense of the word, played, as national tradition would have it, the decisive role. As in the original movement of national awakening, the re-awakening of the 1960s was, in the first instance, an intellectuals' crusade, which progressively gained non-intellectual support until it embraced, at a conservative estimate, some ninety percent of the country's population.

Hitherto unpublished novels began to appear, and new novels were seized upon by the public if they contained so much as a hint of criticism of the "really existent Socialism" that, in the early 1960s, the party hierarchy declared to have been achieved; the once familiar Prague scene of crowds queuing outside bookshops on the days novels by Klíma, Kundera, Škvorecký and the like were first published dates from this time.

Cinematic Revolution

Yet it is not for its novels that "Prague Spring"—loosely understood to mean 1963-64 to 1969-70, for "normalization" did not come fully into operation until the dismissal of Dubček (April 1969)—is remembered, but for its films, and the names of Miloš Forman and Jiří Menzel are, for Czechs, as much a part of the whole phenomenon is that of Alexander Dubček himself.

Prague had the largest film studios in Europe thanks to the entrepreneurial initiative of Václav Havel's architect grandfather who had already constructed the largest cinema in Prague as the central attraction of his Lucerna complex off Wenceslas Square. On a vacant hillside south of Prague named Barrandov, Havel *grand-père* built an up-market residence and leisure complex of villas, restaurants and sports facilities—Czechs' standing in international tennis owes more than a little to the present president's grandfather—to which his son, also Václav, the president's uncle, added film studios and established himself as the Louis B. Meyer of Czech cinema under the First Republic and then under the Protectorate of Bohemia and Moravia, which, after 1948, was the source of Havel family's collective undoing. Barrandov had earlier been used for the production of Nazi propaganda films,

Goebbels' interest in Czech cinema being further fired by his passion for the Czech film actress Lara Baarova.

Prior to the 1960s, the only Czech film to transcend national boundaries was Gustav de Machaty's scandalous *Extasy* of 1933 in which the buxom seventeen-year-old Hedy Kieslerová (later Lamarr) was seen bathing in the nude, though, according to her autobiography, *Ecstasy and Me* (1966), it was the following "sequence of my fanny twinkling through the woods" and the shot of her face in the throes of sexual rapture that got the film banned in the United States and elsewhere the following year. This apart, Czech inter-war cinema was dominated by the comedies, increasingly involving social and political issues, of V & W, and it was the director of the last and best of these (*The World Belongs to Us*, 1937), Martin Frič, who emerged as the leading artistic talent at Barrandov. The Prague Film Academy (FAMU) was established in 1945, and, for a time, "victorious February" did not put an end to the making of films of real quality. Connoisseurs speak warmly of Frič's two-part critique of absolute power, *The Emperor's Baker* and *The Baker's Emperor* (1951), based on the myth of the Golem, and Forman describes Alfred Radok's *Distant Journey* (1949), an early film about the Holocaust incorporating documentary footage, as "one of the undiscovered classics of world cinema"; typically, though, it was no sooner released than it was banned by the authorities, not to be seen again until the late 1960s. Historical subjects came to outnumber contemporary (even "Socialist Realist") ones by more than two to one, the typical "Communist" film of the 1950s being more likely to be about Hus and Žižka than about tractors, steel quotas and the glorious fraternity of Czechs, Slovaks and Soviets at the Battle of Dukla.

In these circumstances, Czech film directors had, in a sense, only to introduce identifiable characters and situations into their films to create something akin to a cinematic revolution. None was better equipped to do this than Miloš Forman (born 1932) whose Czech films are, as he says in his autobiography *Turnaround* (1993), "mostly about trying to see clearly." Born at Čáslav in central Bohemia and educated at Poděbrady where Václav Havel, his junior by four years, was also a pupil, Forman came to Prague in 1949 and first made an impact in a revived production of V + W's *Ballad of the Rags*, a sign of where his artistic and intellectual roots lay. Forman was accepted as a student at FAMU where, for four years, he claims never to have touched a camera or spoken to an actor, was reunited with the precocious Havel through whom he met Seifert and Holan and ended up as assistant to the great Alfred Radok on the original *Laterna magika*. His first full-length film was *Black Peter* (Černý Petr, 1963), a seemingly slight piece in which a young trainee shop assistant is required to spy on customers and denounce any shoplifters. He refuses to turn in one guilty old woman and incurs the wrath of both his employer and his father: no self-respecting Czech cinema goer would miss the implications of the story. For his next major film, *Loves of a Blonde* (*Lásky jedné plavovlásky*, 1965) Forman was inspired by an encounter in the center of Prague with a young woman carrying a battered suitcase who had just arrived from a provincial town where she worked in a textile factory in search of a Prague man who had briefly been her lover and had given her an address that turned out not to exist; after talking to her throughout the night, Forman drove her to the station and she returned to her home-town and the inevitable derision of her fellow factory-workers. From this encounter Forman derives an exquisite modern fable, tender and ironic, not in any obvious sense "political"—though it brings out the tedium of work under "really existent Socialism" and the cramped living conditions endured by most Czechs, several generations packed into one flat— and herein, precisely, lies its force. If in "the west", "the personal is the political" was one of the key slogans in the 1960s, in "the east", to declare that "the personal is *not* the political" was, in a sense, even more radical. "Socialism", the party hierarchy proclaimed, "really exists", but still Andula and her like are lonely, vulnerable and exploited; she has personal emotions and needs that no political regime *per se* can satisfy more than another, her individual identity is not reducible to her "class position" and what is essential about her exists outside and in spite of politics. When everything is politicized, apoliticism becomes a principal weapon of the weak.

Other directors looked back to the experience of war and occupation, but in a spirit very different from the usual fare of Czechoslovak/Soviet solidarity. Both *The Shop on the Main Street* (*Obchod na korze*, 1964) by Jan Kadar and Elmar Klos and Jiří Menzel's *Closely*

Observed Trains (*Ostře sledované vlaky*, 1966), based on a novelette by Bohumil Hrabal, exposed, unforgettably, layers of complicity, cowardice and racism, as well as "small acts" of everyday heroism, among occupied Czechs and, by demystifying the recent past, encouraged audiences further to question the lies of the present: both films deservedly won Oscars for Best Foreign Film in their respective years. Other important directors whose films rarely, if ever, found a showing in "the west" were Věra Chytilová, who created *About Something Else* (*O něčem jiném*, 1963) and *Daisies* (*Sedmikrásky*, 1966) and Jan Němec whose *Report on the Party and the Guests* (*O slavnosti a hostech*, 1966) was widely viewed as a parable of relations between "the party" and its by now predominantly unwilling "guests", the people of Czechoslovakia. All the guests are asked by the host, played by Ivan Vyskočil, who, some claimed, was made up to resemble Lenin, whether they are happy. All but one aver unconvincingly that they are, and the one dissenter runs away from the party to be hunted down by fellow guests assisted by dogs. Again the inveterate decoders of allegories who packed Czech cinemas at the time had more than ample material into which to sink their interpretative teeth.

Still more appetizing was Forman's last, and greatest, film made in Czechoslovakia, *Firemen's Ball* (*Hoří, má panenko!*, 1967). As with *Loves of a Blonde*, the film had its origins in a serendipitous encounter. Frustrated with a recalcitrant screenplay, Forman and two of his closest collaborators, Ivan Passer and Jaroslav Papoušek, decided to take a break in the Krkonoše Mountains and there, in the small town of Vrchlabí one Saturday evening, they happened upon the annual ball given by the local fire brigade: "On Sunday, Papoušek, Ivan, and I just couldn't stop talking about everything that we had seen at the ball. On Monday, we were developing our impressions into what-ifs. On Tuesday, we began writing… six weeks later, we had the final draft of *Hoří má panenko*, or *Firemen's Ball*."

The film was shot in Vrchlabí itself, using local people for almost all of the roles, and develops the events seen at the ball into what Antonín Liehm, one of the most influential intellectuals associated with Prague Spring calls "an extended Gogolian metaphor"— "Hašekian" might have been better—of contemporary Czechoslovakia. All the prizes for the raffle are stolen, the beauty contest for Queen of the Ball, of which the firemen's committee is the leering panel of judges, collapses in chaos, a fire breaks out in a farmhouse nearby and the firemen are too late, too drunk and too incompetent to save it, the farmer is "compensated" with the now useless raffle tickets, and the deputy fire officer is exposed as one of the thieves. When the committee gets round to presenting a ceremonial axe to their former chief (who, though he does not know it, is dying of cancer), all the guests have disappeared with their ill-gotten gains and, lo and behold, even the axe has disappeared from its case. It is a tour de force in 73 minutes, "Aristotelian", as Forman says, in its observance of the classical unities of time, place and action, and, of course, lends itself to all manner of hermeneutic speculation. Is the doomed, doddering fire chief intended to represent "Comrade Number One", First Party Secretary Antonín Novotný? And does the beauty contest— at which the girls compete reluctantly, under pressure from their mothers—symbolize the competitions for jobs and preferment in "Socialist" society? The vanishing lottery prizes were surely a comment on a culture that believed as an item of faith that "he who does not steal from the state steals from his family", but what the fire might stand for, no-one, in 1967, could yet hazard a guess. But the central point of the fable could hardly be missed: those who are supposed to protect their fellow citizens are drunken, incompetent chumps, shoveling snow on to the flames while the farmer, despite all the efforts of the crowd to stop him from watching, gazes on, horror-struck and helpless, at the destruction not just of his livelihood but of his whole world. The villagers are no better, drunken pilferers to the last man and woman, fobbing the victim off with lottery tickets they know to be worthless, and disappearing with their plunder as soon as they can: this truly is a society in which no-one is innocent.

Nonetheless, such is the film's brio that it delighted almost everyone who saw it, not least the people of Vrchlabí, the only dissenters being Comrade Number One and the 40,000 Czech firemen who reportedly threatened to resign if the film was not withdrawn. They got their way and at the end of 1967 *Firemen's Ball* was banned "for all time". "All time" turned out to mean just a few months, for in January 1968 Comrade Number One was overthrown in a palace revolution (though, characteristically, he remained president until

March, when he was replaced by Ludvík Svoboda) and what many had taken to be a definitely cadaverized society began, like the Golem, to show signs of life. *Firemen's Ball* did not exactly predict "the fire next time", but it did suggest that the slow fuse lit in the late 1950s was finally on the point of igniting.

Prague Spring and the Intellectuals

To understand the role of intellectuals and artists in the phenomenon of "Prague Spring", it is necessary to go back from the ousting of Novotný in January 1968 to June the previous year when the Fourth Congress of the Union of Czechoslovak Writers opened at the House of the Slavs (the former German Kasino) on Na příkopě against a background of rumbling discontent with the regime. On the morning of June 27, after Milan Kundera had given a wide-ranging and incisive survey of the role of literature in shaping Czech national consciousness, the playwright Pavel Kohout (born 1928) read out a letter on censorship that Aleksandr Solzhenitsyn had sent earlier that year to the Congress of Soviet Writers, which had refused to discuss it. This act of "provocation" was too much for Jiří Hendrych, the party's ideological supremo who was present as an observer. He stormed out in protest, muttering to Kundera, Lustig and others that they had "lost everything, absolutely everything", presumably referring to the very limited liberalization of the last two or three years. That afternoon Ludvík Vaculík established himself as the writers' leading spokesman, a position he would hold up to and beyond the Soviet invasion, when he spoke on the subject of citizenship and power, arguing bluntly that there were *no* citizens, in the sense of autonomous, self-creating individuals, in contemporary Czechoslovakia, it being the "first law of power" that

> *it reproduces itself in ever more faithful copies, forever homogenizing itself, getting rid of everything alien to itself, till every point is an image of the whole and all parts are interchangeable, so that each peripheral cell of power can for practical purposes deputize for the center and you can swap these peripheral cells around without anything going wrong.*

It is Havel's later concept of "post-totalitarianism" in a nutshell, and it followed, Vaculík continued, that an authentic, creative and self-creating artist is by definition at odds with the self-replicating operations of power: "Just as I cannot believe that power and the citizen can ever see themselves as one, that the rulers and the ruled will ever go to singing lessons together, so I do not believe that art and power will ever cozily enjoy each other's company. They won't; they can't, even." Vaculík was speaking, or feigning to speak, abstractly and generally, but everyone listening, and the many more outside the former Kasino who would get wind of the debate, interpreted his words concrete and particularly, and drew the evident conclusion: the cause of the Czech artist and the cause of the Czech citizen were one and the same. It was an incendiary idea, which would guarantee writers and intellectuals a huge audience over the months and years to come, and one that not even the rigors of "normalization" would ever succeed in extinguishing completely.

Vaculík was roundly denounced the following morning by Hendrych in a specially convened extra-congress address, but the floodgates had been opened, and during the remaining two days of the congress virtually every aspect of the regime's cultural policy came under attack, with writer after writer—Klíma, Havel, Goldstücker, Liehm—rising to condemn censorship and to assert the need for what Jan Procházka called "freedom of creativity". Though the writers did not, at this or any other time, collectively call socialism into question (what some of them felt individually is another matter entirely), the logic of their case was to challenge the party's cultural and intellectual monopoly, and on July 1, the First Secretary himself denounced them in *Rudé právo* for trying to constitute themselves as a "third force" and signaled that there would be "no compromise" with "bourgeois ideology." In late September the ax fell: Hendrych rejected the kind of "abstract freedom" demanded by the writers, whose union, he said, had become a hotbed of "oppositional political conceptions". Vaculík, Liehm and Klíma were all expelled from the party, and *Literární noviny* was placed under the direct control of the Ministry of Culture and Information, at which the existing editorial board resigned en bloc and was replaced by a committee of party nominees. The office of Chairman of the Writers' Union was left conspicuously vacant.

With the provisional silencing of one generation of intellectuals, the torch passed to their putative successors. On October 31, a power failure, the tenth that month, at the student residence at Strahov prompted a candlelit march by students chanting "We want light"—and not just light of the physical variety. The police responded by dousing them and their candles in tear-gas. Thus, in the months prior to the fall of Novotný, a potential coalition was in the making that would provide the most radical element within the multi-stranded phenomenon of "Prague '68": the young and those in their thirties and forties (or older) who, as some of them said, felt young for the very first time in their lives.

With Novotný gone, the Union of Writers moved quickly into position, electing Eduard Goldstücker, the distinguished critic and scholar responsible for the reinstatement of Kafka (see Chapter Three), to its vacant presidency, and in March 1968 launching an independent journal, *Literární listy* (Literary Documents) to counter *Literární noviny* (Literary News), still staffed by Novotný appointees. Edited by Dušan Hamšik, the new journal soon had a circulation of 300,000, a quite incredible figure for a cultural publication, and a sure sign of the solidarity of interests between Czech writers and citizens; never since the heyday of the national awakening had intellectuals been more fully and genuinely the "conscience of the nation", with writers and readers forming a common front of a kind unequaled in twentieth-century Europe.

Most of the writers associated with *Literární listy*, along with most of their readers, would have called themselves Socialists committed to the idea—which was not in fact formulated by Dubček in so many words until late July—of "socialism with a human face", the slogan for which Prague '68 is most remembered. But, with the effective abolition of censorship in April, writers who had never been Communists or who had no faith even in reformed Communism were able, under the chairmanship of Havel, to come together in the Circle of Independent Writers. A Club of Committed Non-Party Members (KAN) was also set up to press for the rehabilitation of the estimated 128,000 victims of "Stalinism". The Writers' Union was in semi-permanent open session at the House of the Slavs, and a three-way split, vividly depicted in Josef Škvorecký's *The Miracle Game* (1972), opened up between the accredited writers of the old order, who were subjected to a merciless grilling, reform Communists and "committed non-Communists" who wanted much more than the limited "reform from above" proposed by Dubček and his colleagues. In Jiří Pelikán, the director of Czech television, the "radicals" (as we shall call them) had a powerful advocate and supporter, and there were proposals to revive the pre-1948 liberal daily *Lidové noviny* (The People's Paper) to compete with the now reformist *Rudé právo*. At the student *Majáles* on May 16, there was criticism of the reformers' timidity that were echoed in *Literární listy* under the by-line of "Dalimil", the joint pseudonym of A.J. Liehm, the foreign affairs specialist Jaroslav Šedivý and, making his first (disguised) appearance in Czech public affairs, Václav Kraus, the future architect of the country's post-1989 market economy.

It was evident that a gap was opening up between the intellectual vanguard and the reformist leadership of the party. Historians of Prague '68 are now at pains to stress the limits of what Dubček and his associates were seeking: "Socialism with a human face", to be sure, but still socialism, and they had no intention, at least at this stage and perhaps not at all, of surrendering the "leading role" of the party and permitting genuine multi-party democracy, let alone of consenting to even a modest privatization of parts of the economy. Asked in 1987 what was the difference between *perestroika* and Prague '68, the Soviet spokesman Gennadi Gerasimov famously replied, "Nineteen years!", thus highlighting both its originality and its limits. But mere reform of Communism was not enough for the radicals, and the issue came to a head with the publication on June 27, in *Literání listy* of a manifesto entitled "Two Thousand Words" drafted by Ludvík Vaculík and bearing the signatures of sixty individuals, scholars, scientists, writers and a number of "ordinary" workers and farmers.

"Two Thousand Words" called for the transformation of reform "from above" into a mass movement of change "from below", involving, if necessary, strikes and popular committees. Ever mindful of how Moscow would react, Dubček and his reformist associates denounced the manifesto's "political romanticism", while the barely if at all reconstructed Stalinists on the Party Presidium scented all-out counter-revolution. On 26 July, *Literární listy* published a further manifesto, this time by Pavel Kohout, calling alliteratively for *Socialismus! Spojenectví! Suverenita! Svoboda!* (Socialism, alliance, sovereignty, freedom) and, naming each member of the Presidium individually, urged them, in the face of up-coming negotiations with the Soviet authorities, to "defend, without concessions, the road on which we have embarked and from which we will never depart alive... We are thinking of you. Think of us!" On July 29, the summit opened at Čierna nad Tisou, a small railway junction on the Slovakia/Ukraine frontier. We need not follow the discussions or trace the rapid escalation of events culminating in the "Warsaw Pact" (i.e. Soviet) "intervention" (i.e. invasion) on the night of August 20-21, 1968. What concerns us is the reaction of the people of Prague to the crisis, and how it relates to the city's political culture. They had not fought in September 1938 or March 1939 or, for that matter, in February 1948. Should they, or could they, have done so in August '68?

Soviet Intervention

Some individuals did, of course, offer physical resistance, and some lost their lives in the process. There were 72 deaths in Czechoslovakia as a whole, with 267 cases of serious injury. The Czech army, although fully armed, made no move, and at no stage—remember that the reformist leaders were in Soviet hands—was there any organized opposition of even a non-physical kind. The one partial exception is almost comically redolent of Hašek's Party of Moderate Progress within the Bounds of the Law (see Chapter Three). At 12 noon on August 23, almost the entire national workforce went on strike—for an hour. The country is invaded, and the people down tools...for the duration of their lunch-break! But outside on the streets, in Prague above all, and in full view, at first, of national and international TV, courage, initiative and imagination were shown as, in a whole host of ways, people registered their revulsion and dismay at the course of events. Prague, in the words of *Svoboda* (August 23), became "one great poster"; "they have guns and rockets," added *Rudé právo* the following day, "our weapons are chalk, pen, word, and the constant ignoring of them!" Protesters took advantage of the Russian they had compulsorily learned at school to inscribe or declaim slogans along the lines of *Ruskiye fashisty, idite domoy!* Škvorecký's account in *The Miracle Game* nicely has a conscientious teacher of Russian going round with chalk correcting the grammar. Street signs, house numbers and nameplates were removed, and mini-skirted girls taunted the largely conscript invading force with expanses of cleavage and thigh unseen in Vishniy-Volochek or Smolensk. As so often in the past, Czechs saw themselves as innocent lambs slaughtered, or about to be slaughtered, by the wolves from the south (Austria), the west (Germany) and now from the east (the Soviet Union), a feeling unforgettably captured in Karel Kryl's omnipresent song of that summer, "little brother, close the gate" (Bratříčku, zavírej vrátka):

Don't sob my little brother
These aren't spooks
Come on, you're a big boy now
These are only soldiers
They arrived in angular
Metal caravans …

Outside's raining and it grown darker
This night shan't be short
The wolf craves the lamb
Little brother! Did you close the gate?

Don't sob my little brother
Don't waste your tears
Swallow the curses
And save your strengths
You mustn't reproach me
If we don't make it

Learn the song
It's not a difficult one
Lean on me my little brother
The road is damaged
We'll stagger on
Can't go back now

Outside's raining and it grown darker
This night shan't be short

The wolf craves the lamb
Little brother, close the gate!
Close the gate!
    (translation by Šarka Dalton)

As in Paris in 1940, some people simply ignored the alien presence among them, and there are reports of hapless invaders reduced to begging for food. It was, says Milan Kundera in *The Unbearable Lightness of Being* (1984), "a carnival of hate filled with a curious (and no longer explicable) euphoria", a mixture of Švejkism and the spirit of *Majáles* in which, like Kundera's Tereza, scouring the streets with her camera to catch the whole thing on film, many Czechs found a bizarre kind of fulfillment, as though the invasion was the apotheosis of the nation's deep-rooted sense of victimhood and of its moral and intellectual superiority over its victimizers. The week after the invasion was, wrote Kundera in December 1968, "the most beautiful week we have ever lived through." Had a nation of Sacher-Masochs attained the ultimate bliss?

If the spirit of carnival really did reign on the streets of Prague in the last week of August 1968, it was soon succeeded by a sense of Lenten reality as, in alliance with the re-emerging old guard and with some disaffected or opportunist reformers, the Soviet Union set out, gradually, determinedly and, in a sense, moderately, to extinguish most, if not everything, that "Prague Spring" had stood for. This it did initially under the cover of the reformists themselves who remained nominally in power until April 1969; the full rigors of "normalization" did not come into operation until after that date. Censorship was re-imposed in September 1968, and the dangerous Jiří Pelikán was removed from the directorship of Czech television. The club of Committed Non-Party Members was banned, as was K231, an organization of those who had been charged and punished as political offenders under the notorious clause 231 of the post-1948 Czech legal code. On the other hand, there were as yet no "screenings" or systematic dismissals, and those who wished to leave the country were permitted to do so. Many thousands duly fled to "the west", and the analogy with the "flight of Bohemia" after the Battle of White Mountain was frequently made, as Škvorecký, Kohout and Forman, followed in due course by Kundera (but not by Havel, Klíma or Vaculík), became modern-day Komenskýs in Toronto, Paris or Frankfurt.

The spirit of resistance flared up again, briefly, at the time of Jan Palach's funeral, in which anything from 100,000 to 750,000 people are said to have taken part, and, most dramatically, at the end of March 1969 when a double Czech victory over the Soviet Union at the world ice hockey championship in Stockholm brought tens of thousands of jubilant Praguers to Wenceslas Square where the Aeroflot offices were ransacked. There were rumors—how could there not be?—that the Soviet team had been ordered to lose to provoke just such a reaction, and the story seemed to be vindicated when, just weeks later, the reformist "rump" of Dubček and Smrkovský was dismissed to make way for Gustáv Husák, a political detainee in the 1950s and at one time closely identified with the reform process, and an assortment of neo-Stalinist *politruks*. In 1967-68, the Golem had awakened from two decades of corpse-like sedation and briefly threatened to bring chaos into the whole Soviet bloc. It was now a matter of plucking the *shem* from its mouth and consigning it not to the dustbin of history (from which things have a nasty knack of re-emerging) but to the attic of total oblivion, for ever.

Prague Normalized

It is next to impossible to write a history of *Praga normalisata*—Škvorecký's scathing term—for the very good reason that the object of the whole process was, as Havel put it in his celebrated (and probably unread) letter to "Dear Dr. Husák" of April 1975, to suspend history and to replace the living, and dangerous, successivity of events with a homogeneous and unchanging "entropic" present. "Normalization" has been well described (by the British political sociologist Abbey Innes) as "living in a melancholic, low-budget, black-and-white, twenty-year-long version of the film *Groundhog Day*," but if the chronology of such an experience is virtually meaningless, so too is the topology, for "normalization" also sought to "entropize" the public space that had erupted so threateningly in 1968 and, if it could not crush all opposition, to drive it inwards and downwards into the privatized sphere.

There is, therefore, no point in surveying, as in previous chapters, the various locations of oppositional culture during the period for the very good reason, once again, that they did not exist. Or, more precisely, if they existed, it was not on public squares or in theaters, but in underground boiler-houses where banned philosopher-stokers discussed Aristotle and Kant, in rancid locker-rooms where, as in Ivan Klíma's *Love and Garbage*, writers in their new guise as dustmen exchange muttered ideas on Kafka, in ill-lit corners of flats where whole novels, like *Love and Garbage* itself, are typed out in multiple copies on onion-thin paper, in private homes where, after giving a password and in dread of police informers and spies, groups of five, ten or fifteen people meet at night to discuss history or politics. Such was what, in his brilliant *samizdat*-published essay "The Power of the Powerless" (October 1978), Václav Havel called a "post-totalitarian system" which "touches people at every step, but it does so with its ideological gloves on", in which, "by pulling everyone into its power structure," ideology "makes everyone an instrument of mutual totality, the auto-totality of society" and in which, unlike old-fashioned, straightforward totalitarianism, no-one, neither ruler nor ruled, actually believes in the system's validity but merely live out the lie of appearing to do so. Indeed, what distinguishes post-totalitarianism from the mere totalitarianism of the past is that the distinction between rulers and ruled is effectively collapsed and "everyone in his own way is both a victim and a supporter of the system." When the system is everywhere and nowhere and when there is no possibility of getting outside of the system in order to resist it, the only option—and it is precarious in the extreme—is to oppose it from within, in the rare gaps or fissures it leaves in its train, and by means that are "existential" or "pre-" (or even "anti-") political rather than political in any conventional sense of the term. In a system founded on a ubiquitous lie, it is necessary, but almost impossible, to "live in the truth", to occupy some if need be microscopic area of veracity and to refuse, come what may, ever to be budged from it.

Havel was too modest and ironic to invoke the Hussite precedent of *Pravda vítězí* in so many words when he embarked upon his own oppositional adventure, but the historical resonance of "The Power of the Powerless" was not lost on the handful of people who, in 1978, were able to read it. *Pravda vítězí* plus Thomas Masaryk's "small acts" (*drobná prace*) plus a dash of Švejkology equals Charter 77, and Charter 77 issues eventually, and with much help from changing external circumstances, in November 1989 and "Velvet Revolution". The moral precedes the political, just as opposition precedes, and makes possible, resistance; the powerless really do have the power to counter "the system" provided they choose, at their peril, to "live in the truth."

But, of course, in 1978, Havel had no idea that his particular set of "small acts" would yield so happy an outcome. "Normalization" had targeted the intelligentsia above all, and its principal effects were as follows:

- 5 million people (59 percent of the adult population) were "screened" after April 1969.
- Of them, 1.5 million were party members and, of these, 500,000 were expelled, reducing party membership to 1.2 million (one in nine of the adult population).
- One-third of all teachers lost their positions.
- Forty research institutions were disbanded or merged ("I'd chuck out even Einstein if his politics were not in order," said the Director of the Nuclear Research Institute).
- The Writers' Union was reconstituted under tight party control in 1972, with 310 members as opposed to 610 in 1968, 475 of whom were suspended in 1969.
- The new union's journal *Literární měsíčník* (Literary Monthly), launched in October 1972, had a circulation of 4,000, as against 150,000 for the old *Literární listy* in 1968.
- The editors of 37 out of 40 influential dailies and weeklies were dismissed, and 40 percent of journalists lost their jobs.
- The works of writers associated with "Prague '68" were removed from libraries, and the names of the writers themselves excised from dictionaries, encyclopedias and reference works (the 1985 edition of *Czech Writers of the Twentieth Century*, 830 pages long, contains no mention of Kundera, Škvorecký, Klíma, Kohout, Lustig, Vaculík or Havel).
- The children of known opponents of "normalization" were denied higher (and sometimes secondary) education.

- Banned writers etc. were re-employed as boilermen, coal heavers, cleaners of all kinds, dustmen, bricklayers and so on (the former student leader Jiří Müller was hired, with nice symbolism, by a fire extinguisher factory; the journalist Věra Štovíčkova was taken on as a charwoman and then fired when her past became known, making her, as she said, "probably the first cleaning woman ever to have been sacked for political reasons."
- At least six "intellectuals", in the broad sense of the term, are known to have taken their own lives (Stanislav Neumann, Jan Alda, Vladimír Burda, Vladimír Heller, Jiří Pištora, Lukáš Tomin).

Samizdat and Opposition

Faced with such extraordinary constraints on their freedom, the first concern of those writers who remained was, naturally, how to get their work published. Some, like Bohumil Hrabal, were, by and large, "tolerated" by the regime while others, banned in the 1970s, were allowed to resume publishing in the 1980s. When, however, the seemingly "apolitical" poet Miroslav Holub (born 1923) published his first collection for ten years, it sold out within days and was not reprinted "due to the shortage of paper". Some writers managed to get manuscripts smuggled abroad where they found exiled publishers, notably the now Toronto-based Josef Škvorecký who, with his novelist wife, set up the famous Sixty-Eight Publishers whose authors eventually included, in addition to the Škvorecký's, Kundera, Klíma, Havel, Seifert, Vaculík, Lustig and Hrabal. Copies of their books were smuggled back into Czechoslovakia where, along with original manuscripts, they were retyped using carbon paper—photocopies were strictly controlled by the regime—to produce multiple copies that were then passed on and retyped yet again, thus reaching an incalculable number of readers; "if the Russians invented *samizdat*," said the émigré editor Pavel Tigrid, "it is undoubtedly the Czechs who perfected the system and made it an art."

Of the several *samizdat* "publishing houses"—Edice Kvart (Quarto), Česká Expedice (Czech Despatch), Edice Popelnice (Ashcan Editions), Krtek a Datel (The Mole and the Woodpecker)—the most famous and prolific was the well-named Edice Pedlice (Padlock Editions) operating under the general editorship of the remarkable

Ludvík Vaculík, which between 1973 and 1987 produced no fewer than 400 typed and bound volumes (plus innumerable copies). Edice Kvart published 120 volumes, largely typed, bound and edited by Jan Vladislav alone who, at ten days per volume, thus devoted 1,200 days to *samizdat* production: arrest and expulsion were his eventual reward. Overall, it is estimated that the "cottage industry" of Czech *samizdat* produced 1,000 volumes in all, plus several long-running reviews, of which *Obsah* (Contents) and *Kritický sborník* (Critical Symposium) were the most widely diffused. It was lonely, exhausting and dangerous work, and not for nothing was the Masarykian doctrine of "small acts" invoked. The "typewriter culture", as it came to be known, was one way, amongst others, of "living in the truth."

The opposition "movement" in normalized Czechoslovakia was concentrated in Prague and Brno, and had virtually nothing in common with the contemporaneous Solidarity in Poland. With no independent trade unions and with its several churches internally divided and in part co-opted by the regime, opposition in Czechoslovakia never had a popular base and consisted, in Barbara Day's telling phrase, of "a bohemia within Bohemia": scattered individuals, usually known personally to each other, meeting and communicating in secret, accepting surveillance as a routine part of their lives. The comparison with the early Hussites or Community of Brethren meeting secretly to take communion "in both kinds" was frequently, and not inappropriately made, with Pilsener and sausage taking the place of the bread and the wine, as "believers" moved between hidden—and eventually not so hidden—chapels both *intra muros* and *extra* (the country cottages that were such a feature of this time.) The network included the house of the Palouš family on Kampa Island (the so-called Kampakademie), the apartment of the philosopher Julius Tomin on Keramická in Letná, and the rented attic bed-sitter of the architecture student Vladimír Prajzler on Krakovská, just off Wenceslas Square. In his apartment on Slovenská in Vinohrady, the philosopher Ladislav Hejdánek organized a seminar almost every Monday night between October and June each year from 1980 to 1989. The seminars were almost certainly bugged, leading one foreign visitor to conclude "if they really do listen in to those seminars, there must be some highly cultivated policemen in Prague by now."

To the "chapels" came regular "missionaries" from abroad, usually sponsored by the Oxford-based Jan Hus Educational Foundation which, between 1979 and 1989, organized over a hundred such visits by philosophers, composers and writers including Richard Rorty (July 1981), Paul Ricoeur (June 1980 and March 1986), Jacques Derrida (December 1980) and, almost every year, Roger Scruton. The Foundation's trustees and patrons included Iris Murdoch, Tom Stoppard, A.J. Ayer, Lady Antonia Fraser, Yehudi Menuhin, and Harold Pinter. The visit of Jacques Derrida was particularly stormy and ended with the philosopher being arrested at Ruzyně airport for "the production and traffic of drugs". Four "packets of brown powder" had been planted in his luggage, and Derrida spent the night in Ruzyně jail before being flown back to Paris, the police's objective being not so much to discredit him personally as to denigrate his host, the philosopher Ladislav Hejdánek. For Czech intellectuals "dreaming about Europe" (in the words of Jiří Dienstbier, Czechoslovakia's first post-1989 Foreign Minister), such visits from "the west" were invaluable in disturbing, be it ever so briefly, the all-encompassing entropy of the post-totalitarian age.

Charter 77

The Jan Hus Foundation apart, none of these groups had a formal organization, being rather loosely coordinated gatherings of like-minded individuals, strengthened rather than weakened by the lack of structures and hierarchies. Nor did Charter 77, launched in the first week of January 1977, ever constitute itself as even an organized pressure group, preferring to describe itself, through its various spokespersons, as a "working human society" embodying a "moral stance" rather than a defined political program. Although it spawned a "Committee for the Defense of the Unjustly Persecuted" (VONS), Charter 77 itself operated exclusively by spoken and written word, and organized no demonstrations, petitions or marches. Of the document's original 247 signatories, 90 percent were resident in Prague, and even when its support grew—750 signatories by mid-1977, 1,000 by June 1980, 1,300 by 1987—it remained heavily weighted towards Prague. It issued some 340 "documents" in the course of its twelve-year existence, some on international rather than narrowly national issues (ecology, nuclear weapons, apartheid), but its principal objective was always to pressurize the regime into actually implementing the Helsinki Accord on human rights to which it had cynically signed up in 1975.

Its signatories came from all walks of life, though with an expected bias towards the intelligentsia and committed members of churches. With its "non-political politics" (Ladislav Hejdánek), Charter 77 came to form what one of its signatories, Václav Benda, called a "parallel polis", a loosely reticulated para-society whose function, in a sense, was to stand hostage for the wider society. Charter 77, said another signatory Vilem Prečan, constituted "a small island of civic activity in the sea of the overwhelming majority of people who had adapted to the situation." In signing the Charter, individuals voluntarily moved out of the proverbial "gray zone" in which most Czechs continued to live, neither supporting nor opposing (save by Švejkian maneuver) a system they considered both repugnant and permanent, and ventured into a far more perilous black and white world which, as it turned out, many found exhilarating and surprisingly easy to inhabit. "They helped me by being so stupid," said ex-teacher Chartist Jan Urban of his former employers, "They made it so easy. The way they acted forced me to explode and the explosion blew me across to the other side of the barricade. One loses one's work and finds that it becomes, strangely, very easy."

Chartists were effectively offering themselves up as potential sacrificial victims on behalf of their as ever mightily cautious fellow citizens, and some did indeed pay with their lives: one young worker-Chartist committed suicide when the pressures on him became too great to bear, and, as we have seen, the death of the philosopher Jan Patočka was clearly linked to his grueling interrogation at the hands of the police in March 1977. Charter 77 had its well-known public individuals, Havel above all, but also the singer Marta Kubišová and the Plastic People's Ivan Jirous (see Chapter Four), whom the regime was able to cast as privileged seekers after publicity. They did indeed command a more fervent audience abroad than among many Czechs themselves, life-long denizens of the "gray zone" who resented the moral high-mindedness of people they saw as considerably better off than themselves.

The Chartists did not "create" the Velvet Revolution, nor did they ever constitute themselves as some kind of alternative government in internal exile, but it was to them, and above all to Havel himself, that Czechs instinctively turned in November-December 1989 to oversee the transition from post-totalitarianism to democracy. As Civic Forum, Charter 77 remained at the forefront of politics until the elections of 1992 swept them, Havel apart, from the scene, somewhat embittered that their courage and sacrifice had been so little recognized, and unhappy, as velvet turned to velcro and Czechoslovakia itself split, that Communist normalization was giving way to another set of norms: the norms of an "ordinary", "western-style" society based on a market economy and parliamentary democracy. Post-1989 Prague may not have been exactly living a lie, but it fell some considerable way short, as we shall see, of the kind of moral and existential authenticity that Havel and others had envisaged.

CHAPTER SEVEN

Martyrs and Puppets

Before we move on to the *dénouement* of November 1989 and to how
life in Prague has developed between then and now, let us pause to
consider a little more closely the two images that, time after time, have
surfaced in this book, so frequently, and indeed so predictably, that they
may be said to belong archetypally to Prague. The city's (and, more
broadly, the country's) obsession with martyrs, on the one hand, and
puppets, on the other, has been frequently noted, and each obsession
has been separately studied. The British scholar Robert B. Pynsent has
written illuminatingly on the subject of "Czech self-definition through
martyrs" (1994), and the image of the puppet and its close relatives (the
automaton, the Golem, the statue, the robot) forms one of the guiding
themes of Angelo Maria Ripellino's *Magic Prague.*

But what, if anything, connects one set of figures with the other?
What qualities are shared by the numerous analogues of the puppet—
the endless dolls in shop windows, the clockwork figures on the Old
Town Hall, the mass-produced *bambini di Praga*, as well as the figures
mentioned above—and the millennium-long catalog of martyrs that
stretches like some kind of apostolic succession from Wenceslas at the
end of the tenth century to Jan Palach and Jan Patočka at the end of
the twentieth, via—to name just the most notable intermediary
figures—St. John Nepomuk, Jan Hus, Dalibor, Johannes Jessenius and
his twenty-six fellow Protestants of 1621, Jan Opletal, Julius Fučík, Jan
Masaryk and Milada Horáková? All those named died violent deaths or
deaths, like Jan Patočka's, accelerated by excessive treatment, but others
whose deaths were premature or emblematic of this or that political
circumstance have also been readily transformed into national martyrs:
Karel Hynek Mácha, Karel Havliček, Karel Čapek and, most recently,
Alexander Dubček whose death (by car accident in October 1992)
seemed to many the almost necessary outcome of almost twenty-five

years as political Man of Sorrows. As the Slovak poet Mihálik wrote in 1969, "On the Mount of Olives Dubček/sweats blood."

If, even setting aside the martyred musicians of Terezín and other victims of fascism and Communism (Josef Čapek, Záviš Kalandra, Jan Zajíc, plus others mentioned below), one adds to these "official" national martyrs an "unofficial" list—perhaps not disproportionately large—of Czech artist-intellectuals who have committed suicide (the composer Jan Jakub Ryba, the architect Bedřich Feuerstein, the poet Konstantin Biebl, and the sculptor Otakar Švec, among others), died prematurely or by accident (Bohumil Kubišta, Jiří Wolker, Otto Gutfreund) or whose deaths were almost certainly hastened by political pressures (František Halas, Karel Teige), then it is evident that the so-called Czech "martyr complex" rests on empirical bases, and is not—or not merely—a figment of the national, or nationalist, imagination. But is there any link, to repeat, with the equally pervasive "puppet complex"? Is the rope from which Fučík, Horáková and Kalandra, among others, were hanged somehow connected with the puppet-master's strings, and the multiple oppressions of the Czech historical experience figured in the stylized violence and jerky manipulated movements of tens of thousands of puppet shows, amateur and professional, private and public? Is the marionette a secularized, miniaturized version of the martyr, and the puppet-show a grotesque rendering of three and a half centuries of control from afar?

Throughout their history, whether as Bohemians, Czechoslovaks or Czechs, the people of Prague have shown a particular propensity to build their sense of collective identity not so much around this or that individual martyr as around a global martyrological tradition. Of course, some martyrs have been more potent than others (Wenceslas, Nepomuk, Hus, Palach), and different regimes or causes have focused on different martyrs (Austro-Catholics on Nepomuk, Czech nationalists on Wenceslas and Hus, Communists on Hus and Fučík, anti-Communists on Jan Masaryk, Horáková and Palach), but the fundamental mechanisms or impulse are the same: it is when gathered symbolically around the body of its martyr(s) that the social, political or national body achieves its maximum sense of collective selfhood. Charles IV understood this when he co-opted and fostered the cult of St. Wenceslas, as did the Austro-Catholics when they virtually invented

St. John Nepomuk as a counter to Hus. The "national awakening" seems one long commemoration of martyrs, and the narrator of Paul Leppin's *Severin's Journey into the Dark* (1914), a German-speaker like the author, recalls encountering as a child "a group of Czech demonstrators who had buried one of their martyrs in the churchyard and were now returning home. A revolutionary song, sung by a thousand voices, advanced with them threateningly," inspiring in the young Severin "a fantastically beautiful terror, mixed with fear and devotion."

"One of their martyrs": it sounds like a regular, almost monthly, event, and out of the communion of mourners and victim rises that great bond of Czechs with each other, music and song, *Ktož sú Boží bojovníci, Kde domuv můj?, Má vlast, Bratříčku, zavírej vrátka*... And is there not something morbidly self-indulgent, some unavowed desire, even need, to be victimized, in this endless obsession with martyrs? "A Czech is only good for martyrdom," says a character in one late nineteenth-century novel quoted by Pinsent, while another describes Czechs as a "nation of flagellants": "Indeed, born suicides. If someone blames you for something, you bend your heads and accept the blame." Nor has the Czech martyr complex abated with time:

> *Oh God, I sighed to myself, the whole world is full of strident symbols. Human torches. Statues of martyrs. Potential martyrs... Sons of martyrs. Mothers of sons of martyrs. Wives of martyrs... Ancient martyrs like that fifteenth-century priest. Fresh martyrs like the boy who poured gasoline on himself...*

Thus Danny Smiricky, Josef Škvorecký's alter ego in *The Miracle Game* (1972), a novel centrally concerned, precisely, with the martyrdom, soon after "victorious February", of the Catholic priest Josef Toufar at Communist hands. One has only to go into almost any Prague church, or any of the city's art galleries, to see what he means and, perhaps, to share some of his weariness at the reiterated theme. Outside of the Iberian peninsula, probably no European city contains more extreme, indeed sometimes virtually pornographic, images of the twisted, bleeding, writhing bodies of holy men and women, as they swoon in exquisite death-agonies and display their mangled body-parts with a relish shocking to even the most jaded Catholic perception.

The Loretta: Images of Calvary

One final example, not so far mentioned: at the Loretta on Hradčany, tucked away in the corner of the cloisters, and easily missed if one does not know it is there, a chapel contains what would be just one more Christ on the Cross were "his" body not so curiously feminine or the black beard sprouting from "his" chin so abnormally abundant. A glance at the guide book reveals that it is not Christ at all, but St. Wilgefortis, Starosta in Czech, daughter to the King of Portugal who, due to be married to the King of Sicily when her only wish was to be a recluse, took a vow of virginity and, through God's intervention, grew a beard that proved not to be to her fiancé's taste; he broke off the engagement. Wilgefortis was then crucified, beard and all, on her father's instructions and, duly canonized, she became the patron saint of unhappily married women.

Is this gruesome image a one-off aberration? Not at all: in the Veletržní Palác is a painting, dating from 1865, by Gabriel Max (1840-1915) of another crucified woman, the beardless St. Julia this time, at whose bloodied feet a suitor or worshipper places the required posy of flowers. The painter Alen Diviš (1900-56) did both a drawing and a painting of St. Starosta, and the date of the painting—1950—is enough to indicate the political resonances of the theme. Indeed, between the mid-1930s and 1970, one Czech painter after another, whatever his or her personal faith, used the Passion as an emblem of the protracted agonies of those times, from František Tichý's *Ecce Homo* of 1940 to Bohuslav Reynck's *Crucifixion* series of 1966-67, via works on similar subjects by Jan Bauch (1942), Alen Diviš (1941, 1946-48, 1951), Václav Chad (1942), Emil Filla (1948), Jiří Balcar (c. 1958) and Antonín Tomalík (1958). It comes as, regrettably, no surprise to learn that Chad was shot, aged 22, by the Gestapo in 1945 and that Balcar committed suicide in 1968. Even (presumably atheistic) Communist poets implicitly likened Julius Fučík to Christ.

But this obsession of recent Czech artists with the Passion went back to at least the late nineteenth century. At the age of eight, Alfons Mucha did a watercolor (1868) of Christ on the Cross, and during the heyday of decadence and symbolism, self-portraits as crucified Christ were almost *de rigueur*. The photographer František Drtikol, famous above all for his female nudes, took a picture of himself clad in seamless robe and crowned with thorns in 1914, and the Symbolist Josef Váchal painted a *Self-portrait as Christ Crucified* in 1906; in a sacrilegious reversal of the image, Jan Zrzavý did a lurid crucified *Antichrist* in 1909, and Bohumil Kubišta memorably painted himself as St. Sebastian in 1912.

It is likely that all of these painters were familiar with Julius Zeyer's widely read *Three Legends about the Crucifixion*, published in 1895. One of the stories has a young Czech poet named Inultus ("Unavenged") meet a Donna Flavia from Milan who wishes to have him painted as Christ "with all the infinite pain that nestles in your heart." Inultus agrees, accompanies her to the studio of a painter named Guido, strips and is attached to a wooden cross, hour after hour, day after day, as, with Donna Flavia watching, Guido paints him. As he poses, "a kind of madness began to take hold of him. His burning fantasy insinuated in him the idea that God had chosen him to redeem by his martyrdom on the Cross the wretched land of Bohemia." For the sake of greater "realism", Donna Flavia has his bonds tightened and he begins to bleed copiously from ankles and wrists, and when, in culmination, Flavia stabs him in the heart, he ecstatically offers his life up for Bohemia: "For you, my people, I give my blood. O my God, accept it as an expiation." This mixture of eroticized Christianity and masochistic nationalism seduced an entire generation, and certainly captivated Zeyer's friend František Bílek (see Chapter Five) who was obsessed, in his own words, by "the idea of the Czech lands as a place of sacrifice where the greatest sacrifices burn with excitement as if on an altar, from the arrival of the Czechs to their fall at White Mountain."

Bílá hora as Calvary, the Czech people as Christ: it is to this commonplace of Czech nationalism that Bílek gives repeated and memorable expression in such sculptures as "Measure" (1917), where a man with a mallet measures up Christ for the Cross and the several variations on "Tilling by the Cross" (1892, 1900) in which the Cross itself becomes a plough to be pushed and pulled through the soil by the toiling Czech people: the reference to the ploughman Přemysl, husband of Libuše and founder of Bohemia's first ruling dynasty, would be obvious to every Czech, then and now, who sees these great wood carvings. There is probably no European country, other than Poland, in which the Crucifixion has preserved a greater artistic vitality, irrespective of the beliefs of the individuals concerned. When Jan Patočka died after police interrogation in 1977, a crown of thorns was placed on his grave by two of the Plastic People of the Universe: believers or non-believers, all were united through the greatest Christian symbol.

Automata and Survivors

To move from crucified Christ and other religious and secular martyrs to puppets, dolls, automata and related simulacra of the human may not be as far as it looks. As we have seen in Chapter Four, there is evidence that Bohemian puppet shows began as miniature Passion Plays, and it is known that puppets were made by carvers of Baroque statuary as a hobby or sideline. Puppets have the same burnished, lacquered appearance as statues, their eyes are blank and unseeing, and their iconic attributes are as fixed as those of a saint. And, as Bohumil Hrabal writes in *Too Loud a Solitude* (1976), "our Catholic statues are full of motion, like athletes who have just spiked a ball over the net or finished a hundred-metre dash or a whirlwind discus throw, their sandstone eyes and arms raised as if on the point of returning God's lob or rejoicing in His victory goal."

The link between martyr and puppet is made explicit in a story by Paul Leppin entitled *Wonderdoll* first published in 1921, but clearly drawing on ancient Prague folklore. On the outskirts of Malá Strana there stands a "peculiar structure of wood and canvas", its outer walls covered with "colorful and fantastic images" in which "blood and terror had run together in mute gestures." It is a traveling waxworks run by a bearded magician containing, according to rumor, "dead people—pale as wax—that could not move an inch (but which) nevertheless breathed and moved their lips as if wanting to say something (as) they gazed with pained, glittering eyes at the visitors, many of whom fainted and had to be carried to the door." There are "severed heads" and "dead emperors and kings with rigid faces, swords in their hands" while "all around on the walls the holy martyrs and the victims of the Inquisition died in horrible torment. The instruments of torture dug into their ashen skin and contorted their mouths into grinning madness."

Most striking of all, though, is golden-haired, flame-eyed Maria the Wonderdoll, clad only in a silk cloth, who, every quarter of an hour, raises her left hand to her breast, bows her head slightly and opens her eyes as though suddenly filled with life. Many a youth falls madly in love with her, "but she could help none of them, for she was made of wax, and in her body wires and spools—not blood—stirred." Hans is one of her swains and one day, "as the severed heads and the martyrs on the walls were whispering amongst themselves," he kneels down before Maria, takes her in his arms and embraces her, whereupon she begins to return his kisses and speak to him of her love, even though "she was only made of wax and had been dead her entire life." He runs away in terror, but the following night returns to the waxworks, crossing Charles Bridge on which the statues themselves come alive as he passes like stone puppets suddenly able to move: "an old bishop shook his weathered head in exasperation and the hound of hell amid the large group of the despairing began to growl. A stone Turk bent down to the boy and called after him." He enters the magician's hut where Maria, more beautiful than ever, is waiting, and together they go up to Hradčany "through the echoing courtyards of the royal palace, past the gloomy doors of St. Vitus Cathedral, past the crucifixes and images of the Blessed Virgin, past old churches and towers." Still embracing, they descend to the Vltava, and there the narrative suddenly ends: "A fisherman found the dead boy in the river downstream from the city. He was holding the beautiful doll from the wax exhibit clutched tightly in his arms." Hans is dead, a martyr to love, an inanimate effigy, but Maria is still "living", opening her eyes and raising her arm every quarter of an hour, just as she has been doing for time immemorial. "In their fear and anger, 'onlookers' cast the enchanted doll back into the river—from the stone bridge into the Vltava—not far from the spot where St. John of Nepomuk died…"

Martyr, puppet, living statue, human corpse, martyr: the story takes us full circle, one figure dissolving into the next in an atmosphere of erotic and religious morbidity and giving us a continuum of images on which martyr and puppet are located at different points but as variant forms of the same basic complex.

Where and how does the Golem fit into the continuum? It too is a kind of statue or puppet, a humanoid form that comes alive when the *shem* is placed under its tongue, a primitive form of the robots of Karel Čapek's *R.U.R.* of 1922, linked also to the rudimentary computer of Václav Havel's 1968 play *The Increased Difficulty of Concentration*. Both Golem and robot—the later word, as we have seen, is linked to the Czech word for serfdom—are slaves that first obey, and then rebel against, their human inventors before, in the case of the Golem, returning to their original corpse-like condition. They are like the statues on Charles Bridge which, in a widespread Prague fantasy, not confined to Paul Leppin, come alive in the middle of the night and promenade through the city: "No one who has failed to see these statues leaving their suicidal pedestals on certain nights not recorded in the calendar, mixing with passers-by and admiring the twelve bridges of Prague, can ever understand my poetry" (Vítězslav Nezval, 1938). The clockwork figures on the Old Town Hall and other automata clearly belong to the same chain of images, effigies of the human that, at regular intervals (like Maria the Wonderdoll), are suddenly invested by an external force that causes them, briefly, to move in a mechanical parody of human gestures. An underlying pattern is beginning to emerge, which may be represented schematically as follows:

"IDEAL"		"REAL"
Martyr	Puppet/Golem/Automaton/Robot	Statue

At one end of the continuum, the martyr is *dispossessed* of his or her soul and transformed into the inanimate simulacrum of the statue at the opposite end, a statue which can, every exceptionally, come back to "life" and cohabit with the living. In between, puppet, Golem, robot and automaton are regularly *possessed* by an animating force that causes them to simulate the living until they return to their original thing—or death-like condition. All the figures "exist" in some kind of frontier-zone between life and death, neither wholly living nor wholly dead. Their center is elsewhere, they are acted on from without, though they do from time to time, but never wholly successfully, rebel against the magician, puppet-master or clockmaker who creates and controls them.

How not to see in all this some kind of transposition of the history of Bohemia: a once powerful kingdom at the center of Europe, dispossessed of its soul at the Battle of White Mountain, and for centuries thereafter relegated to the margins of the Austrian empire, asleep like the Golem until the "national awakening" and then reduced once more, after but twenty yeas of real independence, to its former condition of a pseudo-nation, a satellite? Bohemia: between 1620 and 1918, and again between 1938 and 1989, an object not a subject of history, now and then rebelling but always returning to a state of neither-living-nor-dead in-betweenness, a puppet, a marionette and, just occasionally, a martyr.

And here is the great paradox of the Czech "martyr complex". Historically, Czechs have, or are said to have, shown, in the words of the philosopher Pavel Bratinka in the *samizdat* journal *Paraf* in 1989, a notable "disinclination towards martyrdom", a definite tendency not to resist internal and external domination in the manner of Hus but to oppose it, Švejk-fashion, from within while doing their utmost to avoid violence, confrontation and eventual retribution. Hus may be the ideal, but Švejk is the reality, and, rightly or wrongly, other middle Europeans who have borne the brunt of, and resisted, Austrian-German or Russian-Soviet domination, are more than a little scathing about the Czech survivalist tradition. The Czech army, say the Poles, drills to the chant of *hut-two-three-I-give-up, hut-two-three-I-give-up*, and both Czechs and outsiders point to the failure to fight in 1938-9 and again in 1968 as evidence, not necessarily of cowardice, but of a deep-seated, and historically well tested, urge not to confront, but somehow to neutralize, circumvent or deflect, the intrusions of power. The Czechs,

Jaroslav Durych has written, are a nation of Sancho Panzas without a Don Quixote, anxious to accommodate, to get by, to survive. "Is it not beautiful?" said Edvard Beneš, president of Czechoslavakia at the time of Munich and again after the war, to A.J.P. Taylor in 1945, looking out over Prague from his suite in Hradčany, "the only undamaged city in central Europe and all my doing."

The Czechs' central European reputation as a people of trimmers and tergiversators is not wholly justified, but it has sufficient substance for the accusation to persist. There are no Bohemian equivalent of the Polish uprisings of 1830-31, 1848 and 1863, and no Czechoslovak version of the Hungarian uprising of 1956. 1848 in Prague was a minor skirmish compared with Budapest and Vienna the same year, and if many Czechs enlisted in the Czech Legion between 1914 and 1918, many more fought—apparently willingly—for empire and Emperor; eventual independence owed more to President Wilson than to President Masaryk. As in 1914-8, so in 1938-45: if many Czechs fled and fought with the allies, the "Protectorate of Bohemia and Moravia" notoriously had the highest industrial output in occupied Europe, and Prague, the first European capital to be taken by the Nazis, was also the last to launch any autonomous attempt at self-liberation. In all, 1,694 Czechs were killed in the Prague uprising of 1945, and the reprisals that followed the assassination of Heydrich in 1942 (173 men shot at Lidice, 203 women taken to Ravensbrück, 105 children separated from parents, plus 254 relatives of the assassins executed) did not deter the 25,000 Czech Communists who were killed resisting the Nazis. How many of these were Czechs, as opposed to Slovaks, is not stated in my source, nor are any figures given for non-Communist resisters.

Anti-Nazi resistance notwithstanding, the pattern seems consistent: no organized resistance to the Communist take-over in February 1948, moral and symbolic gestures in August 1968, and only belated and limited activity in November 1989 after Poland, Hungary and the former German Democratic Republic had all overthrown their Communist regimes. For centuries, it seems, Czechs have been willing, if not happy, to live in history's "gray zone", maneuvering, manipulating, adjusting, pretending, above all waiting for something to turn up and for things to get better. Not, on the face of it, a rousing endorsement of either Hus' *Pravda vítězí* or Havel's Living in the Truth...

A cynic might conclude that, puppets of history, occasional but ineffectual Golems all too easily reduced to their ancestral sleep, Czechs have made a cult of "their" martyrs precisely in order to conceal or evade their distinct unwillingness to make martyrs of themselves. For much of their (non-)history, they seem to have been neither living nor dead, geographically at the center of Europe, but historically decentered, reduced to an automatized semi-life on the margins of things. In the martyr, Czechs perceive and revere an ideal of themselves; in the puppet and its equivalents they take a grim pleasure in themselves as they are. Part puppet, part victim, but determined above all to survive, Švejk, says the Marxist philosopher Karel Kosík, is a mixture of both Sancho Panza and Don Quixote, mediating between the ideal and the real, and showing Czechs how, without either totally surrendering their integrity or losing their lives, it is possible to get by in the "gray zone" and eventually come through. Švejk, in this reading, is *homo pragensis*, the city's survivalist instinct made rather too much flesh.

But it was not Švejk, or even the remaining reformers of 1968, who initiated the Velvet Revolution—Švejk never initiates anything, he merely reacts—but a new generation, born in the years just before or just after the Soviet invasion, for whom the whole theory and practice of Švejkism had become increasingly repugnant. This new generation reached out to the "martyrs" of normalization and together they swept the Communists from the stage like the collapsed, stringless puppets they had become. Only then did the city's much larger population of Švejks emerge from their privatized inner world out on to the streets and, as we shall see in the next, and final, chapter of this book, install a new kind of "gray zone" in place of the old.

CHAPTER EIGHT

From Velvet to Velcro: 1989 and Since

The Prague students who organized the demonstration that precipitated the fall of Communism in Czechoslovakia showed an exceptionally keen sense of the city's history and geography. Anniversaries have always been important in Prague, and it was the good fortune of the city's opposition, and the misfortune of the governing regime, that a whole cluster of significant twentieth, twenty-first, fiftieth and seventieth anniversaries fell in 1988-89. On August 21, 1988, the twentieth anniversary of the Soviet invasion, as many as 10,000 mainly young people who had not known the invasion itself had gathered to mark the occasion; the demonstration had no specific objective, nor was it organized by any of the recognized opposition groups, but its symbolism needed no explaining either to the people of Prague or to the government. On October 28, that year, the seventieth anniversary of the founding of the Republic, another demonstration took place, this time more structured, with the aim of marching from Wenceslas Square, via Old Town Square, to Hradčany, the last of which it was prevented from reaching. Early in the New Year, on January 15, 1989, there was the annual attempt to place flowers on the site of Jan Palach's martyrdom; that it was the twenty-first anniversary of his death brought out an exceptionally large crowd, and Havel, among others, was arrested and imprisoned.

That same month, the people of Prague were also alerted to broader developments in central and eastern Europe by the unscheduled arrival of thousands of refugees from the German Democratic Republic in transit to Austria and the Federal republic. "Some had been traveling for days now," wrote Jáchym Topol in his remarkable 1994 novel *City Sister Silver*, "on overcrowded trains, in

Nevada Title Company

Trabants and Wartburgs piled high with junk, on their way out of the cage, on the road to Paradise." Arriving in Prague, the refugees packed into the streets around the Federal German and American embassies in Malá Strana, and there were confrontations with the local police, in which Czech onlookers noisily sided with the fugitives, giving, says Topol, "something of a carnival feel to the Germans' exodus that lingers on to this day, from the moment time exploded, bursting out of that locked-up city, time with its own taste and color that you don't know about until you taste it, until you're there inside the color." "The explosion of time": already in January 1989, the people of Prague were beginning to sense the taste and color of the history—the European history—from which the city had been cut off for twenty years or more. If it was not yet at the center of things, at least Prague felt less on the margins.

November 1989: Theater in Action

The spring, summer and early autumn of 1989 were quiet in Prague, including the first two weeks of November, as one central European Communist regime after another collapsed in what has been called a "reverse domino effect". Transitions from Communism were negotiated under opposition pressure in Poland and Hungary, the Berlin Wall "fell" on November 9, and even Bulgaria was moving towards democratic elections, but still nothing happened in Prague. Finally, unofficial student leaders called a demonstration for November 17, the fiftieth anniversary of the Nazis' execution of nine students in 1939 (see Chapter Six). Not only did the "martyr complex" influence the timing of the demonstration, it also determined its point of departure and planned destination. With a view to marching to Wenceslas Square where Jan Opletal had been shot in October 1939, the students foregathered at the "national shrine" at Vyšehrad. Here they were addressed by their impromptu leaders from the grave of Karel Hynek Mácha, the "founder of Czech poetry" and widely viewed as a "national martyr" from the time of the return of his remains to Prague in 1939: the Velvet Revolution would be a literary-intellectual-theatrical event from start to finish. The students proceeded to march along the Vltava, gathering support as they went until some 50,000 people were involved. Reaching the National Theater, the crowd turned right into Národní třída *en route* for Wenceslas Square: it was though they intended to "take in" as many of the city's national monuments and sites as was possible.

Half way along Národní třída, however, the demonstrators were met by ranks of riot police easily recognizable by their *bílé přilby* (white helmets) reinforced by the *červené barety* (red berets) of the parachute regiment. Committed to the principle of *nechceme násilí* (non-violence) and with the chant of "empty hands" to signal their peaceful intentions, the demonstrators sat down in the street while some of them handed out flowers, sixties-style, to the police. Then suddenly the police charged, and the demonstration turned into what is known, with no little exaggeration, as the *masakr*. A considerable number of demonstrators were injured, but there was no loss of life, though rumors began to spread that a student named "Martin Smid" had been killed by the police. It now appears that both "Martin Smid" and his death were invented by *agents provocateurs*, presumably with a view to inciting the demonstrators to violence which the police would then be justified in repressing.

If this was the tactic, it badly misfired, but the demonstrators were prevented from reaching Wenceslas Square. Under the arches of the Kaňkův dům, not far from the British Council offices on Národní třída, is a bronze relief depicting eight "empty hands" in honor of the demonstration of November 17: no massacre, and no martyrs, but a crucial stage in the toppling of the Communist regime, initiated, it should be stressed, not by Charter 77 or veterans of 1968 but by young people who had been alienated and mobilized as much by the regime's repression of the *alternativní kapely* (alternative rock groups) as by any conventional political program.

It was at this point that the Prague theater was co-opted into the emerging drama to play the part, it has been said, that the Protestant churches had recently played in the toppling of Communism in the German Democratic Republic. While the so-called *masakr* was going on, an injured student from Brno managed to slip away through the streets to a suburban fringe theater called the Junior Klub na Chmelnici—in reality no more than a hall used occasionally for amateur rock concerts—where he knew that the Brno-based Divadlo Na provázku and Ha divadlo (see Chapter Four) were jointly performing a previously banned play, a "living newspaper" called *Rozrazil (Break Through)*. The dramatic arrival of a bleeding student bearing still more dramatic news brought the drama on stage to a standstill, and that night and the following morning, people connected with the theater—actors, directors, authors, stagehands, electricians— telephoned each other to take the unfolding movement a step further. On the afternoon of Saturday November 18, a packed meeting at the Realistické divadlo (Realist Theater) decided to cancel all theater performances until further notice and to open the theaters for public discussion of the political crisis. The next day (Sunday November 19) another meeting at the Činoherní Klub (Drama Club), attended by many signatories of Charter 77 and spokespersons for other dissident groups, set up an umbrella organization called Civic Forum to which Václav Havel was elected chairman. A century and more after the opening of the National Theater, the Prague theater milieu was truly accomplishing its much-vaunted national mission.

From here on things moved with inexorable momentum. On Tuesday November 21, Havel addressed a huge crowd at Wenceslas Square from the balcony of the Melantrich publishing house, an appropriately literary-intellectual site for the (re)union of a writer and

"his" people. On Wednesday November 22, at the initiative of its director, the great scenographer Josef Svoboda (see Chapter Five), the Laterna Magika became Civic Forum's headquarters, and that same evening, at another meeting by the statue of St. Wenceslas, the actor-director Miroslav Macháček committed the National Theater to the dissident cause. Veteran singers of 1968 like Marta Kubišova gave free public concerts, as did the new electrified minstrels of alienated youth, Plastic People, Elektra, Extempore, Stehlik.

With so much public involvement by intellectual-artistic figures, there was a danger that the once fervently "red" suburbs of Žižkov, Nusle and Smíchov would fail to respond, and student and actor "missionaries" were urgently sent out to factories such as Tatra-Smíchov, Kolben-Daněk and Pragation to win over their workforces to "the cause". On the evening of Friday November 24, a week after the mold-breaking student demonstration, Havel again addressed a huge crowd on Wenceslas Square, this time in the company of Alexander Dubček. The combination of new and old oppositional forces was enough to persuade First Secretary Miloš Jakeš to resign later that night in favor of the ex-station master Karel Urbánek, whose inability to put more than two words together in either Czech or Slovak excited the derision of the well-educated crowds. (Among other things, the Velvet Revolution was, or was seen as, the triumph of the smart and the sophisticated over the stupid.)

Over the weekend, there were huge 750,000 strong demonstrations on Letná Plain from which once the gargantuan statue of Stalin had glowered down on to the city. The Prime Minister, Ladislav Adamec, was booed off the platform when he offered to include non-Communists in his cabinet, and on Monday November 27, a two-hour lunch-time strike—shades, once again, of the party of moderate Progress within the Bounds of the Law—was supported by an estimated 57 percent of the population, a figure sufficiently low to suggest that the citizens of Prague were, as ever, playing their cards pretty close to their chests. It was nonetheless enough for parliament to abolish the "leading role" of the Communist party on November 29, thus ending "Marxism-Leninism" as the official state ideology and opening the way to political democracy. Last-ditch attempts by Adamec and others to preserve some kind of power-base for what remained of their party were rejected out of hand by Civic Forum and its supporters, and on December 10, a "Government of National Understanding" was announced by the new (and still Communist) Prime Minister Marián Čalfa.

The principal offices were filled by signatories of Charter 77 and the dissident journalist Jiří Dienstbier was famously summoned from his boiler-house to become foreign minister before returning to keep his boilers burning until a replacement was found. Having sworn in the new government, President Husák resigned, and from the continuing demonstrations the cry "Havel na hrad!", Havel to the castle, arose with a force it was impossible to resist. On December 29, Havel was elected president by a unanimous vote of the Federal Assembly, and his triumph was complete. *Havel je král*, Havel is king: it was evidence of the stability of the city's symbolic geography that the six-week-long movement that brought him to the presidency began, like Bohemia's ancient *králová cesta* or coronation way, at the castle of Vyšehrad and ended in his apotheosis at the castle of Hradčany.

Post-Velvet Prague

The Velvet Revolution presented the Czech situation as a straightforward opposition between heroic, intelligent dissidents versus stupid, mediocre "stalingos" (Jáchym Topol), with the overwhelming majority of the population rallying to the dissident cause at the earliest opportunity. Things were, in reality, much less clear-cut than that, and the new president's first task was to remind "his" people that almost all of them—and, importantly, he did not exempt himself from the charge— had, in one way or another, inhabited the proverbial "gray zone" between outright support of the regime and outright opposition, combining resentful compliance with the familiar Švejkian devices of simulation, manipulation and just getting by. In his New Year address after being chosen as president, Havel spoke of the "decayed moral environment" in which Czechs had lived for the last twenty years (in reality for much longer), during which time "we have become morally ill, because we have become accustomed to saying one thing and thinking another." "In other words," he concluded, "all of us are responsible, each to a different degree, for keeping the totalitarian machine running. None of us is merely a victim of it, because all of us helped to create it together."

It was the kind of situation that might easily have led to a generalized witch-hunt in which erstwhile collaborators, however reluctant their compliance, sought to foist off their guilt on to the abundant supply of ready-made scapegoats: the detested secret police St B, (Státní bezpečnost), party officials, high, middle-ranking and petty, anyone who owed his or her post or privileges or home to the regime, writers who published when others were banned, anyone who worked in the Communist-controlled media, doctors who operated on party members—there really was no end to the possible list. In the event, it was the very open-endedness of guilt that prevented a witch-hunt. The so-called law of "lustration" (*lustrace*), directed essentially against the former secret police, was not passed until early 1991 and was only half-heartedly implemented, to the scandal of many and the relief of many more. The only prominent ex-Communist official to be brought to trial was Miroslav Štěpán, the Prague party leader held responsible for ordering the so-called *masakr* of November 17.

Otherwise, ex-Communists of every position, occupation or hue were able to "re-deploy" themselves in post-Velvet society. The former *nomenklatura* used its secretly accumulated wealth to establish itself in the emerging free-market economy (Prague's numerous casinos are still said to be an ex-Communist monopoly), and ex-secret policemen found that their knowledge, contacts and well-honed information-gathering skills were much in demand under the new dispensation. Many individuals were "outed" as "St B-positive", either as agents, informers or collaborators under coercion, and the discovery that one's wife/husband/lover/son/secretary/employer was part of the immense spider's web of espionage and informing is a recurring theme of post-1989 literature. In general, though, there was an unstated agreement not to push things too far. If Communist power was based, in part, on organized forgetting, post-1989 Czech society has also relied heavily on a tacit conspiracy of oblivion.

Perhaps the first ideal, or illusion, of the Velvet Revolution to succumb to the inexorable restoration of the "gray zone" was Civic Forum's belief that it was a moral, existential movement that somehow transcended mere "politics". Its ascendancy confirmed by the parliamentary elections of June 1990, Civic Forum did not constitute itself formally as a political party until the beginning of

1991 (much to the dismay, incidentally, of President Havel), by which time it was already polarizing into a broadly social-democratic center, led by Foreign Minister and ex-boilerman Jiří Dienstbier, and a free-market right led by the increasingly visible and vocal finance minister Václav Kraus. In April 1991 the split came to a head and resulted in the setting up of two separate parties, the centrist Civic Movement (OH) and the right-wing Civic Democratic Party (ODS). Elections in June 1992 brought the ODS to power, and Klaus, a convinced disciple of Milton Friedman and ardent admirer of Margaret Thatcher, embarked upon dismantling the still largely state-owned economy and replacing it with a vouchers-propelled free-market system. The break with Slovakia in 1993—unconfirmed by referendum and not apparently wanted by either Czechs or Slovaks as a whole—was widely interpreted as being motivated by Klaus's desire to "ditch" the backward eastern portion of the federation in order to facilitate the entrance of its more dynamic western part into "Europe". The ODS remained the leading party after the 1996 parliamentary elections, but lost its overall majority. Further elections brought the new Czech Social Democratic Party (CSSD) under Miloš Zeman to power in 1998, and the new parliament re-elected Havel as president for a further five years. Parliamentary elections in June 2002 confirmed the CSSD as the senior partner in a coalition government, committed to advancing the Czech Republic's entry into the European Union as quickly as possible. Political commentators, meanwhile, observed that the elections represented a victory for "political elites" and a further sidelining of civil society.

After the carnivalesque interlude of November-December 1989, all this reads depressingly, and predictably, like the day-to-day, year-to-year electoral politics of the "Europe" that the former dissidents were so anxious to "rejoin". Melancholy at the return, in a new guise, of the familiar "gray zone" has been strongest among the signatories of Charter 77, almost all of whom—Havel excepted—withdrew from the public arena after the elections of June 1992. In a prescient article published in *samizdat* in September 1989, Jiřina Šiklová predicted that, were the Communist regime to fall, the erstwhile dissidents would quickly lose out to the "gray zone". Having been "out of the system" for so long, Chartists would be at a disadvantage vis-a-vis those who had operated within it. Their unity would soon go and, along with it, "their uniqueness, their moral superiority, their aura of being persecuted and ostracized, a certain non-responsibility for everything that is wrong in politics and society." Correspondingly and conversely, she wrote, "the most will be gained by those who stood aside, not manning either side of the barricades, those who just sat back and waited, that is, those in the gray zone." Šiklová returned to her theme in 1990 to complain that

> last year (the dissidents) were still the Antigones among the silent citizens of Thebes. Today, everyone in Thebes is saying that it would be right to give Polynices a decent burial, and that they had always thought so. When we were dissidents, relationships were clear, the way they are in fairy tales: evil was evil and good was good, and those who were in the opposition were the freest of all.

When we were dissidents... Now everything becomes gray and confused once again, and it is indeed a climate of grayness, monotony and sterility, often figured by the image of atmospheric pollution and environmental blight, that suffuses the post-1989 writing of many ex-Chartists, notably the novels and stories of Ivan Klíma, author of *My Golden Trades* (1992), *Waiting for the Dark, Waiting for the Light* (1994), and *The Ultimate Intimacy* (1996). These novels' mood is not substantially different from that of his *Love and Garbage* of 1986—except, of course, that now the problem is much deeper than a mere political regime. These are books to be read rather than summarized, though their general tone is summed up by the fate of Pavel in *Waiting for the Dark, Waiting for the Light*: a television camera-man in November 1989 recording the "almost sexual" ecstasy on people's faces as they march through the streets, Pavel is by the end of the next year reduced to filming simulated sexual rapture in free Czechoslovakia's booming pornography industry. Even Havel publicly (and controversially) wondered whether he had not, in a way, been personally happier under Communism and, as early as July 1990, confessed to feeling "a sensation of the absurd: what Sisyphus might have felt if one fine day his boulder stopped, rested on the hill-top, and failed to roll back down. It was the sensation of a Sisyphus whose life had lost its old purpose and hadn't yet developed a new one."

"Absurdistan" was the name dissidents had given to Communist Czechoslovakia. Now, writers, artists and theater people, above all, had to engage with a new kind of absurdity characterized by loss of status, loss of role, loss of audience and, in not a few cases, loss of income as well. The huge lines waiting outside bookstores to purchase new publications—a common sight in Communist Prague—were rarely seen now. It was as though when nothing was permitted, everything was read; now that everything was permitted, nothing, or very little, was read. The refusal to return to Czechoslovakia of the country's two most famous writers-in-exile, Škvorecký and Kundera, was taken by many as symptomatic of the current social, political and artistic impasse, as was the death (by accidental or voluntary defenestration) of Bohumil Hrabal in 1997. With Forman also electing to stay in the United States, the overwhelming majority of films showing in Prague cinemas were of American origin.

Yet despite the preponderance of foreign films in Czech cinemas, there are signs that the local film industry is undergoing a renaissance, notably through the work of Jan Svěrák, the director of the Oscar-winning *Kolya* (1996), discussed further on pages 229-230. Most recently, his *Dark Blue World* (*Tmavomodrý Svět*, 2001), tells the story of two Czech airmen who flee to Britain in 1939, join the RAF together, and then become estranged when they both fall in love with the same Englishwoman, played by Tara Fitzgerald. Only one survives the war, full of guilt that, despite their rivalry, his comrade died trying to save him. On his return to Czechoslovakia, the survivor finds that his Czech fiancée has married and that even his dog has forgotten him; to complete his dereliction, he is imprisoned after "Victorious February" on the catch-all charge of "cosmopolitanism", i.e. of having spent the war years in Britain and not the Soviet Union. The film was hugely successful, taking over 30 million crowns in is first month alone, and has revived interest in a period that, at one time, seemed to have disappeared in the collective post-1989 conspiracy of oblivion.

Despite such successes, the performing arts in general have experienced a lean time since 1989. Even the theater, the most dynamic and, because of state subsidies, the most prosperous art form in Communist Prague, began to feel the pinch of the free-market system. Already in spring 1990, theater attendances were reported to be dropping, and the famous E.F. Burian Theater Company, dating back to Burian's original D34 project (see Chapter Four), closed at the end of the 1990-91 season. If its collapse could be attributed in part to its (and the late Burian's) Communist past, the same could not be said of Otamar Krejča's Theater beyond the Gate and Karel Kříž's Labyrinth Theater (formerly the Realist Theater), both focuses of opposition before 1989, which expired in 1994 and 1998 respectively, unable to withstand the double blow of audience decline and the withdrawal of state subsidies.

The alternative theater tradition is kept alive by the Theater Viola (opposite the Nová scéna on Národní třída) and the Theater Ungelt on the square of that name behind Týn Church, but the pre-1989 sense of almost conspiratorial solidarity between performers and audience cannot readily be recreated in the absence of external constraints. Jean-Paul Sartre famously said that French people—and French writers in particular—had never been freer than under German occupation. Czech writers, artists and theater people may not have been free under the Communist regime, but they knew how too exploit their unfreedom creatively, knowing that it gave them a role and a bond with their publics. It would be naïve to look for that kind of community in present-day Prague.

Changing Faces

"La forme d'une ville change plus vite, hélas, que le coeur d'un mortel." (The form of a city changes, more quickly alas, than the heart of a mortal). Thus Baudelaire—much admired by Czech modernists—on the transformation of his native Paris in the mid-nineteenth century. To this "mortal heart", returning to Prague in 2002 after an interval of almost thirty years, it seemed that precisely the opposite had occurred in its case. The form of the city had remained remarkably constant, at least in its core of Staré Město, Nové Město and Malá Strana, while its human content had changed enormously, not least in the huge number of tourists thronging daily along the Hradčany-Charles Bridge-Old Town Square axis. True, as Jáchym Topol has written in his novella *A Trip to the Train Station* (1995), the city is changing, but less in respect of its form than in the use existing buildings are put to:

Old broken walls were torn down, ads pasted up over cracked, mysterious maps in the roughcast plaster, sidewalks were newly paved, barriers of sheet metal and wood that had stood for years vanished overnight. New owners took charge of dilapidated buildings and tried to convert them into hotels, pubs, wholesale glass and crystal shops, travel agencies. Pants, coats, wooden toys, hot dogs, newspapers, gingerbread and gold were sold on the street out of ground-floor apartments, and the idea of declaring income was a joke. Nothin' sleazy 'bout money, said the sleazeballs, and they parceled up the streets and squares to fit their stands. On the periphery of the city and in the outlying districts, new centers sprang up around discos, mini department stores, new bars and restaurants.

To a remarkable extent, the city has indeed, in Topol's words, "peeled off its stern and gloomy face of the past, the mask of rotting Bolshevism, and replaced it with a thousand others." It is an incomparably more cheerful place to be than in 1970 and 1973, the dates of the present writer's first visits, but, insofar as it increasingly resembles any other "western" capital city, in certain respects less interesting, or interesting to the extent—the very considerable extent—that the past is visible in the present. The architectural fabric of the central areas has changed hardly at all, but every other secessionist or modernist building on Wenceslas Square or Na příkope seems now to house a branch of Marks & Spencers, Gap or Next, while, for members of the new elite, local or foreign, there is no shortage of high-class international fashion: Hugo Boss on Jungmannovo náměsti, Red or Dead on Myslíkova, Gianni Versace at Celetná 7, a couple of doors up from where Hermann Kafka opened his haberdashery in 1896. How he would respond to his son's face or profile on everything from table mats to T-shirts and coffee mugs is anyone's guess.

More striking is the enrichment (to some) or the dilution (to others, including the far-right Republican Party led by Miroslav Sládek) of the remarkably homogeneous and monolingual population of post-1945 Prague. Some Vietnamese and Laotians had come to Prague in the 1970s and 1980s under government sponsorship, but it was the "explosion of time" in 1989—first manifested in the arrival of East German refugees mentioned above—that brought to Prague an unprecedented number of foreigners, not so much (with the exception of the Roma—gypsies—from Slovakia) from adjacent middle European countries but from further afield: Romanians, Bulgarians, Bosnians, Croatians, Ukrainians, Russians, Armenians, Chinese. Most of these were, initially, seeking to move on to "the west", but since Germany, in particular, refused to take immigrants from what it defined as a "safe" country, a category now including Czechoslovakia, a high proportion of the new arrivals remained in the country. By 1994, there were (excluding Roma) 100,000 foreigners with long-term or permanent rights of residency in the Czech Republic, 5,000 with applications pending, and an estimated 15,000 illegal immigrants; 90 percent of all these were from former Communist countries, and a high proportion came to Prague, and to the decaying suburbs of Žižkov and Smíchov in particular.

Žižkov and Smíchov had also had pockets of Roma for several decades, but the pockets became whole communities after 1989 when Roma, fleeing harsh treatment and poor prospects in Slovakia, fled to the western part of the federation, many of them undoubtedly hoping to move still further west. Like other arrivals, however, they found themselves blocked and, after the Velvet Divorce, denied citizenship rights if they had a criminal record over the previous five years. Many of them did, and this so-called "Romany clause", which did not apply to other categories of immigrant, was widely interpreted as a device to marginalize the Roma population, better still to persuade it to move back or on. Now numbering about 250,000 in the Czech Republic as a whole, Roma are almost automatically associated by ethnic Czechs with crime (particularly pick-pocketing and mugging), social parasitism, violence and disease. It is as though, having refrained (with good reason) from scapegoating each other, Czechs are now engaged in projecting all their fears, guilt and frustrations on to a displaced out-group from "the east". Unable or unwilling to go back to Slovakia, Hungary or Romania, Roma are prevented from moving onwards by careful screening at Ruzyně airport where, for example, the British immigration service set up an office in 2001 in order, in the words of the British ambassador, to stop "the continued, systematic abuse of our immigration and asylum system by some Czech citizens." He, and everyone else, knew that, by "some Czech citizens", he meant Roma, 1,223 having applied for asylum in Britain in the first six months of the year. In one ten-day period in December 2001, 85 people, almost all of them Roma, were prevented from boarding British-bound flights at Ruzyně.

The Underside
Still more alarming to Praguers is the city's growing importance as a hub of international crime. And conceivably of international terrorism as well, for in the autumn of 2002 Czech newspapers were full of the several visits that Mohammed Atta apparently paid to Prague in the months preceding September 11. Some of the much-touted "mafias" are local Prague outfits, but the more serious operations are run by

Albanians, Russians and Ukrainians who quickly moved into the vacuum created by the overthrow of the totalitarian regime and were able cannily to exploit the opportunities opened up by full-scale privatization. The large number of Chinese restaurants in Prague, many with never a customer to be seen, are pointed to as evidence of "triad" involvement, and every new addition to the hotchpotch of refugees and migrants is believed to bring with it its quota of criminals. The smuggling of drugs, cigarettes, people and arms (that traditional Czech export) is the principal activity, so widespread in its ramifications that two top British specialists in organized crime were recently seconded to the Czech Interior Ministry. Within Prague itself, organized prostitution involving women of every nationality and none ("I noticed the movement of nations began in the brothels," says the narrator of Topol's *City Sister Silver*) flourishes both in city's innumerable sex-clubs, openly advertised in the press, and around the old Hussite church of St. Martin-in-the-Wall (see p.12) and the adjoining Perlová and Na Perštýně streets. There are also alleged paedophilia rings, and an avalanche of pornography was one of the first consequences of the abolition of censorship after November 1989. None of all this— especially prostitution—was exactly unknown under the previous regime, but, like everything else, it has become more public, more garish, more visible.

This entire underside of Prague life is vividly, extravagantly, captured in Jáchym Topol's novel *City Sister Silver* referred to several times before. Born in 1962, Topol is the son of the well-known playwright Josef Topol (born 1935) and is, by birth and upbringing, very much a member of that intellectual elite whose hopes, dreams, failures and sufferings, both in love and in politics, sometimes seemed the only theme of the Czech literature written between the early 1960s and the fall of Communism. Topol junior might well have followed this well-trodden literary tradition, but has broken with it decisively in terms of subject, setting and language alike. Published in 1994, *City Sister Silver* is set in "bad old Prague 5", in other words the working-class suburb of Smíchov, in the "years 1, 2, 3 (1990-92) when we came crawlin outta the Sewer (forty years of Communist rule, also known as the 'pre-days'), slowly and cautiously, so the air wouldn't get us right away." With the fall of the "stalingos" and the "explosion of time", everything that had been held underground or kept to the margins moved to the surface and center of things: "chrome-domes" (skinheads) and "hitlers" (neo-Nazis), junkies, criminals, prostitutes, and wave upon wave of migrants/refugees, "Yugos", Kazakhs, Armenians, Azeris, Cambodians, all of them hoping to get to the "desirable states" and for whom even Prague is some technological, consumerist paradise: "Look! The Bulgarian cried. The supermarket doors opened all by themselves!" Also disgorged by the Sewer is the "little entente" of weirdoes and drop-outs, the "Knights of the Secrets", whose lives in the crannies and crevices of Smíchov provide the proliferating, dislocated "plot" of the novel: Bohler, Micka, David, Lady Laos, Černa, above all the anonymous cacoglossic narrator himself.

But *City Sister Silver* is remarkable not only for exploring the underside of Prague life that had previously been excluded even from *samizdat* literature, but for doing so in the "dog-language" of Smíchov and Žižkov themselves, a kind of creolized Czech full of neologisms, puns and imported nonce-words, a "tongue that was to have been dropped, but its time has yet to come", the convulsive language of a convulsive rebirth into history: "I knew that Czech had exploded together with time." Here, for example, is how Topol (and his brilliant translator Alex Zucker) breathes new life into the classic Prague theme of puppets, automata and toys, fresh specimens of which arrived in the city's shop windows with the explosion of time:

> *Toyfils [cf German Teufel = Devil] filled the shelves, and those freaks were alive! They busily communicated amongst themselves, the Thinking Machines whirling about spewing flames at frightening speed, Draculas jockeying Spiders, Gargoyles of Zador bearing down on the valiant Batman, the Mutant King and the Purple People-Easter chatting away in the corner, and that stupid Barbie, the robot clone, may AIDS drag her into its pestilent grave!*

While *City Sister Silver* may lack the structure and coherence of the finest Prague art, it marks a radical and welcome departure from the kind of writing that dominated Czech fiction from the early 1960s until 1989. In contrast to the hesitations of the theater and cinema, still to redefine their role within the new context, Topol has daringly opened up a way forward with his "blather, babel, and babylon", "a sort of lesser pornography with a humanist spin, and Pragocentric to boot."

City of Tears

Prague is without doubt one of the most beautiful cities in Europe, its central core virtually unaffected either by war damage or post-war "development". Of almost uninterrupted interest from Hradčany in the west to Náměstí Republiky in the east and from Josefov in the north to Vyšehrad in the south, it contains, within the space of three or four square miles, four individual sites which must, by any standards, count among the finest in Europe: the castle-cathedral complex on Hradčany itself, Charles Bridge, Old Town Square and the Old Jewish Cemetery. But it has been one of this book's principal objectives to suggest that there is much more to Prague architecturally than the Baroque treasure-house of international tourism, and if it prompts some of its readers to hunt out Plečnik's Church of the Most Sacred Heart in Vinohrady or Gočar's Czech Legionnaires' Bank on Na poříčí, then it will not have been written in vain, for these are great buildings which deserve to be far better known than they are.

In addition to its clutch of great architects (Polívka, Janák, Chochol and Novotný as well as Plečnik and Gočar), Prague has produced and/or inspired some of the most interesting modern painting and sculpture created outside the great modernist centers of Paris, Barcelona and Vienna (Bílek, Kubišta, Gutfreund and Toyen), fostered one of the most remarkable collective artistic endeavors of the twentieth century (Devětsil) and, in cubo-expressionism, rondocubism, social civilism and poetism, given an invigorating local twist to pan-European art movements. It has made a major art of photography (Rössler, Sudek, Štyrský, Medková) and, through Teige and Kolár, opened up new possibilities for the combination of image and text. In parallel with the Prague School of Linguistics, the best Prague art of the twentieth century has shown an impressively consistent preoccupation with combining imaginative freedom with coherence of form. At certain times, notably in the 1960s, Prague theater was the equal of any in Europe, and in Radok, Krejča and Svoboda produced three of the great scenographic innovators of the twentieth century. Somewhat earlier, the Liberated Theater represented arguably the most successful attempt anywhere in Europe to translate the spirit of Dada on to the stage. For a tragically brief period, again in the 1960s, Prague was producing films as interesting and moving, if not as technically innovative, as anything being made in Paris at that time.

Finally, Prague is without question one of the great classical music centers of Europe, with, in addition, a distinctive local jazz scene and, in the 1980s, a clutch of rock musicians who, as much as Charter 77, opened the way for the Velvet Revolution of November 1989. Just as there is more to Prague architecture than the Gothic and the Baroque, more to twentieth-century Prague painting than the over-hyped Alfons Mucha, so there is more to Prague music than the *New World Symphony* and *Má vlast*, and if, once again, any reader is prompted by this book to track down the music of Jaroslav Ježek, Vítězslava Kaprálová or the eclectic jazz master Jiří Stivín, one of its various objectives will have been achieved.

In literature, the record is perhaps rather more mixed, and it is important not to equate "Prague" with "Czechoslovakia", for while most Czech writers have inevitably gravitated to Prague and written about it, not all are necessarily "Prague writers" in a truly visceral sense. This is particularly true of the three most prominent post-war Czech novelists—Hrabal, Kundera and Škvorecký—all of whom have lived in Prague (Hrabal for the best part of his life), set novels partly or wholly in Prague and treated Prague themes, but whose inspiration remains, in the best sense of the word, provincial rather than metropolitan. None of Kundera's "Prague novels" is as totally persuasive as his "Moravian" masterpiece *The Joke*, and Škvorecký is really much more the novelist of small town Bohemia than of the Mother of Cities itself. On the other hand, the vision of Hašek is Prague to the core, even when Švejk's "anabasis" takes him not only round Bohemia but into Russia as well, and, since the 1960s, Kafka's Pragocentricity has been as comprehensively studied as it was comprehensively neglected before.

Yet there is still no great "Prague novel" or "Prague novelist" in the sense that, whatever their origins, Dickens was a London and Balzac a Paris novelist before all else. No Czech novelist has yet done for Prague what Alfred Döblin's *Berlin Alexanderplatz* (1929) did for Berlin or Carlo Emilio Gadda's *That Awful Mess on the Via Merulana* (1957) for Rome: namely, create a synoptic image of the whole of the city rather than focus obsessively on one of its parts, in the case of Prague fiction its intellectual and professional elite. Perhaps, given the huge breakthrough made by *City Sister Silver*, that lacuna will shortly be filled.

If one turns to the poetry of Prague—or to that portion of it that has been translated—there is a similar sense of possibility as yet unfulfilled. Of the three outstanding figures, Nezval, Seifert and Holan, Nezval's poetry has weathered no better than that of any other European surrealist poet. Its declamatory tone soon wearies, and its cascading images seem not so much hallucinatory as approximate, hurtling one after the other in inexhaustible profusion, yet failing to hit home either individually or collectively. Take the opening lines of "City with Towers" (1936):

> *o hundred-towered Prague*
> *city with fingers of all the saints*
> *with fingers made for swearing falsely*
> *with fingers made of fire & hail*
> *with a musician's fingers*
> *with shining fingers of a woman lying on her back*
> *with fingers brushing up against the stars on night's abacus*
> *with fingers from which the evening gushes fingers tightly clasped*
> *with fingers without nails*
> *with fingers of the smallest babes & pointed blades of grass*
> *with maytime fingers & with fingers out of graves*
> *with beggar women's fingers & an entire form at school with thunder &*
>   *lightening fingers*
> *with purple crocus fingers*
> *with fingers up in the Castle & on old women playing harps*
> *with fingers made of gold*
> *fingers through which a black bird whistles & a storm*
> *with fingers of naval harbors & of a dancing school for girls*

And so on for a further forty-odd lines that take in (along with "fingers of asparagus", "fingers of the inquisition", "fingers on which a bee has landed") "fingers of a chimney sweeper and the chapel of the Loreta", "fingers of a coral morning and of the view from Petřín

Tower", "hacked off fingers of the rain and of Týn Church on the glove of twilight"—so many fingers (and occasional thumbs) that the much-vaunted "magic" or "mystery" of Prague has somehow slipped between them. With Seifert the problem is not so much a surfeit of images as a lack of them. In his discursive, charming way, he *tells* us how beautiful his native city is ("It is mine/and I also believe it is miraculous") and how "without /her ancient voice/I would be silent/as the bird/called the kiwi" ("View from Charles Bridge", 1983) while never quite articulating what that "ancient voice" is telling him or what precisely is "miraculous" about his "gallant city, bravest of the brave/eternally enshrined in mankind's story." Paradoxically, it is the obsessively inner-directed poetry of Vladimír Holan, so much more precise in its imagery than that of either Nezval or Seifert, ("Above Valdštejn Palace/male stains shone on the sheet of the moon"), that best captures what it feels like to be in Prague rather than above it, among the walls, the weeds, the lampposts, looking up to Hradčany, like K. to his castle, for an impossible deliverance.

City of Tears (Seifert), *Rainy-fingered Prague* (Nezval): it is the melancholy of Prague, as much as its beauty, that haunts the imagination, or, rather, the melancholy beneath its beauty, that sense of a suffering, centuries-long, that has never really been confronted or expressed but rather repressed, evaded and denied, leaving the city still somehow suspended, as so often in the past, between life and death, like the inevitable puppets, statues and other such effigies whose presence can sometimes eclipse that of the living human beings on the streets. It is this sense of a city in limbo that is captured to perfection in one of the finest novels about Prague by a non-Czech writer, the French novelist Sylvie Germain's *The Weeping Woman on the Streets of Prague* (1992). Here an anonymous, limping woman, forever in tears, makes a series of unscheduled "apparitions", like some negative Madonna, on the streets of the city. A vast, unfinished being, part female Golem, part Comenian pilgrim in drag, her tears are the tears of humanity itself, endlessly flowing back into the stones and cobbles from which she has sprung. Or else, the city has been drained of all life, as it seemed to be to Patrick Leigh Fermor when he visited Prague in the course of his famous walk from London to Paris in 1934. Recognizing, in *A Time of Gifts* (1977), that he had evoked only the city's architecture, he wrote:

I seem to have cleared the streets. They are as empty as the thoroughfares in an architectural print. Nothing but a few historical phantoms survive; a muffled drum, a figure from a book and an echo of Utraquists rioting a few squares away—the milling citizens, the rushing traffic vanish and the voices of the bilingual city sink to a whisper.

On the one hand, the city contains "an unusual array of grand and unenigmatic monuments" whose very familiarity makes Prague seem curiously remote. On the other, it is "scattered with darker, more reticent, less easily decipherable clues", moments when "very detail seemed the tip of a phalanx of inexplicable phantoms." Ghosts, enigmas, mysteries, an oppressive, even sinister, sense of "history (pressing) heavily upon it"—everything, it would seem, except a living, breathing, active city. Perhaps it is this sense of human absence that makes Jindřich Štyrský's totally depopulated photographs by far the most telling visual record of twentieth-century Prague.

Prague is a city inhabited by death as no other in Europe: there are even, or so Angelo Maria Ripellino tells us, "sweets that both look like and are called little coffins (*rakvičky*)", a distillation, as it were, of what he elsewhere calls "the inordinate gloom and tyranny of the city on the Vltava." Visiting Prague in August 1934, André Gide wrote, somewhat predictably, of a "glorious, painful and tragic city," sustained by "a sort of mystical vehemence," its beauty not so much marred as enhanced by the rain that seems to have fallen throughout his visit. But beneath his hotel window a less poetic melancholy is revealed, and one that seems to go to the core of the city's double experience of tragedy and denial: "Mute gathering of a crowd around an unfortunate news-dealer who is weeping, in a recess of a wall, turning his back to life, his face hidden in his upraised arm, a picture of the blackest despair." Two years later, in the otherwise exalting if tragic summer of 1936, Albert Camus spent a miserable week in the city, trying to find some kind of "homeland" in its "sumptuous Baroque churches" but "emerging emptier and in deeper despair after this disappointing encounter with myself", then wandering along the Vltava and spending hour after hour "in the immense silent and empty district of the Hradchin [Hradčany]." "At sunset in the shadow of its cathedral and palaces my lonely step echoed along the streets," but, back at his hotel, he learns that in the room next to his a man has been found dead, undetected by anyone for several days: "A man no different from many others, short and fat. He had doubtless been dead for some time. And life had gone on in the hotel, until the waiter had had the idea of calling him. He had arrived in this hotel without suspecting anything and he had died alone." Mute, anonymous death, death not in Venice but in Prague, death without tragic catharsis, the tragedy of the absence of tragedy...

Sixty years on, and the pall of melancholy seems not greatly to have lifted, at least on the evidence of Jan Svĕrák's exquisite and hugely successful film *Kolya* (1996). At fifty-five and a bachelor, Louka, a cellist banned from performing with the Prague Philharmonic for unspecified reasons (we are at the very tail-end of Communist rule), makes some kind of living by playing at cremations and picking out in gold lettering the names on headstones in Prague's principal cemetery. To pay off his debts, he contracts an arranged marriage with a Russian woman who, having obtained Czech citizenship, promptly absconds to "the west", leaving Louka with ultimate responsibility for her five-year-old son Kolya, who speaks only Russian. With all the subtlety, irony and pathos that one associates with the great Czech films of the mid-1960s, Svĕrák explores the developing relationship between Louka (played by his own father Zdenĕk Svĕrák, who also wrote the script) and Kolya, along with the decidedly mixed reaction of his fellow Czechs towards his newly acquired "son". With Kolya in tow, Louka earns his crust at the crematorium, accompanying his off-and-on girl-friend Klara to the strains of Dvorak's heart-rending setting of "The Lord is my Shepherd", while sometimes allowing his bow to play unscheduled glissandi up her skirt as the oven doors open and the coffin glides in. In one of the film's most poignant moments, Kolya stages a mock cremation of his own with the aid, almost inevitably, of Louka's home puppet theater. As Louka practices his cello, Kolya, reciting Psalm 23 to himself, places one of the puppets in a shoe box, wraps it in a pair of black lace panties left by one or another of Louka's girl-friends, draws a black cross on the lid and pushes the "coffin" through the puppet theater curtains, closing them afterwards like the crematorium doors. Louka is questioned by the police concerning his sham marriage—that one of his interrogators is called Novotny is no accident at all—and, when a social worker threatens to "repossess" Kolya and return him to the USSR, "father" and "son" take to the road in Louka's dilapidated Trabant, ending up in one of Bohemia's spa-towns where Louka gets a job in a café orchestra.

It is here, away from the capital, that Louka hears the news of the November 17 demonstration: like the Czech people as a whole, he has missed yet again the rendezvous with history. He and Kolya return to Prague and take part, belatedly, in the anti-regime demonstrations and marches, finding themselves alongside Louka's erstwhile interrogators who have deftly switched sides. Louka is reinstated in the orchestra and, with the word *Pravda vítězí* half visible behind him, takes part in the great performance of *Má vlast* conducted by the returned maestro Rafael Kubelík.

Cemeteries, gold, puppets, music: *Kolya* is nothing less than an anthology of Prague themes, with windows, the panorama from Petřín tower and the modern labyrinth of the underground, where "father" and "son" are separated from each other, thrown in for good measure. And what of the little boy who, through living with Louka, has become almost a Czech? In the wake of the Velvet Revolution, he is reunited with his mother and, together, they return to "the west". The departure lounge doors close behind them like those of the crematorium, leaving Louka, like the Czech people, free of all ties, wondering what he will do with the rest of his life, already faintly nostalgic for the trials of unfreedom. With Kolya he has known the greatest joy of his life, but, like all Prague joys, it has been stolen from death and, with its passing, the old melancholy returns:

> *Joy!*
> *There is joy, there really is.*
> *And he felt it not as something merciless*
> *which rushes on us [...]*
> *no, what he felt was a quiet, simple, unfounded joy,*
> *given rather than granted for an hour,*
> *the joy of a man walking over a bridge*
> *who will go on singing for ever ...*

But it was enough for the wind to toss a withered leaf
at his feet
And the bridge was overloaded.
> (Vladimír Holan, "Eodem anno pons ruptus est")

❋   ❋   ❋

In early February 2003, Václav Havel's second, and constitutionally final, term as president of the Czech Republic came to an end, with the Czech parliament struggling to elect a successor with the necessary majority. In the last weeks of his presidency, admirers of Havel, full of nostalgia for the clarities and certainties of the now far distant Velvet Revolution, erected a huge red neon heart on the scaffolding encasing one of the towers of Hradčany, within view, presumably, of the president's apartment. The heart was no gratuitous symbol, but rather closely associated with the Havel himself (it is something of a trademark). Shortly afterwards, a group of Prague students climbed up the scaffolding, removed or obscured the left half of the heart-shaped outline and mounted a single red lamp beneath the remaining right half, thus neatly transforming the heart into a question mark. It was a typical Prague gesture, drawing on that tradition of deconstructive humor that finds a way of turning every sign on its side, if not on its head. (Take the famous statue of the Soviet tank in Smíchov painted a lurid pink by the situationist artist David Cerný in—with equally Czech caution— the summer of 1991.) Out of official celebration and commemoration the modified icon creates a counter-text of opposition and irony. It also enables this book on the most secret, ambiguous—and often the most magical—European city to conclude on a suitable note of interrogation and dubiety.

❋   ❋   ❋

Further Reading

Only works in English are cited and the place of publication, unless otherwise stated, is London. The titles of individual novels etc. have not been included here. Dates are those of the actual editions used.

General

The best general book on Prague is without doubt Angelo Maria Ripellino's *Magic Prague* (Picador, 1994). It is not, however, the easiest of reads, and anyone wanting a good historical overview of the city would be advised to begin with Peter Demetz, *Prague in Black and Gold. The History of a City* (Penguin, 1997), with the proviso that, like *Magic Prague*, it effectively stops in 1948. Derek Sayer's *The Coasts of Bohemia. A Czech History* (Princeton: Princeton UP, 1998) is a first-rate cultural history, strongly Pragocentric, and particularly good on the construction of Czech national identity; again, it does not take the story up to the present, halting around the mid-950s. Of the numerous guides to the city I have found Rob Humphreys's *Prague. The Rough Guide* (2000) especially valuable: accurate, informative, and embodying a provocative and individual view of the city.

Chapter One

The collective work *Prague. Eleven Centuries of Architecture* (Prague: PAV Publishers, 1996) by Jaroslava Staňkova and others is an authoritative guide to all aspects of the city's architecture. *Charles Bridge* (Gallery of the City of Prague, 1991) by Karel Neubert and others is an exceptionally detailed architectural and iconographical study that has been extensively drawn on here. Plečnik is the subject of two impressive monographs: Peter Krečič, *Plečnik. The Complete Works* (Academy Editions, 1993) and Damjan Prelovšek, *Jože Plečnik, 1872-1957. Architectura Perennis* (New Haven, CT: 1997). The Prague of Rudolf II is fully studied in R.J.W. Evans, *Rudolf II and His World. A Study in Intellectual History 1576-1612* (Thames and Hudson, 1997) and in Thomas Da Costa Kaufmann, *The School of Prague. Painting at the Court of Rudolf II* (Chicago: Chicago UP, 1988). Werner Kriegeskorte, *Arcimboldo* (Cologne: Taschen, 2000) is a perceptive and well-illustrated study of this exceptional painter.

Chapter Two

Most studies of German-speaking Czechs focus on the so-called Sudetenland Germans. An exception is Gary B. Cohen's thorough and insightful *The Politics of Ethnic Survival. Germans in Prague 1861-1914* (Princeton: Princeton UP, 1981). There are useful essays on ethnic politics in Czechoslovakia in *Bohemia in History*, edited by Mikuláš Teich (Cambridge: Cambridge UP, 1998); Helena Krejčová's "Czechs and Jews" (pp. 344-63) is a particularly valuable overview. "Prague— City of Three Peoples" by Hans Tramer (*Leo Baeck Institute Year Book*, IX (1964), pp. 305-39) gives a vivid sense of pre-1914 Prague. For a history of Jews in pre-modern Prague, see Otto Muneles (ed.), *The Prague Ghetto in the Renaissance Period* (Jewish State Museum in Prague, 1965). The best introduction to the question of the Golem is the chapter (pp. 158-204) in Gerschom Scholem's well-known study, *On the Kabbalah and its Symbolism* (Routledge and Kegan Paul, 1965). The Golem as literary theme is well studied in Arnold L. Goldsmith, *The Golem Remembered, 1909-80. Variations on a Jewish Legend* (Detroit: Wayne State UP, 1981). Joza Karas, *Music in Terezín 1941-1945* (Stuyvesant, NY: Pendragon Press, 1985) is the best study of the whole subject of Terezín as well as of its remarkable musicians.

Chapter Three

There is an immense critical and biographical literature on Kafka. As a biography, Ronald Hayman's *K. A Biography of Kafka* sets Kafka well in the context of Prague literary life, and, of the many critical introductions to his work, both Erich Heller, *Kafka* (Fontana/Collins, 1974) and Anthony Thorlby, *Kafka. A Study* (Heinemann, 1972) are among the clearest and most insightful. More challenging and contentious is Gilles Deleuze and Félix Guattan, *Kafka. Toward a Minor Literature*, (Minneapolis: Minnesota UP, 1986). *Franz Kafka and Prague* (Prague: Vitalis, 1998) by Harald Salfellner is by far the best of several works on that subject. The standard English-language biography of Hašek is *The Bad Bohemian. The Life of Jaroslav Hašek, Creator of the Good Soldier Švejk* by Cecil Parrott (Bodley Head, 1978).

Chapter Four

The best overview of theater in Prague is Jarka M. Burian's *Modern*

Czech Theater. Reflector and Conscience of a Nation (Iowa City: Iowa UP, 2000). For a shorter introduction, see Barbara Day, "Czech Theater from the National Revival to the Present Day", in *Theater Quarterly*, 11: 7 (August 1986), pp. 250-74, and also her preface to *Czech Plays. Modern Czech Drama* (Nick Hern Books, 1994). The National Theater project is exhaustively studied in Stanley B. Kimball, *Czech Nationalism. A Study of the National Theater Movement 1845-83* (Urbana: University of Illinois Press, 1964). On puppetry, see Alice Dubská, *Czech Puppet Theater over the Centuries* (International Institute of Puppet Arts in Prague, no date) which takes the story as far as 1945. Brian Large's *Smetana* (Duckworth, 1970) gives a lively overview of Czech musical nationalism in the nineteenth century. On jazz in Czechoslovakia, see Josef Škvorecký's introductory essay to *The Base Saxophone* (Chatto and Windus, 1978).

Chapter Five

There are a number of general works on Czech modernism, principally exhibition catalogues, that can be strongly recommended: *Devětsil. Czech Avant-Garde Art, Architecture and Design of the 1920s and 1930s* (Museum of Modern Art, Oxford, 1990), *Czech Modernism 1900-1945* (Museum of Fine Arts Houston, 1990) and, for a somewhat earlier period, *Poetry and Ecstasy. Prague 1900* (Van Gogh Museum, Amsterdam, 1999). For secessionist architecture in Prague, see *Prague and Art Nouveau* (Prague: V RAJI, 1995) by Marie Vitochová and others. A selection of Karel Teige's writings is to be found, together with a valuable introduction and examples of his photomontages, in Erich Dluhosch and Rotislav Švácha, *Karel Teige 1900-51. L'Enfant Terrible of the Czech Modernist Avant-Garde* (Cambridge, Mass: MIT Press, 1999). On individual artists, see *František Bílek, 1872-1941* (City Gallery of Prague, 2000), Karel Srp, *Jindřich Štyrský* (Prague: Torst, 2001) and the same author's *Toyen* (City Gallery of Prague, 2000). On modernist poetry, Alfred French's *The Poets of Prague. Czech Poetry between the Wars* (Oxford: Oxford UP) is useful but dated. There are English translations of poetry by Nezval (*Antilyrik and Other Poems*, Los Angeles: Green Integer, 2001) and Seifert (*The Early Poetry of Jaroslav Seifert*, Evanston, Ill: Northwestern UP, 1999, and *The Poetry of Jaroslav Seifert*, North Haven, CT: Catbird Press, which also contains extracts from Seifert's autobiography *All the Beauties of the World*).

Chapter Six

There is a massive bibliography on Communism in Czechoslovakia, and most studies focus strongly on Prague. The atmosphere of the immediate post-1948 period is movingly captured in Heda Margolius Kolavy's *Prague Farewell* (Indigo, 1997), centered on the trial and execution of her husband in 1952; Milan Kundera's *Life is Elsewhere* (Faber, 2000) is also full of insights into the early period. On the phenomenon of "Prague Spring", Gordon Skilling's monumental *Czechoslovakia's Interrupted Revolution* (Princeton: Princeton UP, 1976) has not been superseded, but may be complemented by Kieran Williams, *The Prague Spring and its Aftermath. Czechoslovak Politics 1968-70* (Cambridge: Cambridge UP, 1997). The role of writers and intellectuals in the making of Prague '68 is well studied in Vladimír Kusin, *The Intellectual Origins of the Prague Spring. The Development of Reformist Ideas in Czechoslovakia 1956-1967* (Cambridge: Cambridge UP, 1971) and in Dušan Hamšík, *Writers against Rulers* (Hutchinson, 1971). Kusin continues his story in *From Dubček to Charter 77. A study of "Normalization" in Czechoslovakia 1968-78* (Edinburgh: Q Press, 1978), which may be complemented by John Keane's lively *Václav Havel. A Political Tragedy in Six Acts* (Bloomsbury, 1989). Gordon Skilling, *Samizdat and an Independent Society in Central and Eastern Europe* (Macmillan, 1989) has a typically well documented chapter on Czechoslovakia, and Barbara Day's *The Velvet Philosophers* (Claridge Press, 1989) is an authoritative study of the Jan Hus Foundation by one of its principal organizers; both books convey a powerful sense of intellectual life under "normalization". Havel's essay "The Power of the Powerless" is reproduced in *Open Letters. Selected Prose 1965-1990* (Faber, 1992), and his political philosophy is discussed in detail in Aviezer Tucker, *The Philosophy and Politics of Czech Dissidence from Patočka to Havel* (Pittsburgh: University of Pittsburgh Press, 2000). Holan's *A Night with Hamlet* is available in a bilingual Czech/English edition with translations by Jamila and Ian Milner (Prague: Academia, 1999), who also translated his *Selected Poems* (Penguin, 1971). The Czech cinema of the 1960s is perceptively discussed in Mira and Antonín J. Liehm, *The Most Important Art. Eastern European Film after 1945* (Berkeley: University of California Press, 1977) and, from a more personal point of view, in Josef Škvorecký, *All the Bright Young Men and Women. A Personal History of the Czech Cinema.*

Chapter Seven

The whole discussion of puppets and related images is greatly indebted to Ripellino's *Magic Prague*, especially sections 66-68. The Czech "martyr complex" is discussed fully in the concluding chapter of Robert B. Pynsent, *Questions of Identity. Czech and Slovak Ideas of Nationality and Personality* (Budapest: Central European University Press, 1994), and there is much to be learned, on this and related themes, from Ladislav Holy's *The Little Czech and the Great Czech Nation. National Identity and the Post-Communist Social Transformation* (Cambridge: Cambridge UP, 1996). A selection of Paul Leppin's stories has been published under the title of *Others' Paradise*, in a translation by Stephanie Howard and Amy R. Nestor (Prague: Twisted Spoon Press, 1995).

Chapter Eight

The best study of the overthrow of Communism and the transition to democracy is Bernard Wheaton and Zdeněk Kavan, *The Velvet Revolution. Czechoslovakia 1988-1991* (Boulder, CO: Westview Press, 1992). Post-1989 politics are explored in Carol Skalnik Leff, *The Czech and Slovak Republics. National versus State* (Boulder, Co., Westview Press, 1996), and the "Velvet Divorce" is trenchantly discussed in Abby Innes, *Czechoslovakia. The Short Goodbye* (New Haven, CT: Yale UP, 2001). There is a chapter on the *lustrace* in Tina Rosenberg, *The Haunted Land. Facing Europe's Ghosts after Communism* (Vintage, 1995). Finally, Jáchym Topol's *City Sister Silver* is published by Catbird Press (North Haven, CT, 1995) and Sylvie Germain's *The Weeping Woman on the Streets of Prague* by Daedalus Books (Sawtry, Cambs, 1998).

Index of Literary & Historical Names

Index of Places and Landmarks